DEFINING ISSUES IN PENTECOSTALISM

 **McMaster Divinity College Press**
Theological Studies Series

VOL. 1 Steven M. Studebaker, ed., *Defining Issues in Pentecostalism: Classical and Emergent*

DEFINING ISSUES IN PENTECOSTALISM
Classical and Emergent

EDITED BY
Steven M. Studebaker

☙PICKWICK *Publications* · Eugene, Oregon

DEFINING ISSUES IN PENTECOSTALISM
Classical and Emergent

McMaster Divinity College Press Theological Studies Series

Copyright © 2008 Wipf and Stock Publishers. All rights reserved. Except for brief quotations in critical publications or reviews, no part of this book may be reproduced in any manner without prior written permission from the publisher. Write: Permissions, Wipf and Stock Publishers, 199 W. 8th Ave., Suite 3, Eugene, OR 97401.

McMaster Divinity College Press
1280 Main Street West
Hamilton, Ontario, Canada
L8S 4K1

Pickwick Publications
Wipf and Stock Publishers
199 W. 8th Av.e, Suite 3
Eugene, OR 97401

ISBN 13: 978-1-55635-843-2

Revised Standard Version of the Bible, copyright 1952 (2nd edition, 1971) by the Division of Christian Education of the National Council of the Churches of Christ in the United States of America. Used by permission. All rights reserved.

Cataloging-in-Publication data:

Defining issues in Pentecostalism : classical and emergent / edited by Steven M. Studebaker.

    xiv + 208 p. ; 23 cm.

    Includes bibliography.

    McMaster Divinity College Press Theological Studies Series

    ISBN 13: 978-1-55635-843-2

    1. Pentecostalism. 2. Pentecostal churches—Doctrines. 3. Holy Spirit—Biblical teaching. I. Studebaker, Steven M. II. Title. III. Series.

BR1644 D40 2008

Manufactured in the U.S.A.

To Clark H. Pinnock

An early Charismatic voice

and theologian of the Holy Spirit

at McMaster Divinity College

Contents

List of Contributors ix
Acknowledgments xiii

Introduction: The Dynamism of Pentecostal Theology 1
Steven M. Studebaker

PART I **Defining Issues in Pentecostal Theology:
Classical and Emergent**

1 Baptized in the Spirit: Towards a Global Pentecostal Theology 13
Frank D. Macchia

2 The Inviting Spirit: Pentecostal Beliefs and Practices
regarding the Religions Today 29
Amos Yong

3 Beyond Tongues: A Pentecostal Theology of Grace 46
Steven M. Studebaker

4 This Spirit is God: A Pentecostal Perspective on the Doctrine
of the Divine Attributes 69
Andrew K. Gabriel

PART II **Defining Issues in Pentecostal Biblical Studies:
Classical and Emergent**

5   *The Charismatic Theology of St. Luke* Revisited
    (Special Emphasis upon Being Baptized in the Holy Spirit) 101
    Roger Stronstad

6   Paul's Experience and a Pauline Theology of the Spirit 123
    Cynthia Long Westfall

7   Spirit and Suffering in Contemporary Pentecostalism:
    The Lukan Epic Continues 144
    Martin William Mittelstadt

Epilogue 175
Clark H. Pinnock

Pentecostal Studies Resource Guide 178
Martin William Mittelstadt

Modern Authors Index 197
Subject Index 203

Contributors

Andrew K. Gabriel (Ph.D. candidate McMaster Divinity College) is adjunct faculty at Emmanuel Bible College in Kitchener, Ontario, where he teaches theology, philosophy, and Greek. He also instructs students at Tyndale University College and Seminary in Toronto. He is the author of several articles and essays related to Pentecostal theology, including "Beyond the Cross: Moltmann's Crucified God, Rahner's Rule, and Implications for the Doctrine of God," *Didaskalia* 19 (2008), forthcoming, and "Pneumatological Perspectives for a Theology of Nature: The Holy Spirit in Relation to Ecology and Technology," *Journal of Pentecostal Theology* 15.2 (2007): 195–212. He is a licensed minister in the Pentecostal Assemblies of Canada.

Frank D. Macchia (D. Theol. University of Basel) is Professor of Theology in the School of Religion of Vanguard University, Costa Mesa, California. He is the past President of the Society for Pentecostal Studies and currently edits the Society's journal, *Pneuma*. He is a member of the Faith and Order Commission of the National Council of Churches, and has served in the Reformed/Pentecostal dialogue. He has published seminal articles and books on Pentecostal theology, the most recent of which is *Baptized in the Spirit: A Global Pentecostal Theology* (Zondervan, 2006). He is ordained with the Assemblies of God.

Martin William Mittelstadt (Ph.D. Marquette University) is Associate Professor of New Testament in the Theology Department of Evangel University, Springfield, Missouri. He focuses on the relationship between the Spirit and suffering in Luke–Acts and recently published *Spirit and*

Suffering in Luke–Acts: Implications for a Pentecostal Pneumatology (T&T Clark, 2004). He is an ordained minister with the Assemblies of God and holds memberships in the Society for Pentecostal Studies and the Pentecostal Peace Fellowship.

Clark H. Pinnock (Ph.D. University of Manchester) is Professor Emeritus of Systematic Theology at McMaster Divinity College, Hamilton, Ontario. He is a prolific author who has made major contributions to Pentecostal/Charismatic theology, notably *Flame of Love: A Theology of the Holy Spirit* (InterVarsity Press, 1996), and to Evangelical theology, such as *Most Moved Mover: A Theology of God's Openness* (Paternoster, 2001), *The Scripture Principle* (Harper & Row, 1984), and *A Wideness in God's Mercy: The Finality of Jesus Christ in a World of Religions* (Zondervan, 1992). His current projects are in the areas of the atonement and the interrelationship between contemporary science and theology.

Roger Stronstad (D.Div. Christian Bible College) is the Biblical Theology Director at Summit Pacific College in Abbotsford, British Columbia. He was a member of the executive of the Society for Pentecostal Studies for four years, culminating in his Presidency in 1994. Over his 33 years at Summit Pacific (formerly known as Western Pentecostal Bible College), he has written and taught extensively on various themes related to Pentecostal thought and practice, with an emphasis on the charismatic theology of Luke–Acts. His books include *The Charismatic Theology of St. Luke* (Hendrickson, 1984), *Spirit, Scripture, and Theology: A Pentecostal Perspective* (APTS Seminary Press, 1995), and *The Prophethood of All Believers* (Sheffield Academic Press, 1999).

Steven M. Studebaker (Ph.D. Marquette University) is Assistant Professor of Systematic and Historical Theology at McMaster Divinity College, Hamilton, Ontario. He is an active member in the Society for Pentecostal Studies and the author of several articles on Pentecostal theology and the forthcoming book, *Jonathan Edwards' Social Augustinian Trinitarianism in Historical and Contemporary Perspectives* (Gorgias Press, 2008). He is ordained with the Assemblies of God.

Cynthia Long Westfall (Ph.D. University of Surrey) is Assistant Professor of New Testament at McMaster Divinity College, Hamilton, Ontario.

She is a recognized expert in the area of discourse analysis of the New Testament and on the book of Hebrews and also specializes in Jewish Christianity, the General Epistles, and Johannine Literature. She has published several articles and essays, and the book *A Discourse Analysis of the Structure of Hebrews: The Relationship between Form and Meaning* (T&T Clark, 2006). She has been co-chair of the Biblical Greek Language and Linguistics Section of the Society of Biblical Literature for several years and she has recently served as co-chair of the Evangelicals and Gender Section of the Evangelical Theological Society.

Amos Yong (Ph.D. Boston University) is Professor of Systematic Theology and Director of the Doctor of Philosophy Program in the School of Divinity at Regent University, Virginia Beach, Virginia. He is the First Vice-President of the Society for Pentecostal Studies and the author of many articles and books, the most recent of which are *Hospitality and the Other: Pentecost, Christian Practices, and the Neighbor* (Orbis Books, 2008), *Theology and Downs Syndrome: Reimagining Disability in Late Modernity* (Baylor University Press, 2007), and *The Spirit Poured Out on All Flesh: Pentecostalism and the Possibility of Global Theology* (Baker Academic, 2005). He is a credentialed minister with the Assemblies of God.

Acknowledgments

Several people need to be recognized for their roles in the organization of the Pentecostal Forum held at McMaster Divinity College on February 10, 2007, and the subsequent transformation of the papers presented there into the present book.

Stanley E. Porter, the President of McMaster Divinity College, and Dennis L. Hillis, the South Central Ontario District Director of the Canadian Bible Society, originally brainstormed the idea of McMaster Divinity College hosting a conference on Pentecostalism.

Jeff Clarke, Associate Director of Admissions at McMaster Divinity College, and Clark H. Pinnock, McMaster Divinity College Professor Emeritus of Systematic Theology, took the initial idea for a conference and developed it by designing the actual format and inviting the presenters. Jeff Clarke especially deserves recognition for his exceptional coordination of the myriad of details involved in planning and executing the conference. Under his leadership, several student volunteers from the Divinity College (Daniel Abernot, Robert Higgins, and Melissa Phillips) were indispensable in taking care of the on-site concerns of the Forum attendees.

McMaster Divinity College also deserves recognition for providing the facilities and financial resources to make the Forum possible (particular thanks go to Patricia Webb, Director of Advancement at McMaster Divinity College).

We appreciate all those who attended and participated in the discussions at the conference and trust that the presentations on different areas of Pentecostal thought enriched and stimulated them.

We are thankful for the presenters who took time to write papers (and subsequently revise for publication), travel, spend time away from families, and disrupt their schedules to be a part of making the Pentecostal Forum and this book possible.

We appreciate McMaster Divinity College Press and Wipf & Stock Publishers for recognizing the value of publishing the essays presented in this volume. In this respect, Lois K. Fuller Dow provided necessary editorial assistance in the final stages of the preparation of the manuscript. Nikola Caric and Jon Stovell (students and research assistants at McMaster Divinity College) served during the earlier stages of editing. When Roger Stronstad was, unfortunately, unable to attend the conference due to urgent last minute concerns, Nik read his paper for him.

Introduction:
The Dynamism of Pentecostal Theology

Steven M. Studebaker

The rise and global expansion of Pentecostalism is one of the seminal stories of Christianity in the twentieth century and first years of the twenty-first century. Pentecostalism in its various forms has attracted more than 590 million adherents.[1] Within the span of a century, Pentecostalism grew from scattered bands of revival seekers to a global movement that comprises nearly one third of Christians worldwide. Illustrative of its growth, the first Pentecostal Forum held at McMaster Divinity College on February 10, 2007 (at which the essays that comprise this book were originally presented) was one of the best attended academic conferences in the history of the Divinity College. Also, the number of Pentecostal students at McMaster Divinity continues to increase so that now, apart from Baptists, they are the largest confessional group in the College's student body. Without joining the triumphalism that sometimes accompanies the quotation of such statistics, the spectacular growth of the movement makes it one of the leading issues for contemporary consideration by Christian church leaders and scholars. Moreover, the historic significance and evolution of the movement invites theological assessment and reflection.

Although a relatively young movement in Christian history, Pentecostalism has passed through several transformations. The modern Pentecostal movement has three primary historical forms that now co-

---

1. Barrett and Johnson, "Missiometrics 2006: Goals, Resources, Doctrines of the 350 Christian World Communions," 28.

exist. These are Classical Pentecostalism, the Charismatic movement, and the Third Wave or Neocharismatic movement. Classical Pentecostalism effectively began January 1, 1901, when Agnes Ozman (1870–1937) experienced a baptism in the Holy Spirit with the sign of speaking in tongues. The Azusa Street Revivals of 1906–1909 and 1911–1912, led by William J. Seymour, launched Pentecostalism as a worldwide movement. The distinguishing belief of Classical Pentecostalism is that Spirit baptism is a post-conversion experience for empowered ministry, evidenced by speaking in tongues. Classical Pentecostalism represents the first form of modern Pentecostalism. Representative denominations include the International Pentecostal Holiness Church, Church of God in Christ, the Church of God (Cleveland), the Assemblies of God, the Pentecostal Assemblies of Canada, and the International Church of the Foursquare Gospel.

The Charismatic movement was the first major development in Pentecostalism. Charismatics share much in common with Classical Pentecostals, but they are unique in that they come from mainline Protestant denominations and the Catholic Church, and although they affirm Spirit baptism, they are less stringent on speaking in tongues as its initial evidence. For the first half of the twentieth century, the North American Pentecostal movement remained a distinct subgroup within Protestant Christianity. However, in the 1950s, Christians within the traditional mainline Protestant churches and Catholic Church not only came into the Pentecostal experience, they remained within their churches. Prior to the Charismatic renewal, church leaders and congregants who participated in Pentecostalism most often left their traditional churches and joined Pentecostal ones. Important figures in the Protestant side of the Charismatic movement have been Harald Bredesen (1918–2006), who was a Lutheran minister, and Dennis Bennett (1917–1991), who was rector of St. Mark's Episcopal Church in Van Nuys, California. Upon his forced resignation after receiving Spirit baptism and speaking in tongues, he served as vicar in St. Luke's Episcopal Church in Seattle, Washington. The Catholic Charismatic renewal began at Duquesne University, Pittsburgh, PA and the University of Notre Dame, South Bend, IN in 1967. Throughout the 1970s, the renewal spread from America to Europe, Australia, Latin America, and Korea. Early leaders in the movement included Ralph Martin (1942–), Stephen Clark (1940–), and Cardinal

Léon-Joseph Suenens (1904–1996), who was the papal representative to the Catholic Charismatic movement.

The early 1980s saw the emergence of the most recent development within Pentecostalism: the Neo-charismatic movement or "Third Wave" (the first and second waves being Classical Pentecostalism and the Charismatic Renewal). Key leaders in the rise of the "Third Wave" are C. Peter Wagner (1930–), who coined the term to refer to the spread of charismatic experience and spirituality in Evangelical churches, and John Wimber (1934–1997), who founded the Vineyard Christian Fellowship in Anaheim, CA, which is the movement's most visible organization. Wimber popularized the "Signs and Wonders" ministry that he advocated while lecturing in Wagner's course at Fuller Theological Seminary in the 1980s. The emphasis on spiritual renewal through the Holy Spirit without the traditional Pentecostal doctrine of Spirit baptism appealed to Christians within Evangelical churches in North America and Britain. Neocharismatics are often more interested in charismatic manifestations—e.g., "Signs and Wonders"—for church growth than in the Classical Pentecostal emphasis on Spirit baptism and speaking in tongues for empowered witness. Neocharismatics generally have no clear connection to traditional Pentecostal and Charismatic Renewal churches, but nevertheless embrace charismatic forms of spiritual experience and worship. Familiar manifestations of the Neocharismatic movement are the "Toronto Blessing" led by former Vineyard pastor John Arnott (1940–), the Brownsville Revival led by pastor John Kilpatrick in Pensacola, Florida (although the revival occurred at an Assemblies of God church, which is a Classical Pentecostal denomination, it reflects the ethos of the Neocharismatic movement), cell churches, prayer and spiritual warfare movements, new church networks such as the "apostolic churches" and restoration of the fivefold ministry offices, and the Alpha Course.

Pentecostalism is a movement that continues to evolve and is perhaps now at its most dynamic stage. Confronted with the reality and prospect of change, some will ask: can we not simply reclaim the doctrine and practice of our tradition? Others may wonder, why bother with the past? And yet still others seek an alternative response and believe that perhaps the best way to respond to the demands of being both Christian and Pentecostal in the changing world involves a synthesis of both concerns; that is, we remember and resource the past to answer the new demands facing contemporary Christian thought and life.

The consideration of the relationship between the past and present forms of Pentecostalism highlights the dynamism and contextual nature of Christian faith and practice. In an important respect, these two characteristics of the Christian life are interrelated. The contexts of Christianity are not static and, therefore, the ways of embodying its faith are fluid. This does not collapse into religious relativism, because the Christ who calls and the Spirit who empowers to follow are the same. But at the same time, the way that Christ's call lays hold of persons, and the form that Spirit-enabled discipleship takes, are open-ended. The Apostle Paul, empowered by the Holy Spirit, took the gospel of Jesus Christ to the marketplaces of the leading commercial and cultural cities of his time. William J. Seymour implicitly critiqued the ethnic and intra-Christian prejudices of the early twentieth century by preaching and practicing a racial and confessional transcendent love. Sharing the gospel of Christ and transcendent love are enduring Christian values, but the way the Spirit leads contemporary Christians to enact these in the mission fields of the suburbs, urban areas, marketplaces, and cultures of the present world, will look different than it did for our forerunners. We need to grasp that, as is the world in which we live, Pentecostalism is dynamic and in flux.

The dynamism of the present world is also the source of challenge and excitement for the Christian. Why is the current circumstance a challenge? First, because we realize that the world in which we live now is not the world of earlier generations. Pentecostals, like other Christians, must face the current cultural conditions. We live in a culture described in terms such as postmodern, post-Christendom, post-Christian, and perhaps post-churched. The churches in which we serve are not those of earlier generations. The Pentecostal movement in which many of us participate is not the same as it once was. For example, the International Pentecostal Holiness Church was a denomination of small rural churches in the southeastern region of the United States for most of the twentieth century, but it is now an increasingly global and urban church.

Second, the shifting nature of contemporary life presents the challenge of discipleship. The call of Christ to fellowship with God comes to us in the particular circumstances of our lives and we seek to respond to that call within those circumstances. The challenge for Pentecostals (and again, all Christians) is to bring their unique way of following Christ to *authentic* and *credible* expression in the light of the current cultural circumstances. What does it mean to be a Pentecostal Christian in the twenty-first century? The way contemporary Pentecostals answer that question will look somewhat different than it did for past ones. It will not do to unreflectively ape the practices of the past; this is traditionalism that fails to see that Christ calls people to follow him in their world and their culture and not the world of an idealized past.

Despite their recent appearance in the history of Christianity, Pentecostals are particularly prone to romanticizing the past. Pentecostals want to get back to Acts and recapture the glorious revivals of the early days of Azusa Street. Of course, the attempt to recapture biblical forms of ministry and life is appropriate, but not if it reifies, decontextualizes, and treats these as transcendent ahistorical models. For instance, many Pentecostals church leaders would laugh at the idea of casting lots to select church leaders (as the disciples of Jesus did in Acts 1:15–26), but unreflectively rush to adopt so-called "Apostolic" and five-fold ministry paradigms (Eph 4:11). It is not so much that there is something wrong with calling a church leader "apostle," but they forget that people were called "apostle" probably for no other reason than it was the idiom that best captured their sort of activity. The danger is to rip these categories from their historical and cultural background (and subsequent ones from other supposed "golden ages") and ontologize them so that they become transcendent ideals and forms. Sharing the gospel and nurturing the church are perennial Christian concerns, but the specific forms, titles, and ways these are accomplished emerge from, and should be tailored to, specific contexts. Please do not misunderstand me; I am not dismissing the achievements and practices of the past. Remember that my title is professor of Systematic *and* Historical Theology; one of my primary areas of research is on Jonathan Edwards, an eighteenth century Puritan theologian. Thus, I am committed to the value of Church history for the on-going life of the churches. However, contemporary Pentecostals misunderstand and ultimately do not honor their past heroes of the faith, both biblical and historical, by unblinkingly and woodenly repeating their theologies and practices. We honor them and emulate them when we *do what they did*. Filled with the Holy Spirit, they brought the gospel to bear on their world, and proclaimed what it meant to be a faithful disciple of Jesus Christ in their day. Thus, the contemporary and contextual focus of Pentecostal theology does not marginalize the insights of its traditions. On the contrary, the tradition instructs and shows the way in which those who have gone before sought to give authentic and credible witness to Christ and to the central ideas that give shape to the narrative of Christian redemption.

Notwithstanding the challenges, the dynamism of the current cultural context is also exciting for the Christian. We are mindful that Christ did not remove his followers from the world, but called them to follow him *in* the world (John 17:15–19). The story of the first Christians recorded in the book of Acts is not an account of cultural isolationism. Quite the contrary, the Spirit-empowered disciples of Christ took the gospel from the locked doors of an upper room in Jerusalem to the very center of their cultural world—Rome. Consequently, being a Pentecostal is an adventure of the Spirit in which we seek to follow the Christ of discipleship in the present world and time.

In light of these considerations, the essays in this book, which discuss central Pentecostal biblical and theological categories, are an effort to assess and mine the Pentecostal past for resources to discern an appropriate Pentecostal witness to the work of the Spirit in the present. This in turn points the way toward the future of Pentecostalism. The title of this book, *Defining Issues in Pentecostalism: Classical and Emergent*, indicates its purposes. In one sense, *defining* refers to the task of identifying the historical or classical issues that have defined Pentecostalism. In this respect, defining is descriptive. However, from the perspective of defining the emergent concerns within Pentecostalism, it is also prescriptive because the book seeks to identify and propose the embryonic theological trajectories that will characterize the future of Pentecostalism.

Most of the essays blend respect for the past and engagement with the present. Although they treat a classical issue within Pentecostalism, they offer a new way of thinking about it. For example, Amos Yong explores the relationship between Pentecostalism and the World Religions through a re-reading of Luke–Acts—the classical texts of Pentecostalism. Martin Mittelstadt shows that the traditional reading of Luke–Acts that emphasizes the charismatic nature of the gift of the Holy Spirit should be supplemented with a reading that highlights the Spirit's role of empowerment in suffering. Thus, he draws on the classical biblical texts of Pentecostal theology to show the Spirit's role in suffering, which is a dimension of Christian spirituality that North American Pentecostals often overlook in their thirst for charismatic power and gifts. Cynthia Long Westfall explores possible correlations between the pneumatology of Pauline literature and Paul's charismatic experience in Luke–Acts. Her work provides Pentecostals with a way to overcome the discontinuity they tend to assume between Pauline literature and Luke–Acts. Thus, the essays mine the traditional Pentecostal biblical and theological sources and categories, but deliver a fresh theological yield from them.

The authors of the essays represent some of the best Pentecostal scholars, as well as those now emerging. For example, Roger Stronstad and Frank Macchia are among the most established and respected Pentecostal theologians today. Amos Yong is one of the most prolific and theologically-gifted young theologians within Pentecostalism. Andrew Gabriel (a Ph.D. student at McMaster Divinity College) reflects the new generation of Pentecostal scholars. The authors, therefore, embody the ethos of the book, as they represent classical and emergent scholarship within Pentecostalism. Moreover, most of the authors come from the ranks of Pentecostal churches. Thus, the authors are not only analyzing, and at times critiquing, Pentecostalism, but are doing so from within the movement. Cynthia L. Westfall is an exception as she is not part of a self-styled Pentecostal or charismatic church, although she does embrace charismatic experience. Nevertheless, Pentecostals will find her piece quite "Pentecostal." Her voice is important because she illustrates an important dimension of the many tongues of Pentecost (Acts 2:1–12). Pentecost was not mono-chromatic but diverse from the beginning. The Spirit moves and speaks in a variety of ways and through many people. With that in mind, hearing her contribution is of the essence of Pentecostalism, because it is openness to the tongues of the Spirit.

The essays come under theological and biblical sections with an epilogue by Clark H. Pinnock. The first section on Pentecostal theology includes four essays. First, Frank Macchia treats the key theological themes that have emerged historically as distinctive to Pentecostal theology. He answers the question: can one discern from this history a coherent theology distinctive to the Pentecostal movement, or must we speak of different Pentecostal theologies and significantly different "Pentecostalisms?" He narrates the history of Pentecostal theological identity in terms of Spirit baptism and the loss of this identifier in the advent of modern studies of the movement and then mounts an argument for its retrieval as a meta-metaphor that embraces and integrates alternative approaches to Pentecostal distinctives. His presentation of the unique theological issues that have shaped the Pentecostal and Charismatic movements sets the context for the following essays that address specific classical and emergent theological issues within Pentecostalism.

Second, Amos Yong proposes a Pentecostal theology of religions. Historically, Pentecostals have embraced an exclusivistic stance with regard to their understanding of other religions. Yet, when Christian beliefs and practices are seen in their interconnectedness, the exclusiveness of Pentecostal beliefs seems to be complemented by a more inclusive set of postures and practices. Through a re-reading of Luke–Acts, the Pentecostal "canon-within-the-canon," Yong suggests a model of "the inviting Spirit," which underscores how the many tongues of Pentecost open up toward many different practices with regard to the Pentecostal encounter with other faiths in a post-9/11 context.

Third, Steve Studebaker engages the tendency of traditional Pentecostal pneumatology to focus on the related issues of baptism in the Holy Spirit as an experience subsequent to salvation, speaking in tongues, and spiritual gifts. The intention is to emphasize the importance of the Spirit for Christian thought and life. Indeed, Pentecostalism often sees itself as redressing a marginalization of the Spirit found in other Christian traditions. The irony is that the Pentecostal practice of seeing the primary work of the Spirit as an experience of spiritual ecstasy and ministry empowerment *supplementary* to the salvation already provided by Christ extends the subordination of the Spirit found more broadly in other Christian traditions. Studebaker maintains that Pentecostal theology can transcend the limited parameters of its traditional pneumatology and embrace a more comprehensive pneumatological vision of redemption.

Fourth, Andrew Gabriel proposes a Pentecostal revision of the divine attributes. Along with classical theism, Pentecostals have tended to neglect the triune nature of God in their understanding of God's attributes. While theologians have begun to integrate Christological implications into their revisions of classical theism, they have regularly ignored the Holy Spirit when modifying the classical doctrine of God. In an effort to be more adequately trinitarian, Gabriel proposes a Pentecostal perspective on the doctrine of God by advocating for, and exploring, the potential of a pneumatological approach to the doctrine of the divine attributes.

The second section on Pentecostal biblical studies includes three essays. First, Roger Stronstad maintains that the Pentecostal interpretation of Luke–Acts is one of its hallmark characteristics. He provides a sophisticated example of the Classical Pentecostal interpretation of Luke–Acts with a new twist. He makes a case for the Christian and converted status of the Roman Centurion Cornelius prior to Peter's visit in Acts 10. He draws on a redactional-critical method to demonstrate that Luke–Acts advances a theology of the Spirit of charismatic gifting in contrast to Pauline literature's presentation of the Spirit of salvation. The emphasis on charismatic gifting in Luke–Acts provides the biblical categories to support the traditional Pentecostal doctrine of Spirit baptism as a work distinct and subsequent to salvation.

Second, Martin W. Mittelstadt also works in Luke–Acts, which is the favored source for the Pentecostal emphasis on the Holy Spirit as the source of empowered ministry and charismatic gifts. However, he approaches these classical texts for Pentecostal theology from the overlooked perspective of the Spirit of suffering and opposition. He maintains that the Holy Spirit not only empowers Jesus and the disciples for ministry, but also enables them to bear the hostility and persecution that invariably accompanies their witness to the gospel. Jesus and the disciples' experience of the Spirit of empowered ministry and suffering in Luke–Acts is the paradigm for the ongoing history of the church. The Spirit who constitutes and empowers the ministry of the church is the Spirit who empowers its faithfulness in the midst of rejection and affliction. Thus, Mittelstadt complements the Spirit of charismatic gifts with the Spirit of suffering.

Third, Cynthia L. Westfall engages the trend of Pentecostal scholarship that assumes a dissonance between Paul's and Luke's pneumatology. She undertakes to connect Paul's experience of the Spirit in Acts with Pauline pneumatology. Although baptism in the Holy Spirit does not feature prominently in Pauline literature, perhaps the themes of new creation, the church as the temple of the Holy Spirit, and the filing, gifts, and fruits of the Spirit are specifications of the broader metaphor of Spirit baptism. Her study promises to illustrate points of continuity in place of the discontinuity presupposed in traditional Pentecostal biblical studies.

The above essays provide students with an excellent introduction to the significant past and present theological trajectories and latest developments within Pentecostal theology. Many excellent works on Pentecostalism are available, but because of their length and/or limited scope, they are suitable only for courses devoted to Pentecostalism.

Consequently, they are not often used for the more common introductory theology courses offered by many Christian colleges, universities, and seminaries. The present volume gives professors desiring to introduce students to Pentecostalism a concise and accessible introduction to its seminal historical and contemporary issues. Moreover, the book's focus on North American Pentecostalism heightens its value as an introductory text because so many theological students first encounter Pentecostalism in its North American variety. Thus, an introduction focused on the issues significant for the North American genre of Pentecostalism serves them well. The addition of the Pentecostal Studies Resource Guide also adds tremendous value to this book for students. The guide provides an annotated bibliography and direction to electronic resources.

Bibliography

Barrett, David B. and Todd M. Johnson. "Missiometrics 2006: Goals, Resources, Doctrines of the 350 Christian World Communions." *International Bulletin of Missionary Research* 30 (2006) 27–30.

PART I

Defining Issues in Pentecostal Theology:
Classical and Emergent

1

Baptized in the Spirit: Towards a Global Pentecostal Theology

Frank D. Macchia

Introduction

The subtitle of my contribution, "Towards a Global Pentecostal Theology," might seem presumptuous. After all, there is no single theology for Pentecostalism globally. If anything, Pentecostalism globally is widely diverse theologically. Yet, the issue of whether or not there is a coherent message that is more or less constant throughout the diversity of Pentecostal movements globally cannot be dismissed out of hand. It is the purpose of this paper to explore this issue. The central question is, "Does Pentecostalism have a chief theological distinctive or a theologically distinctive message?" If so, how may we develop it in a way that brings many different Pentecostals to the table in conversation?

Spirit Baptism and Tongues: The Early Concern

I will start with an assumption that I believe the research will bear out, namely, that the dominant theological concern of Pentecostalism from the early decades of the Movement to the present was an experience called the "baptism in the Holy Spirit," especially as accompanied by speaking in tongues and other spiritual gifts. If one were to purchase a book by a Pentecostal theologian prior to the 1970's on the most cherished doctrine among Pentecostals, it would most assuredly be about Spirit baptism. The fact that such is no longer the case needs to be addressed, as I will below. At this point let me state my agreement with Pentecostal historian Grant

Wacker that early Pentecostal literature shows an overwhelming majority interest in Spirit baptism.[1] Such has, in my view, remained the case on a grassroots level throughout the decades of the Pentecostal movement. Korean Pentecostal theologian, Koo Dong Yun, notes accurately that "out of a number of intriguing characteristics of the Pentecostal-Charismatic Movement, 'Baptism in the Holy Spirit' . . . represents the most distinctive doctrine."[2] I thus concur with Allan Anderson that "a fundamental presupposition of all Pentecostal theology is the central emphasis on the experience of the baptism in the Holy Spirit."[3]

There is no question but that Spirit baptism has been thrust forward as a theological concern in its own right due to the focus on it among Pentecostals worldwide. We should not neglect to note that the Pentecostals borrowed the category from Holiness revival movements. However, the Pentecostals and the Charismatics were the ones who brought the topic to prominence as a subject of theological discussion and debate.

The fact is, however, that Spirit baptism is no longer widely regarded by scholars of Pentecostalism as the dominant theological distinctive of the Pentecostal movement. The reason for this, put simply, is the challenge of theological diversity discovered among Pentecostal groups both historically and globally by Pentecostal historians. This diversity has to do both with how Spirit baptism itself is understood as well as the range of theological beliefs found among Pentecostal churches. I will explain.

In their focus on Spirit baptism, Pentecostals were inspired by the Holiness Movement, which described a post-conversion experience of "sanctification" (or consecration to God) as a "Spirit baptism." John Fletcher had wedded John Wesley's quest for Christian perfection with the revivalist's penchant for crisis experience to arrive at an understanding of sanctification as a "second blessing," or a "baptism in the Holy Spirit" subsequent to regeneration (or conversion-initiation). Meanwhile, a view of Spirit baptism as a post-conversion empowerment for witness was current in the Keswick revivals in England in the late 19th century, attracting adherents from a more Reformed theological influence, like D. L. Moody. The earliest Pentecostals adopted this Keswick view of Spirit

---

1. Shared with me in personal conversation.
2. Yun, *Baptism in the Holy Spirit*, 23.
3. Anderson, *Zion and Pentecost*, 244.

baptism as empowerment but detached it formally from the Fletcherian view of sanctification as the needed third blessing (conversion, sanctification, and Spirit baptism as empowerment for witness). Most early Pentecostals ended up turning to John the Baptist's prediction that Jesus would "baptize in the Spirit" (Matt 3:17), and to the fulfillment of this experience among the earliest followers of Jesus in Acts 1:8 and 2:4–5, to argue that Spirit baptism was not formally sanctification but rather a "charismatic" experience that empowers Christians for witness (e.g., Acts 1:8), especially in greater openness to extraordinary gifts (*charismata*) of the Spirit, such as speaking in tongues, prophecy, and divine healing. Spirit baptism was power for witness given to the sanctified life.

Four developments, however, complicated this picture and added considerable variety to how Spirit baptism was understood among Pentecostals. First, though many early Pentecostals sharply distinguished Spirit baptism from sanctification in polemics against the Holiness Movement, they tended, when away from these polemics, to speak of Spirit baptism as a sanctifying experience of the love of God poured into our hearts, using Rom 5:5 as their proof text.[4] As a consequence of this trend, Singaporean Pentecostal pastor, David Lim, even speaks of Spirit baptism as "vocational sanctification."[5]

Second, there was an argument among early Pentecostals as to whether or not the sanctification experience advocated within the Holiness Movement (*à la* John Fletcher) was still necessary. Under the influence of William H. Durham (of Chicago), believers coming into the Pentecostal Movement from outside the strict boundaries of the Holiness Movement regarded sanctification as accomplished by the "finished work" of Christ on the cross and thus available to believers from the moment of initial faith in Christ. Among these "finished work" Pentecostals, Spirit baptism, as a post-conversion empowerment for witness, simply followed conversion rather than conversion and then sanctification as a distinct experience. Arguably, the close connection between Spirit baptism and the sanctified life grew weaker in this wing of the Pentecostal Movement.

Third, a movement erupted within the nascent Assemblies of God denomination, populated by "finished work" Pentecostals who followed

---

4. E.g., Bell, "Believers in Sanctification," 3. See my discussion of this with other examples from early Pentecostal literature in Macchia, *Baptized in the Spirit*, 80–82.

5. Shared with me in personal conversation.

William H. Durham, that interpreted Spirit baptism as the crowning moment of a conversion-initiation process involving repentance, faith, and water baptism, after the pattern of Acts 2:38. This movement, called today Oneness Pentecostalism due to its Christocentric and modalistic understandings of the Trinity, represented a marked departure from the typical Pentecostal understanding of Spirit baptism as a post-conversion revival experience.

Even the Oneness Pentecostals, who regarded Spirit baptism as intimately connected to water baptism as part of a conversion-initiation complex, have not held to a single view of Spirit baptism, since some have conceived of the relationship to water baptism more loosely than others.[6] Furthermore, some Trinitarian Pentecostal groups (e.g., in Chile and Germany) have associated Spirit baptism with Christian regeneration, apart from water baptism.

Fourth, the doctrine of speaking in tongues as initial evidence of Spirit baptism has been variously interpreted among Pentecostals. Many early Pentecostals considered tongues the means by which the world would be evangelized (through xenolalia, i.e., miraculously speaking unlearned foreign languages). This passion soon waned (understandably). Others considered tongues an in-depth praise or groaning in the Spirit opened up through Spirit baptism. Some Pentecostals outside of U.S. Pentecostal denominations do not regard tongues as necessary for Spirit baptism to be experienced. Even within the U.S., where the doctrine of tongues as evidence of Spirit baptism has strongest support, various understandings of the doctrine may be found. For example, the prominent pastor Jack Hayford, of the International Church of the Foursquare Gospel, has written of Spirit baptism as opening up the capacity or privilege of in-depth prayer in tongues but has refused to see tongues as absolutely necessary to the Spirit baptismal experience.[7] Pentecostal founder William J. Seymour viewed tongues as the Bible evidence that the powerful experiences of the Spirit among Pentecostals were bringing together people from all races and nations to share the goodness of God with the world, a view shared by others in the early days of the movement.[8] More recently, Murray Dempster has written of tongues as the chief sign that God is breaking

---

6. Fudge, *Christianity without the Cross*.
7. Hayford, *Spiritual Language*, 89–107.
8. Seymour, "Same Old Way," 3. See also Hezmalhalch, "Among the Indians," 3.

down barriers between people, the renewal of language signifying the creation of a new humanity in Christ.[9] I would regard tongues speech as the first "ecumenical language" of the church, which calls into question the adequacy of human speech to capture the divine mystery and lodges an implicit protest against any effort to make one language or cultural expression determinative for how the gospel is to be understood or witnessed to in the world. The Pentecostal doctrine of tongues as symbolic of Spirit baptism implies that the Spirit's redemptive and empowering work is to be experienced and expressed in a vast diversity of tongues that groan for the redemption to come (Rom 8:26), revealing the ultimate inadequacy of human thought and speech to express the divine mystery. Many Pentecostals today who lift up glossolalia as a mark of the experience of Spirit baptism, however, have lost touch with this early ecumenical (and I hasten to add, Lukan) perspective concerning glossolalia. How "glossocentric" Spirit baptism is in our understanding of the experience and how the connection between Spirit baptism and tongues speech is to be defined is by no means settled among Pentecostals globally.

In general, this diversity of viewpoints concerning Spirit baptism opens up the question as to what purpose it serves to speak of Spirit baptism as the dominant Pentecostal theological distinctive if there has been little agreement as to what the doctrine might mean. Whether the issue is sanctification, conversion-initiation, or tongues as evidence, Spirit baptism has been interpreted in various ways within Pentecostalism.

The second point to consider when noting the dominant Pentecostal attention paid to the metaphor of Spirit baptism is the fact that Spirit baptism is not the only distinctive doctrine of the Pentecostal movement historically or globally. Divine healing and the Second Coming of Jesus have also received a great deal of emphasis among Pentecostal groups. Divine healing was waning at the turn of the twentieth century among Evangelical and Holiness churches right about the time that the Pentecostal movement spread. One is tempted to conclude that Pentecostalism spread in part as a haven for those passionate about healing. The healing doctrine also reveals the somewhat "material" understanding of salvation among Pentecostals. Salvation is not only of the soul but also for general well being in this life. This assumption is widespread among Pentecostals today globally, leading increasing numbers toward an exaggerated "health

---

9. Dempster, "Church's Moral Witness," 1–7.

and wealth" gospel that promises prosperity and good health to all of the redeemed. Though this trend seems extreme to many, it is rooted in an impulse that is quite distinctively Pentecostal.

Furthermore, the pre-millennialist (especially dispensationalist) second coming doctrine that became popular among Evangelical churches (especially among Baptists and Presbyterians) near the turn of the twentieth century had a tremendous influence on early Pentecostals and in a significant way continues to do so. Though early Pentecostals were more concerned with transforming the world through witness and missions than predicting the time of Christ's return, they shared the fervency for Christ's soon return with their early Evangelical peers. They were convinced that the Pentecostal revival was ushering in the latter days. The urgency for missions gripped them deeply, since the gospel was to go out to all the earth before Christ returned.

The question raised by the importance that topics like healing and eschatology played in Pentecostal experience and belief is whether or not there is a distinctive message among Pentecostals that is coherent. Are we just left with a cafeteria of doctrinal emphases among Pentecostals that have been variously interpreted? Due in part to the diversity of belief that has been discovered by Pentecostal scholarship, Spirit baptism no longer enjoys the attention it once warranted among theological spokespersons of the Pentecostal Movement. Even the significant efforts by New Testament scholars Robert Menzies and Roger Stronstad to focus on the unique charismatic pneumatology of Luke in order to open up fresh possibilities for viewing Spirit baptism as prophetic or charismatic inspiration has received no significant response from the most prolific among contemporary Pentecostal theologians, who have focused on broad pneumatological themes toward the construction of an ecumenical pneumatology.[10] Not since Harold Hunter's and Howard Ervin's books on Spirit baptism, written nearly three decades ago, has there been a constructive effort at elaborating on the doctrine by a Pentecostal systematic theologian. This was the occasion for the writing of my recent book.[11]

Both issues, the diversity of viewpoints concerning Spirit baptism and the diverse range of doctrines emphasized among Pentecostals, raise the question as to whether there is a Pentecostal movement to

10. Stronstad, *Charismatic Theology* and Menzies, *Empowered for Witness*.

11. Hunter, *Spirit Baptism* and Ervin, *Baptism in the Holy Spirit*. Note my book: Macchia, *Baptized in the Spirit*.

speak of. Are we forced to refer to various "Pentecostalisms" rather than to "Pentecostalism" in the singular? This question is profoundly theological as well as phenomenological. If the Lutherans had justification, the Calvinists election, and the Wesleyans sanctification, what did the Pentecostals have? Is there a theological distinctive typical of global Pentecostalism?

Experience and Oral Theology: Walter J. Hollenweger

Walter J. Hollenweger's research revealed a vast doctrinal diversity among Pentecostals worldwide and even within the U.S., both now and from the beginning of the movement. His classic, *The Pentecostals*, fell like a bombshell in the late sixties and early seventies upon geographically sheltered Pentecostal groups surprised by the doctrinal diversity of the movement globally. In essence, Hollenweger sought coherence in what is distinctive to Pentecostalism, not in a point or points of doctrine (since for him no such coherence existed), but rather in experience and how this is expressed. I will explain.

Hollenweger not only diversified the doctrinal distinctives of Pentecostal theology, he shifted what was most distinctive about Pentecostal theology from doctrinal points to religious experience and how this was expressed orally and narratively. He wrote that "talk of 'the doctrine' of the Pentecostal churches is highly problematic. What unites the Pentecostal churches is not a doctrine but an experience and this can be interpreted and substantiated in many different ways."[12] Hollenweger thus sought to describe Pentecostal distinctives experientially and in terms of how Pentecostals bring their experiences to expression narratively. He wrote in another context concerning the diversity of Pentecostal theologies, "A description of these theologies cannot begin with their concepts. I have rather to choose another way and describe how they are conceived, carried and might finally be born."[13] Hollenweger was taken with the typically non-Western ways in which Pentecostals experienced God and expressed theological truth, namely, through visions, bodily healing, and stories, rather than primarily through rational discourse and abstract propositions. This shift in focus from doctrine to experience and in theological method made Spirit baptism seem like an accident of his-

12. Hollenweger, "Azusa Street to the Toronto Phenomenon," 7.
13. Hollenweger, "Theology of the New World," 228.

tory, that is, a holdover from the Holiness Movement that was not at all significant to what is most distinctive about Pentecostal theology. The narrow and ecumenically irrelevant understanding of Pentecostalism as a revivalist "tongues movement" was replaced in Hollenweger's work with a Pentecostalism that seemed ecumenically relevant, at the forefront of a way of doing theology that is not burdened with post-Enlightenment standards of rational discourse.

While recognizing the value of Hollenweger's approach to Pentecostal theology, it is also important to note that doctrinal issues cannot be so easily detached from the symbolic framework that shapes how a movement experiences God and expresses theological truth, as George Lindbeck has shown us.[14] Furthermore, Spirit baptism is not only a doctrine, but a metaphor that can function imaginatively in ways other than doctrinal conceptualization. Of course, we cannot deny that there was doctrinal diversity early on and historically among Pentecostals globally. But this diversity does not necessarily mean that there was not some kind of coherent, doctrinal vision among Pentecostals. It is to this issue that we now turn.

Towards Doctrinal Coherence: Donald Dayton and D. William Faupel

Donald Dayton and D. William Faupel accepted the fact that Pentecostals were diverse doctrinally and, therefore, not just about Spirit baptism and tongues. However, they were not willing to forsake the possibility of a conceptually-coherent doctrinal distinctive throughout global Pentecostalism. They both, in their own way, showed that there was a theologically coherent understanding of God's redemptive work through Christ and the Holy Spirit in early Pentecostal theology that remained typical of the Movement. Dayton showed that early Pentecostal theology advocated a four-fold devotion to Jesus as Savior, Spirit Baptizer, Healer, and Coming King.[15] D. William Faupel highlighted the final eschatological element of this four-fold gospel as what was decisive.[16] Pentecostalism was mainly about the latter rain of the Spirit to restore the gifts and power of Pentecost to the church in order to empower global mission before

14. Lindbeck, *Nature of Doctrine*.
15. Dayton, *Theological Roots of Pentecostalism*.
16. Faupel, *Everlasting Gospel*.

Christ's soon return. Pentecostals viewed the church as a "missionary fellowship," which (as Grant Wacker noted) was "riding the crest of the wave of history" toward the end of the latter days of the Spirit.

Steven J. Land's seminal effort at writing a Pentecostal theology follows Faupel's shift of emphasis from Spirit baptism to eschatology within the context of the four-fold gospel. Interestingly, Land's, *Pentecostal Spirituality*, devotes no more than a few pages to Spirit baptism, marking a significant departure from past Pentecostal theological polemics. He explicitly takes issue with Dale Bruner's description of Pentecostal theology as "pneumatobaptistocentric" (Spirit baptism centered). Land regards Bruner's description as "missing the point altogether" concerning what is really distinctive about Pentecostal theology, which is, in Land's view, the sanctification of the affections as part of an eschatological passion for the Kingdom of God yet to come.[17] Through the work of Dayton, Faupel, and Land, the four-fold gospel and eschatology virtually replaced Spirit baptism as the dominant theological distinctive of Pentecostalism.

The Current State of Pentecostal Theology

It seems that we can no longer return to the old assumption that Pentecostalism is *only* about "Spirit baptism and tongues." We have arrived rather at two options concerning that which is most distinctive to Pentecostal theology. The first option is to follow Hollenweger in positing a theologically diverse Pentecostal Movement united principally by a holistic experience of the Spirit and an oral or narrative way of doing theology. Our second option is to assume a distinctive doctrinal coherence to Pentecostal theology that revolves around the four-fold gospel (following Dayton) or around an eschatological fervency for the soon return of Christ that involves notions of Spirit baptism, healing (and other spiritual gifts), and missionary zeal (following Faupel and Land). Either way, Spirit baptism has lost its role in scholarship as the dominant theological concern of the Pentecostal Movement. Just when the Pentecostals have effectively raised the issue of Spirit baptism to the level of theological discussion and debate they seem to be backing away from the importance that the doctrine has held for them historically and globally.

In reflecting on this situation in scholarship, it seems to me that theological diversity within Pentecostalism should not be used to eclipse what

17. Land, *Pentecostal Spirituality*, 62–63.

Pentecostals do typically hold in common concerning Spirit baptism. I agree here with Simon Chan that Pentecostals are not in agreement over the details of their distinctive beliefs but that, nevertheless, "what comes through over and over again in their discussions and writings is a certain kind of spiritual experience of an intense, direct, and overwhelming nature centering on the person of Christ which they schematize as 'baptism in the Holy Spirit.'"[18] Despite their diversity of Spirit baptism theologies, Pentecostals typically regard Spirit baptism as an empowering experience connected in some way to their witness to Jesus Christ, especially in a way that assumes participation in spiritual gifts. This emphasis on empowerment is present, for example, among both Trinitarian and Oneness Pentecostals. As Thomas Fudge notes, Spirit baptism for Oneness Pentecostals "is the quintessential Pentecostal experience in which the individual is empowered by God."[19] Furthermore, though Spirit baptism has been accompanied historically by other theological components of the "Apostolic" or "Full" gospel, such as divine healing and eschatology, I do not find it convincing as a historical thesis that Spirit baptism was just one concern among others and held no special prominence over other concerns. A reading of the literature over the history of the Pentecostal movement will show, I believe, an overwhelming concern with both the experience and the doctrine of Spirit baptism as that which is most distinctively Pentecostal. Though Spirit baptism is defined within a broader theological devotion to Jesus as the one who imparts new life as Savior, Healer, and Coming King, it is my view that Spirit baptism is the "crown jewel" of all Pentecostal experiential and doctrinal concerns.

Where do we go from here? Given the diversity of views among Pentecostals on Spirit baptism, can we construct a doctrine of Spirit baptism that brings a variety of Pentecostal voices to the table? Can we do this in a way that also opens up neglected features of the biblical message of redemption? This challenge will occupy us for the remainder of the paper.

Spirit Baptism and Eschatology: Towards Constructive Dialogue

The challenge as I see it for the future of Pentecostal theology is to maintain the focus on Spirit baptism as the chief theological distinctive of

---

18. Chan, *Pentecostal Theology*, 7.
19. Fudge, *Christianity without the Cross*, 117.

Pentecostalism, while leaving "breathing room" for a diversity of nuances and interpretations among Pentecostal movements globally. If Pentecostal theology is to remain true to its global diversity and to its historic focus on the metaphor of Spirit baptism, it will need, in my view, to expand the boundaries of the metaphor beyond the narrow limits of only one perspective on the doctrine. Moreover, to be true to Pentecostal distinctives, this expanded view of Spirit baptism must have a strong eschatological component and be connected to healing or the renewal of creation as well. It is my conviction that a fresh look at the New Testament can provide Pentecostal theologians with just such an expansive and integrated appreciation for the baptism in the Holy Spirit. Let us proceed throughout the remainder of this essay to explore what such a newly constructed Pentecostal focus on Spirit baptism might look like.

Two things strike me as I read the New Testament use of the verb to "baptize" in the Spirit. First, Spirit baptism is the most distinctive belief about Jesus shared by the New Testament writers. All four Gospels begin by announcing Jesus as the coming Spirit Baptizer. John links Jesus' role as Spirit baptizer to his divinity, since in John 20:22 Jesus "breathes" the Spirit forth as God did in Gen 2:7. The Logos is said to be "God" in John 1:1 because "in him was life" (John 1:4), the very life of God poured forth to redeem and to sanctify. Luke also has Jesus refer to himself as the Spirit Baptizer in Acts 1, and Luke understands this identity to mean that Jesus will "pour forth" the Spirit once he has ascended to the Father (Acts 2:33). Though Paul only mentions Spirit baptism once in the letters that we have from him (1 Cor 12:13), he assumes throughout that Jesus' significance is in the fact that the Spirit is accessed through him, more specifically, by faith in him (Gal 5:1–5).

This New Testament concentration on Jesus as the Spirit Baptizer or Mediator of the Spirit is all the more remarkable considering the fact that the Messiah's role in imparting the Spirit to others is unique to the New Testament, not having any explicit precedence in Jewish Messianic expectation. In the Old Testament, for example, the Messiah bears the Spirit (Isa 61:1–3). Nowhere does it state in the Old Testament, however, that he will pour it forth upon others. I have thus argued elsewhere that later high Christological claims of Christ's deity arose historically from the assumption that Jesus has poured or breathed forth the Spirit for new life, something presumably only God can do.[20] This idea places Spirit baptism at the core of the distinctively Christian understanding of Jesus in the New Testament.

Oddly, Spirit baptism has played no significant role in Christian dogmatics or theological discussions on Christology or other theological loci. Not even in discussions on water baptism (where Spirit baptism is sometimes mentioned) is there a discussion of Spirit baptism in its own right. A notable exception would be Karl Barth's extensive discussion of the metaphor in the concluding fragment of his *Church Dogmatics*.[21] This lack of attention to the metaphor is due in part to the atrophy of pneumatology in the West. We are simply not accustomed to speaking of God's redemptive work in the world principally through a pneumatological metaphor.

Second, what strikes me further as I look at the New Testament teaching about baptism in the Spirit is that the metaphor functions in the New Testament in a way analogous to how it functions among Pentecostals globally, namely, with a certain amount of fluidity and multidimensionality. The overall rubric that seems to tie all of the conceptions together in the New Testament is eschatology, namely, the inauguration of the Kingdom of God through the bestowal of the Spirit. In Matt 3, for example, John the Baptist is said to teach and preach the message of the Kingdom of God (Matt 3:2), and it is in this context that Jesus is featured as the Baptizer in the Spirit. John the Baptist saw himself as standing on the edge of the end of the world announcing the Messiah's act of "baptizing in the Spirit" (only the verb form is used) as the final act of salvation. John knew that his water baptism did not have the power to bring down the Spirit and to end the age. The prophets of old said in effect, "We circumcise the foreskin but God will circumcise the heart." So John uses similar prophetic rhetoric to say in effect, "I can baptize in water unto repentance but the Messiah will baptize in the Spirit unto judgment and purgation/restoration." John's baptism was preparatory, namely, to gather the repentant together in preparation for the final judgment and restoration, but "apocalyptic transcendence" belongs to the Messiah alone. Only from him will the wind of the Spirit blow away the chaff and store the wheat into barns. That the Messiah will be anointed of the Spirit is

---

20. Macchia, *Baptized in the Spirit*, 107–12.
21. Barth, *Church Dogmatics*, IV/4.

foretold. But insight into the Messiah's role to dispense and baptize in the Spirit is unique to John the Baptist.

Consistent with our eschatological theme, the opening of the heavens at Jesus' baptism is a typical sign depicting an apocalyptic revelation. In Matt 3, the descending of the dove is reminiscent perhaps of the Spirit brooding upon the waters of creation and the sign of new creation in the story of Noah. Jesus is being commissioned here to usher in the Kingdom of God in power to make all things new: "If I cast out demons by the Spirit of God, the Kingdom of God has come upon you" (Matt 12:28).

It seems clear that Spirit baptism in the Synoptics is granted broad eschatological implications that cannot be exhausted in any version of Christian initiation. Interestingly, Donald Hagner notes insightfully that the church connected to the Gospel of Matthew saw parallels between its Christian baptism and Jesus' Jordan experience. But this church also recognized the unique eschatological undertones in the complex of events at the Jordan that await fulfillment at the end of salvation history.[22] I believe that Hagner's insight can be applied quite broadly. The vision of Spirit baptism foretold by John the Baptist and depicted in Jesus' Jordan experience pointed to final judgment and to the final sanctification of the entire creation.

John also connects Jesus as the Spirit Baptizer with entering the Kingdom of God (John 3:5). Luke as well has Jesus refer to his role as the Spirit Baptizer in Acts 1, in the context of Jesus' teaching concerning the Kingdom of God (Acts 1:3–5). The disciples are in Jerusalem when Jesus pours out the Spirit, the city associated in Judaism with the inauguration of the Kingdom. After the Spirit is poured out upon the disciples, Luke informs us that the Spirit is to be poured out upon all flesh (Acts 2:17), which I interpret as ultimately fulfilled eschatologically in the new creation in which "God will be all in all" (1 Cor 15:28) and Christ will "fill the whole universe" with his presence through the Spirit (Eph 4:10). Paul refers in 1 Cor 12:13 to a "baptism in the Spirit" "into" (or, better, "for the purpose of") "one body" (or, as the NIV states accurately, "so as to form one body"). The unity and *koinonia* of the Spirit among the faithful thus functions to foreshadow the Spirit's work among all flesh towards the creation of a new humanity, or even a new creation. This new humanity and new creation are eschatologically the goal of Spirit baptism.

---

22. Hagner, *Matthew 1–13*, 58.

Interestingly, Pentecostalism has implicitly connected Spirit baptism to the culmination of God's Kingdom in history. As Faupel and Land have noted, Pentecostals have classically believed in a "latter rain" of the Spirit that will bring the divine outpouring of the Spirit to all peoples before the end comes. I agree with Faupel and Land that eschatology is thus a vital element in the Pentecostal full gospel, but as a context for interpreting Spirit baptism rather than as a component to be viewed alongside Spirit baptism (and in competition with it). Some Pentecostals and Charismatics have begun to interpret Spirit baptism consciously along the lines of the eschatological work of the Spirit. I have attempted to develop this theme as a way of bringing together various Pentecostal views of Spirit baptism at the ecumenical table.

What I have in mind as the chief theological distinctive of the Pentecostal movement is a concentration on Spirit baptism eschatologically defined so as to leave "breathing room" for various Pentecostal and Charismatic accents. Though the typically Pentecostal focus on empowerment and spiritual gifts will be maintained, there will be enough flexibility to the Spirit baptismal metaphor to include Paul's understanding of the metaphor as that which constitutes the unity of the church as a communion of saints, as well as in regeneration through faith in Christ. One can also view the goal of the doctrine in broadly transformationist terms. This expansion of the boundaries of Spirit baptism allows Pentecostal theologians to maintain a focus on the chief theological distinctive of the Pentecostal Movement without narrowly defining that distinctive as "empowerment plus tongues." Also, it will allow Pentecostals to relate constructively with other ecclesiastical traditions from the standpoint of a pneumatological concentration.

Conclusion

Pentecostalism is a movement that has helped to bring the neglected metaphor of Spirit baptism back to the center of our understanding of God's redemptive work in history. Especially in the light of the well-known *Geistvergessenheit* (forgetting or abandonment of the Spirit) in the West, Spirit baptism can emerge as a powerful metaphor of the pneumatological substance of God's redemptive work through Christ. What would it mean, for example, to develop a Christology from the core belief that he is the one who mediates the Spirit? What would it mean further to define soteriological categories like justification by faith from the conviction that the Spirit expands the circle of the Son's favor with the Father in order to include humanity too? What about an ecclesiology from the conviction that the church is constituted by the outpouring of the Spirit? Should Pentecostal theologians abandon their central theological distinctive and give up the possibilities of a Pentecostally-inspired systematic theology? Why not expand the Pentecostal understanding of Spirit baptism so that it can function as an aid in the formation of a uniquely Pentecostal contribution to theology? It is my hope that this constructive task will form the next chapter in the debate among Pentecostal theologians as to what indeed is theologically distinctive about the Pentecostal Movement.

Bibliography

Anderson, Allan. *Zion and Pentecost: The Spirituality and Experience of Pentecostal and Zionist/Apostolic Churches in South Africa*. Pretoria: University of South Africa Press, 2000.

Barth, Karl. *Church Dogmatics*. Vol. 4, pt. 4. Ed. G. W. Bromiley and T. F. Torrance. Edinburgh: T&T Clark, 1969.

Bell, E. N. "The Believers in Sanctification." *Christian Evangel* 59 (September 19, 1914) 3.

Chan, Simon. *Pentecostal Theology and the Christian Spiritual Tradition*. Sheffield: Sheffield Academic Press, 2003.

Dayton, Donald W. *Theological Roots of Pentecostalism*. Grand Rapids: Zondervan, 1988.

Dempster, Murray. "The Church's Moral Witness: A Study of Glossolalia in Luke's Theology of Acts." *Paraclete* 23 (1989) 1–7.

Ervin, H. M. *Conversion-Initiation and the Baptism in the Holy Spirit: A Critique of James D. G. Dunn's Baptism in the Holy Spirit*. Peabody, MA: Hendrickson, 1984.

Faupel, D. William. *The Everlasting Gospel: The Significance of Eschatology in the Development of Pentecostal Thought*. Sheffield: Sheffield Academic Press, 1996.

Fudge, Thomas. *Christianity without the Cross: A History of Salvation in Oneness Pentecostalism*. Parkland, FL: Universal Publishers, 2003.

Hagner, Donald A. *Matthew 1–13*. WBC 33A. Dallas: Word, 1993.

Hayford, Jack. *The Beauty of Spiritual Language: My Journey toward the Heart of God*. Dallas: Word, 1992.

Hezmalhalch, T. "Among the Indians at Needles, California." *The Apostolic Faith* 5 (January, 1907) 5.

Hollenweger, Walter J. "From Azusa Street to the Toronto Phenomenon: Historical Roots of the Pentecostal Movement." In *Pentecostal Movements as an Ecumenical Challenge*, ed. Jürgen Moltmann and Karl-Josef Kuschel, 3–14. Concilium 3. London: SCM, 1996.

———. *The Pentecostals*. 2d ed. Peabody, MA: Hendrickson, 1988.

———. "Theology of the New World, III: The Religion of the Poor Is Not a Poor Religion." *Expository Times* 87 (1976) 228–32.

Hunter, H. D. *Spirit Baptism: A Pentecostal Alternative*. Lanham, MD: University Press of America, 1983.

Land, Steven J. *Pentecostal Spirituality: A Passion for the Kingdom*. Sheffield: Sheffield Academic Press, 1993.

Lindbeck, George. *The Nature of Doctrine: Religion and Theology in a Post-Liberal Age*. Philadelphia: Westminster Press, 1984.

Macchia, Frank D. *Baptized in the Spirit: A Global Pentecostal Theology*. Grand Rapids: Zondervan, 2006.

Menzies, Robert P. *Empowered for Witness: The Spirit in Luke–Acts*. Sheffield: Sheffield Academic Press, 1991.

Seymour, William J. "The Same Old Way." *The Apostolic Faith* 1 (September, 1906) 3.

Stronstad, Roger. *The Charismatic Theology of St. Luke*. Peabody, MA: Hendrickson, 1984.

Yun, Koo Dong. *Baptism in the Holy Spirit: An Ecumenical Theology of Spirit Baptism*. New York: University Press of America, 2003.

2

The Inviting Spirit: Pentecostal Beliefs and Practices regarding the Religions Today

Amos Yong

Introduction

Historically, Pentecostals have not differed much from the exclusive theological beliefs of evangelicals (and fundamentalists) with regard to other religions and people of other faiths. However when Christian beliefs and practices are seen in their interconnectedness, the exclusiveness of Pentecostal beliefs is in some cases offset by a more inclusive set of postures and attitudes. The first two parts of this essay will present these two trajectories: 1) Pentecostal beliefs (theologies) regarding other religions and 2) Pentecostal missions (practices) vis-à-vis people of other faiths. The final section will present, through a re-reading of Luke–Acts (the Pentecostal "canon-within-the-canon"), a model of "the inviting Spirit" that provides a more coherent framework for Pentecostal beliefs and practices regarding other faiths. Central to this view will be an underscoring of how the many tongues of Pentecost open up toward many different practices with regard to the interfaith encounter today.

Pentecostalism and Exclusivism in Theology of Religions

At the heart of modern Pentecostalism is the experience of the Holy Spirit who empowers the Christian witness: "but you will receive power when the Holy Spirit has come upon you; and you will be my witnesses in Jerusalem, in all Judea and Samaria, and to the ends of the earth" (Acts 1:8).[1] This Lukan promise of the Spirit of God enabling the spread of the gospel to the ends of the earth is, from the Pentecostal point of view, what makes possible the Great Commission (Matt 28:19–20). Further, since it is Jesus who promises to send the Holy Spirit, and since "There is salvation in no one else, for there is no other name under heaven given among mortals by which we must be saved" (Acts 4:12), not only does the gospel itself center on the person and work of Jesus Christ, but the purpose of the gift of the Spirit is precisely to enable the proclamation of Christ so that all may be saved.

Pentecostal exclusivism regarding the non-Christian religions is less a primary theological dogma and more a by-product of the evangelical and missionary commitment characteristic of the movement's ethos since the early days of the revival.[2] In saying this, I mean only that for the most part, and up until recently, Pentecostal theologians have not given serious and extensive thought to theological reflection on the religions on their own terms. Rather, Pentecostal ideas about the religions have been generally imbibed from evangelical (and fundamentalist) sources, and put into the service of legitimating Pentecostal missions. We can see this trend at work by looking at a representative textbook of systematic theology in use at a major Pentecostal seminary.[3]

The first thing to notice is that there is no sustained discussion about other religions in its almost 700 pages. Rather, the eighteen chapters explicate the theological loci as developed in evangelical texts in systematic theology, with the exception of focused discussions on Pentecostal themes such as the baptism in the Holy Spirit, spiritual gifts, and divine healing. Yet if one reads carefully, there is at least an implicit theology of religions throughout the text.

One of the first references to religion in the main text defines it as "the search for the ultimate," and as "the human search for God."[4] Citing Augustine (rather than Barth), this sets the tone for the rest of the volume to distinguish religion, as human efforts to seek after God, from Christian

---

1. All scripture quotations will be from the NRSV unless otherwise noted.

2. E.g., Goff, *Fields White unto Harvest*.

3. Horton, *Systematic Theology*. I focus on this text only because I am affiliated with the Assemblies of God denomination and therefore most familiar with the broader context behind this book.

4. Horton, *Systematic Theology*, 40–41.

faith, in which God takes the initiative to reach out to human beings. Thus whereas the one true God has revealed himself to humankind, false religions are the result of the tendencies of human beings "to create fictitious gods that are easy to believe in, gods that conform to their own life-style and sinful nature."[5] In fact, against theories in the history of religions that posit an evolution of religion from polytheistic to monotheistic traditions, it is asserted that the original revelation gives way through processes of syncretism to the multitude of religions.[6]

Unsurprisingly, then, many of the references to the religions are found in the chapter on divine revelation. Following the Reformation distinction between general revelation, which provides knowledge of God's existence but is non-salvific, and special revelation, which mediates God's saving offer in Christ, the text says that the latter reveals the God of the Bible who stands "in stark contrast with the gods of polytheistic paganism."[7] More precisely, only special revelation is uncontaminated by sin, the fall, and the devil's mechanisms; in contrast, general revelation has been received by fallen human beings only to suppress the truth in unrighteousness, according to St. Paul in Romans 1. Hence we are cautioned against "seeing the human experience of the supernatural in non-Christian world religions as valid divine revelation. These religions do not speak with the voice of God but rather of Satan and his demons (see 1 Cor 10:20)."[8] Rather than preserving the truth of general revelation, "one must recognize these religions as serious distortions of God's true revelation. Persons seeking after God in false religions are not to be applauded as 'good enough.' The wrath of God is directed at them for their idolatry (Rom 1:18, 23–32)."[9] Hence God is justified in condemning the ungodly in other faiths not because they have not heard the special revelation of the gospel, but because they have suppressed and distorted the truth of general revelation that has been made known to all people.[10] Throughout, then, the authoritative revelation of God as preserved in the Bible is contrasted with the claims of other faiths as found in human figures (like

---

5. Horton, *Systematic Theology*, 117.
6. Horton, *Systematic Theology*, 118–19.
7. Horton, *Systematic Theology*, 67.
8. Horton, *Systematic Theology*, 68.
9. Horton, *Systematic Theology*, 74.
10. Horton, *Systematic Theology*, 75.

Sun Myung Moon or Joseph Smith) or even other texts considered sacred (such as the Koran).[11]

Elsewhere in the volume, we find a passing reference to Christian Science, Hinduism, Buddhism, and other New Age movements and trends. The context here is the discussion of the nature of sin, and the point being made is to illustrate the claim that some people, and the religious traditions to which they belong, "believe sin and evil are not real but merely illusions that may be overcome by right perception."[12] The related view of cosmic dualism, the idea that there are eternally opposed good and evil forces with the latter manifest in the impurity of material reality, is also to be found in non-Christian religions like Gnosticism, Manichaeism, and Zoroastrianism. In the contemporary scene, "In many versions of Hinduism and Buddhism, and their New Age offspring, evil is reduced to an amoral necessity."[13] These religious traditions are hence reduced to their false views about sin. When set in the wider context of the book, readers (students) are led to draw the conclusion that this results from non-Christian suppression and distortion of the truth.

There may be one final implication regarding the religions in the chapter on the mission of the church. Amidst the discussion of the Christian mission to the world, there is the statement that "The proclamation of Christ and His offer of salvation is not just an affirmation to ponder and dialogue about—it requires a decision (Matt 18:3)."[14] The inference here may be to the practice of interreligious dialogue, much more common in mainline Protestant circles, and the concern is that dialogue focused on understanding has displaced evangelistic and kerygmatic proclamation focused on repentance and conversion.

As already noted, this survey shows that Pentecostals have not developed a theology of religions per se; rather, their discussions of other religions occur in passing, during discussions of the more established theological topics. Further, we should also point out that there is nothing substantively "Pentecostal" in the views regarding other religions in the preceding observations. These are fairly standard claims made about other religions that can be found in the wider conservative Christian theologi-

---

11. Horton, *Systematic Theology*, 83.
12. Horton, *Systematic Theology*, 257.
13. Horton, *Systematic Theology*, 258.
14. Horton, *Systematic Theology*, 591.

cal world. Finally, that the bulk of the comments about the religions is to be found under the doctrines of revelation and of sin is no coincidence: if general revelation cannot save, and if false religions are connected to false views regarding sin that humans need to be saved from, then the centrality and urgency of the Christian mission to the non-Christian religions is all the more accentuated.[15]

The Pentecostal-Charismatic Movement and Inclusive Postures and Practices vis-à-vis the Religions

I now want to turn to Pentecostal missiologies in order to observe Pentecostal practices regarding mission and evangelism in multireligious contexts involving people of other faiths. Taking for granted that Pentecostal mission practices include evangelistic proclamation directed toward repentance and conversion, I want to highlight instead other trajectories that suggest a more inclusive and even dialogical view. As we proceed through this survey, the question I wish to pose up front is whether or not such practices are merely pragmatically (evangelistically) motivated or whether there is a deeper theological foundation upon which they might rest.

I begin with the work of Allan Anderson, one of the foremost missiologists of Pentecostalism today and currently Reader in Pentecostal Studies at the University of Birmingham (UK).[16] In a recent book on world Pentecostalism, Anderson calls for a more intentional Pentecostal theological engagement with other faiths. He reasons, first, that Pentecostal spirituality itself provides a platform for observing similarities and differences between religious traditions at the level of phenomenology, piety, and affections; and second, that it is precisely Pentecostal experience and practices that are more easily translatable into missionary contexts

---

15. I suspect that these generalizations hold true across the spectrum of Pentecostal systematic theological texts, as they do among this genre of books produced by the charismatic renewal movement. I have in mind here efforts such as by Duffield and Van Cleave, *Pentecostal Theology*; Hart, *Truth Aflame*; and Williams, *Renewal Theology*. However, to be honest, I have not re-read every word in the many pages of these volumes to confirm this claim.

16. See his latest work on early Pentecostalism and missiology, Anderson, *Spreading Fires*. My thanks to him for sharing a pre-publication draft of this book with me and inviting my critical comments.

permeated by other cultures and religions.[17] In fact, Anderson suggests that the global spread of Pentecostalism has been made possible precisely because its spirituality provides multiple points of contact with other religious cosmologies, spiritualities, and practices.

Anderson had already argued this point in detail in one of his first books (in 1991) on African religion and spirituality, *Moya*. "Moya" or "umoya," from the Sotho and Nguni languages of southern Africa, where Anderson had lived for most of his life at that point, can be loosely translated as "wind" and "spirit." From this, Anderson noted the congruity between the African and the Pentecostal "spirit" worldviews. The similarities observed regarding concepts of spiritual power and manifestations, the charismatic giftings of tongues and prophecy, spirit possession on the one hand and exorcism of evil spirits on the other, and rites designed to engage and even "manipulate" the spirit world, led Anderson to see greater continuity rather than discontinuity between Pentecostalism and traditional African religions. He concluded then that "The Holy Spirit has sanctified for his use religious expressions which are found in traditional Africa!"[18]

A central aspect of this continuity for Anderson was found in the holistic view of the universe in both Pentecostalism and in traditional African religions, with a concomitant holistic soteriology. By "holistic," Anderson meant the interconnections between the spiritual and the material worlds in both traditions, and the interrelatedness between religious beliefs and spiritual practices. At this level, Pentecostal Christian exclusiveness with regard to other religions had to be tempered, not undermining the absoluteness of Christ, but lifting up instead the points of contact that allowed for the much deeper enculturation and contextualization of the gospel in an African context. In other words, Pentecostal claims to exclusivity lay more at the rhetorical level of proclamation than at the practical level of missionary engagement.

The "holistic charismatic missiology" of Anglican missiologist Andrew Lord displays some similar features to that proposed by Anderson.[19] Lord understands "holistic" to refer to the interrelated saving work of God expressed in bodily healing, social reconciliation, and

---

17. Anderson, *Introduction to Pentecostalism*, 200–203, 235–37, and 282–84.
18. Anderson, *Moya*, 123.
19. Lord, *Spirit-Shaped Mission*.

ecological redemption. Because of this multidimensional soteriology, Lord proposes a pneumatological perspective that bridges the saving work of God in the present (in the church) with that of the future (in the coming kingdom). In this framework, Lord's concern is to articulate a dynamic, multifaceted, and contextualized missiology that is sensitive to the many arenas, forms, and structures in which the Holy Spirit is present and active.

Precisely for these reasons, the Christian mission is not only *to* people of other faiths, but also *with* them. Lord affirms the evangelistic mandate that is focused on proclaiming Christ through the body of Christ. At the same time, "we realise that the Spirit is already at work, in creation and in those of other faiths"; more precisely, "we may be moved alongside others of all faiths or none in social action, in protest for justice, in environmental concern."[20] Note that Lord's immediate context is the multi-faith society of Great Britain, and he no doubt recognizes that the British increasingly need to cooperate across faith lines in social, economic, and political initiatives. However, I also suggest that Lord is articulating theologically what Pentecostals have long been putting into missionary practice, whether that is in hospitals, orphanages, and rescue missions focused on meeting the physical needs of all people, in the public sphere involving politicians serving in office, or in the social domain involving activists engaged in civil rights and other grassroots movements. In each of these areas, interreligious relations are involved, either at the level of Pentecostals serving people of other faiths or at the level of Pentecostals working alongside people of other faiths to address and engage political, social, and environmental issues that are "larger" than what any one religious tradition can handle on its own.

Before moving on, I want to make some brief remarks about the work in theology of religions by Pentecostal missionary Veli-Matti Kärkkäinen.[21] Given his globe-trotting experiences (raised in Europe, educated in part in the U.S.A., and having served as a missionary to Thailand), Kärkkäinen has long been convinced that Christian theology must be ecumenical and global in its orientation. An early essay took up the question about the relationship between Christian missions and

---

20. Lord, *Spirit-Shaped Mission*, 102–3.

21. Kärkkäinen spent four years (1990–1993) as a Pentecostal missionary in Thailand. For a more in-depth discussion of Kärkkäinen's life and theological project, see Yong, "Whither Evangelical Theology?"

theology of religions, asking specifically what Pentecostal perspectives might contribute to the discussion.[22] More recently, Kärkkäinen has published two volumes in theology of religions, one introductory survey text, and the other a preliminary attempt to develop a trinitarian approach to the topic.[23] While Kärkkäinen in no way compromises his Christian convictions about the uniqueness of Christ, like Lord (while not citing Lord), he surmises that within a trinitarian framework, the idea of the one God constituted perichoretically by the three divine persons provides a theoretical model for understanding how the many religions of the world exist as communities of difference that may anticipate the eschatological unity-in-diversity of the kingdom of God.[24] But what is his main point behind this proposal? The "cash value," I suggest, is that for Kärkkäinen, a trinitarian theology of religions is able to respect and honor religious others and the differences they represent even while not negating the scandal of Christian particularity. In other words, such a theological approach underwrites the interfaith dialogue, both in terms of the mutual learning that takes place and in terms of the efforts to speak persuasively across religious lines.[25]

I suggest that Kärkkäinen's trinitarian theology of religions underwrites not only the kinds of interfaith dialogues that theologians have long been participants of, but also the ecumenical discussions that have been going on even longer. Put alternatively, sustained Pentecostal reflection on theology of religions emerges out of the recognition that we have long been involved in such ventures, but have lacked the theological rationale to justify such practices.[26] And it is not just formal interreligious dialogues that need theological justification, but also the kinds of dialogical relationships that exist in our globalizing world, wherein we now encounter neighbors and co-workers of other faiths, where religious diversity denotes not many religions each in their own parts of the

---

22. Reprinted as ch. 14 in Kärkkäinen, *Pneumatological Theology*.
23. Kärkkäinen, *Theology of Religions* and *Trinity and Religious Pluralism*.
24. Kärkkäinen, *Trinity and Religious Pluralism*, esp. 175–80.
25. Kärkkäinen, *Trinity and Religious Pluralism*, 180–81. On this point, see also the essays by Pentecostal pastor-scholar, Tony Richie: "Pentecostal in Sheep's Clothing," "Azusa-era Optimism," "God's Fairness," "Precedents and Possibilities," and "Neither Naïve nor Narrow."
26. That has been the motivation behind my own work in theology of religions; see Yong, *Discerning the Spirit(s)* and *Beyond the Impasse*.

The Inviting Spirit 37

world but many religions existing alongside one another in many parts of the world, and where, in our post-9/11 context, the practices of a small handful of people may have drastic reverberations for many religious communities.

The question I have in view of the preceding is whether Pentecostals will remain motivated only pragmatically in their practices relative to people of other faiths or whether we see the need for a more flexible and nuanced theology of religions commensurate with the many kinds of interfaith practices already at work in our time. A pragmatic response would say, for example, that our contextualization projects, social-political actions, and interfaith dialogues are all subservient to the ultimate goal of missions and evangelization, and that therefore they are accidental to the fundamental Christian practice of evangelism. In this framework, there is no need to rethink the exclusivistic theology of religions since these more dialogical practices are "back doors" to accomplish the mission of taking the gospel to the ends of the earth.

I suggest, however, that the missiological proposals of Pentecostals like Anderson, Lord, and Kärkkäinen represent an emerging consensus that classical Pentecostal exclusivistic theologies of religions are not necessarily completely wrongheaded, but that they need to be expanded precisely in order to keep up with the richness and multifacetedness of our interfaith practices. In this case, Pentecostal theological beliefs are being reformulated based on Pentecostal mission practices. There is an implicit acknowledgment that the reduction of "other religions" to the negative side of the ledger of general revelation and Christian salvation provides insufficient theological rationale for Pentecostal interfaith engagements in our time.

Transforming Pentecostal Theology of Interreligious Encounter: Many Tongues and Many Practices

I wish to sketch here a more flexible, nuanced, and expansive Pentecostal theology of religions captured in the motto: "many tongues and many interreligious practices."[27] Rather than undermining the exclusive Christological claims of Christian faith or evangelistic zeal of Pentecostal missions, I hope to enrich Pentecostal mission theology precisely by

---

27. I provide much more extensive argumentation for this, with full documentation, in the forthcoming Yong, *Hospitality and the Other*, esp. chs. 4–5.

making explicit on Pentecostal grounds a theology of interreligious dialogue and theology of interreligious social engagement. To do so, I will focus briefly on four pericopes in Luke–Acts, the Pentecostal "canon-within-the-canon."[28]

I begin with the launching of Jesus' public ministry at Nazareth (Luke 4). Here, Jesus himself announces, "The Spirit of the Lord is upon me, because he has anointed me to bring good news to the poor. He has sent me to proclaim release to the captives and recovery of sight to the blind, to let the oppressed go free, to proclaim the year of the Lord's favour" (Luke 4:18–19). The major point to note here is the central argument of Lord's missiology: that Christian mission involves, but is not limited to, the proclamation of the gospel; rather a holistic missiology recognizes that the Christian mission is empowered by the Holy Spirit (Acts) to do precisely what Jesus did through the same Spirit's power (Luke): meeting the needs of the poor, healing of bodies, delivering those oppressed, marginalized, and disenfranchised to the underside of society for whatever reason, and establishing the peace, justice, and righteousness promised for the ancient Hebrew year of Jubilee (the "year of the Lord" of this text).[29] Many different practices are involved in fulfilling these missionary commitments, as well as, might I suggest, many different tongues. Thus the Lukan narrative shows Jesus forgiving sins, raising the dead, healing the sick, feeding the hungry, challenging the complacency and hypocrisy of the religious authorities, and violating purity, ritual, and religious laws (even to the point of dying the death of a condemned criminal).

The parable of the Good Samaritan (Luke 10:25–37) provides a concrete illustration for how this Lukan soteriology might be worked out in a religiously plural world. As I have already provided more extensive commentary on this parable elsewhere,[30] let me make only three summary observations pertinent for our purposes. First, note that the main characters of this parable, Jews and the Samaritan, represented two religious traditions. But whereas those "in the know" (the Jews) failed to be neighbors to the man left fallen on the wayside by robbers, the "religious outsider" (the Samaritan) proved his neighborliness by showing hospitality to the religious stranger. Second, the Samaritan reveals the

---

28. I defend this methodological approach for Pentecostal theology in Yong, *Spirit Poured Out*, 83–86.

29. Helpful here is Prior, *Jesus the Liberator*.

30. See Yong, *Spirit Poured Out*, § 6.1.2.

The Inviting Spirit

second most important commandment—loving one's neighbor—in action, and not by proclamation but by the gift of hospitality. Hence, the Samaritan shows how the Spirit's empowerment of Jesus' salvific ministry is extended to those who would wish to be his disciples (as did the lawyer who originally questioned Jesus). What was needed was the works of love and hospitality, and it was these that mediated the saving work of God to those needing salvation. Finally, note also that in this case, the Good Samaritan becomes an interreligious dialogue partner for the Jews. On the one hand, the faith tradition of the "outsider" becomes a means through which the "insiders" (Jews) are reminded about the greatest commandments; on the other hand, the "outsiders" and "insiders" in effect have switched positions—the Samaritan host is now the "insider" knowing the truths and practicing the commandments—but yet without any "conversion" taking place. In short, the religious other is now the means through which God's saving presence and activity is mediated to the people of God. The implications of this for interreligious praxis are profound.

Turning now to the book of Acts, the wide range of the Spirit's ministerial empowerment in the life of Jesus cannot be underestimated, especially not if we read this book together with the Gospel of Luke. The second Lukan volume tells the story of how the promise of the Father (Luke 24:49) is fulfilled in the lives of Jesus' followers through the outpouring of the Holy Spirit (Acts 2). With this gift, the earliest Christians "began to speak in other languages, as the Spirit gave them ability . . . about God's deeds of power" (Acts 2:4, 11b). If in fact God was doing a "new thing" on the Day of Pentecost, such could only be communicated through a new language, more precisely, through many new languages of the Spirit. But new tongues produce new practices. We can see this in part in the formation of the new community of faith in which all things were owned and shared in common and in part in the new practices of table fellowship inaugurated by these followers of Jesus.

From this, I suggest that the many Pentecostal tongues should be understood not only linguistically with regard to the many people groups mentioned in the Pentecost narrative (Acts 2:9–11), but also culturally with regard to what they represented and socially with regard to this new work of God breaking barriers between men and women, young and old, slave and free (Acts 2:17–19). Here, the particularistic starting point of Christian faith in Jesus of Nazareth not only opens up to the multidimensionality of salvation manifest in his ministry but also "inaugurates an 'inclusive' history"[31] in the life of the early church. Part of the debate among the early Christians concerned how to understand what it meant to be followers of Christ as "day by day the Lord added to their number those who were being saved" (Acts 2:47b). The expansion of the church to include Hellenistic widows and their families, Samaritans, Gentiles like the Ethiopian eunuch, and godfearers like Cornelius and his household—many of whom were first proselytes to Judaism and later came to be followers of Jesus—all combined to shape the many tongues and practices of a diversified community under the confession of Jesus as Lord.

Last (but not least) for our purposes, I want to call attention to the narrative of St. Paul's shipwreck on the island of Malta (Acts 28:1–10). In this context, it was Paul (and his seafaring colleagues) who experienced salvation through the hospitality of the Maltese islanders (Acts 28:2, 10). While it is an argument from silence to conclude that no explicit evangelistic proclamation to the island's "barbarians" (βάρβαροι, Acts 28:2!) took place, apparently not even during the "long time" that they waited to see if Paul would escape death from the snake bite (vv. 5–6), this silence at least suggests that such was not the first priority for guests (even missionary ones!) cast ashore in a strange land, and that Luke himself did not think such an activity was sufficiently noteworthy to be included in his narrative. To be sure, Paul indeed "visited him [Publius] and cured him by praying and putting his hands on him" (Acts 28:8b), but he did so as a personal guest indebted to the hospitality of this chief official. First century hospitality protocols shaped the interreligious interactions between Paul as guest and the islanders as hosts.

Space (and time) constraints prevent us from further textual or narrative considerations, but enough has been said to warrant the following three summary observations. First, contemporary Christians following in the footsteps of Jesus and the early church should recognize that a similarly wide range of tongues and practices mark our identity and missionary endeavors. This is especially the case if we take seriously the empowerment of the Spirit first given to Jesus, but since the Day of Pentecost also available to his disciples, to release those oppressed and to proclaim God's year of Jubilee in the lives of the poor, the marginalized, and the disenfranchised on the underside of history. I note further that

---

31. Lochman, "Zeal for Truth," 110.

while some of these tasks might be accomplishable by Christians working alone (on their own), most of the wider-scale social, political, and economic factors underlying poverty, injustice, and oppression will resist parochial efforts of engagement. Only a cooperative venture across political, cultural, and religious lines can fully challenge and perhaps redeem these structurally broken realities. By this I do not intend to embrace all interreligious ventures uncritically, but to provide a wider soteriological framework, what Andrew Lord might call a holistic view, for reconsidering especially practices of social engagement that involve people of many faiths. In these cases, believers in Christ would be invited by the Spirit of God to participate in the mission of God manifest in the life of Christ. What this involves would be many interreligious tongues and the many interreligious practices that, from the Christian perspective, could be understood as orchestrated by the Spirit of God for the healing, reconciliation, and redemption of the world.

Second, I suggest that the "inclusive history" inaugurated by the outpouring of the Spirit on the Day of Pentecost has implications for how we understand and engage the diversity of religions in our time. The fact is that religions are not one thing beside social, cultural, and linguistic traditions; rather religions at least overlap with these other domains of human experience, if they are not actually constituted by them. Hence we never meet religious others apart from their social, cultural, and linguistic configurations, and these latter structures may provide us at least with points of contact, if not windows, into their religious worlds. This means that the earliest converts to Christ also shifted religious allegiances, but did so in ways that were not only discontinuous but also continuous with their previous religious identities. Becoming new creatures in Christ did not mean for Jews their ceasing to be Jews; rather, it meant that in light of their new following after the way of Jesus, their Jewishness was set into a new configuration, partly in extension but partly also in repudiation of their former religious beliefs and practices. Similarly, might I suggest that even at the level of Christian conversion, we do not cease dealing with interreligious issues, since part of what is involved in any conversion to Christ is an invitation into a process of redefining what that means for the broad spectrum of one's previous religious commitments.[32] It also means

---

32. Here I do not mean to elide over the differences between Judaism and other faiths vis-à-vis conversion to Christianity; my point, however, is that religious conversion inevitably involves both continuities and discontinuities, and that point holds across

that converts to Christ from other religious traditions will be learning both a new language and a new set of practices, commensurate with their newfound Christian faith.

Finally, the many tongues and many practices of the Spirit are meant to facilitate the salvation of the world, understood in its broadest senses, precisely because it is such a diversity (even plurality) of approaches that is needed to engage the fullness of the missionary task. Our response must be to be discerning about the many situations in which we find ourselves since it is such discernment that dictates which tongues (e.g., interreligious dialogues) and which practices (e.g., socio-economic-political engagements) are most viable. In the situations where we find ourselves as guests of those in other faiths, for example, there are certain codes of conduct that are more and others that are less appropriate; similarly, even when we are hosts to people of other religions, there will be an etiquette governing the extension of hospitality no matter in what culture we find ourselves. When hosting guests on one's "home turf," one can be bold in proclaiming the kingdom and preaching Christ (Acts 28:30–31); when on Mars Hill one rightly engages in philosophical-religious rhetoric and discussion;[33] or when shipwrecked on Malta one appropriately receives hospitality, even if at the hands of pagans and barbarians. Hence we are both those invited (guests) and also invitees (hosts), playing out different roles in different places and times, but always participating redemptively in the hospitality of God and thus already extending such an invitation to others, precisely through entering into relationship with them. For this very reason, the flexibility of such interreligious praxis is not political correctness read back into the New Testament; rather, it represents the Pentecostal commitment to being led by the Spirit that is but an extension of the Pentecost principle of many tongues and many practices (cf. 1 Cor 9:19–23).

---

the interreligious spectrum. For discussion of some of the issues, see Lamb and Bryant, *Religious Conversion: Contemporary Practices and Controversies*.

33. I have not commented on this text of Acts 17 precisely because it has long been debated in theology of interreligious dialogue literature. I agree with the interpretation of Kilgallen, "Acts 17:22–31," especially in his argument that the invitation to conversion in Paul's speech is nevertheless couched in and engaging of Hellenistic religious and philosophical discourse and assumptions.

Conclusion: The Inviting Spirit and Pentecostal Interreligious Postures/Practices Today

In this essay, I have not intended to overturn Pentecostal theological exclusivism regarding the person and work of Christ; rather, I have taken my cues from Pentecostal missiologists to seek a more robust theological platform capable of grounding the broad range of our interreligious practices in the twenty-first century. Without denying the importance of kerygmatic proclamation, we have seen that a more flexible set of attitudes and postures must be cultivated so that our missionary practices can be appropriate to the many different interreligious contexts of our time. On the one side, in democratically free countries like the U.S.A. and Canada, there is public space for street evangelism (although I suppose in Canada, that takes place only when the weather heats up!); but at North American meetings like the American Academy of Religion, this will have to give way to more sophisticated forms of interreligious dialogue and apologetics.[34] On the other hand, even if we stay in the democratic world, there are numerous other interreligious contexts in which street preaching, while legal, is politically and even religiously unwise. Such might be the case in Nigeria, where Muslim-Christian relations have been on edge over the last twenty-five years, or in Sri Lanka, where the Christian minority has to be as wise as serpents and as harmless as doves in the face of a hostile Sinhala Buddhist nationalist movement.[35] Yet in no case I can think of will hospitality be an inappropriate form of interreligious practice.

The Spirit who has been poured out on all flesh is the inviting Spirit in at least three different senses. First, the Spirit of God and of Christ invites all people to enter into God's hospitality manifest in the redemptive salvation of Christ. Second, the inviting Spirit empowers our own participation in the redemptive hospitality of God so as to carry out the mission of Jesus to all people, including those in other faiths. Finally, however, the inviting Spirit enables us to receive the redemptive hospitality of God through our interactions with others—whether Samaritans, barbarians, or those in other religious traditions. So we go forth in many tongues and many practices, encountering perhaps an even more bewildering diversity of tongues and practices in the process, inevitably being transformed through this encounter on the one hand, but maybe also serving

---

34. E.g., as articulated by Griffiths, *Apology for Apologetics*.
35. I discuss these cases in some depth in Yong, *Hospitality and the Other*, ch. 1.

as instruments in the hands of the inviting Spirit for the redemption of the many tongues, tribes, peoples, and nations on the other hand. Is this not the Christian hope anticipated in the promise of the eschatological outpouring of the inviting Spirit in these last days (Acts 2:17)?[36]

Bibliography

Anderson, Allan. *An Introduction to Pentecostalism: Global Charismatic Christianity.* Cambridge: Cambridge University Press, 2004.

———. *Moya: The Holy Spirit in an African Context.* Pretoria: University of South Africa Press, 1991.

———. *Spreading Fires: The Missionary Nature of Early Pentecostalism.* London: SCM, 2007.

Duffield, Guy P. and Nathaniel M. Van Cleave. *Foundations of Pentecostal Theology.* Los Angeles: L.I.F.E. Bible College, 1983.

Goff, James R., Jr. *Fields White unto Harvest: Charles F. Parham and the Missionary Origins of Pentecostalism.* Fayetteville, AR: University of Arkansas Press, 1988.

Griffiths, Paul J. *An Apology for Apologetics.* Maryknoll, NY: Orbis, 1991.

Hart, Larry D. *Truth Aflame: Theology for the Church in Renewal.* Rev. ed. Grand Rapids: Zondervan, 2005.

Horton, Stanley M., ed. *Systematic Theology: A Pentecostal Perspective.* Rev. ed. Springfield, MO: Logion, 1995.

Kärkkäinen, Veli-Matti. *An Introduction to the Theology of Religions: Biblical, Historical, and Contemporary Perspectives.* Downers Grove, IL: InterVarsity Press, 2003.

———. *Toward a Pneumatological Theology: Pentecostal and Ecumenical Perspectives on Ecclesiology, Soteriology, and Theology of Mission.* Edited by Amos Yong. Lanham, MD: University Press of America, 2002.

———. *Trinity and Religious Pluralism: The Doctrine of the Trinity in Christian Theology of Religions.* Burlington, VT: Ashgate, 2004.

Kilgallen, John J. "Acts 17:22–31: An Example of Interreligious Dialogue." *Studia Missionalia* 43 (1994) 43–60.

Lamb, Christopher and M. Darrol Bryant, ed. *Religious Conversion: Contemporary Practices and Controversies.* London: Cassell, 1999.

Lochman, Jan Milič. "The Zeal for Truth and Tolerance: Spiritual Presuppositions of Christian Ministry." *The Princeton Seminary Bulletin* 5:2 (1984) 106–17.

Lord, Andrew. *Spirit-Shaped Mission: A Holistic Charismatic Missiology.* Waynesboro, GA: Paternoster, 2005.

---

36. Thanks to Clark Pinnock and Steve Studebaker for their invitation to present a draft version of this paper at the Pentecostal Forum at McMaster Divinity College on 10 February 2007. Professor Pinnock was a theological mentor to me from a distance when I first began my journey in academia in the early 1990s. I am also grateful to Jeff Clarke for arranging McMaster hospitality for this event. Finally, thanks to my research assistant, Doc Hughes, for his help with various aspects of this essay.

Prior, Michael. *Jesus the Liberator: Nazareth Liberation Theology (Luke 4.16–30)*. The Biblical Seminar 26. Sheffield: Sheffield Academic Press, 1995.

Richie, Tony. "Azusa-era Optimism: Bishop J. H. King's Pentecostal Theology of Religions as a Possible Paradigm for Today." *Journal of Pentecostal Theology* 14:2 (2006) 247–60.

———. "God's Fairness to People of All Faiths: A Respectful Proposal to Pentecostals for Discussion regarding World Religions." *Pneuma* 28 (2006) 105–19.

———. "Neither Naïve nor Narrow: A Balanced Pentecostal Approach to Christian Theology of Religions." *Cyberjournal for Pentecostal/Charismatic Research* 15 (2006). No pages. Online: http://www.pctii.org/cyberj/cyberj15/richie.html.

———. "A Pentecostal in Sheep's Clothing: An Unlikely Participant but Hopeful Partner in Interreligious Dialogue." *Current Dialogue* 48 (2006) 9–15.

———."Precedents and Possibilities: Pentecostal Perspectives on World Religions: An Introduction to Theology of Religions." *Pneuma Review* 9:2 (2006) 70–71. (This is an "article in brief" that directs readers to the full online version, http://www.pneumafoundation.org/article.jsp?article=/article_0042.xml.)

Williams, J. Rodman. *Renewal Theology*. 3 vols. Grand Rapids: Academie Books, 1988–1992.

Yong, Amos. *Beyond the Impasse: Toward a Pneumatological Theology of Religions*. Grand Rapids: Baker Academic, 2003.

———. *Discerning the Spirit(s): A Pentecostal-Charismatic Contribution to Christian Theology of Religions*. Journal of Pentecostal Theology Supplement Series 20. Sheffield: Sheffield Academic Press, 2000.

———. *Hospitality and the Other: Pentecost, Christian Practices, and the Neighbor*. Maryknoll, NY: Orbis, 2008.

———. *The Spirit Poured Out on All Flesh: Pentecostalism and the Possibility of Global Theology*. Grand Rapids: Baker Academic, 2005.

———. "Whither Evangelical Theology? The Work of Veli-Matti Kärkkäinen as a Case Study of Contemporary Trajectories." *Evangelical Review of Theology* 30 (2006) 60–85.

3

Beyond Tongues: A Pentecostal Theology of Grace

Steven M. Studebaker

Pentecostalism arose and continues to see itself, at least in part, as a renewal movement within the Church. One of Pentecostalism's more significant contributions is to correct the tendency in other Christian traditions to marginalize the experience of the Spirit and the charismatic gifts. Early within the movement, Spirit baptism as a subsequent experience to salvation, for the purpose of empowered ministry and charismatic gifting, evidenced by speaking in tongues, became the chief way to express in theological terms Pentecostal experience and spirituality. Although the doctrine of the subsequence and normative experience of tongues may not be a hallmark of Pentecostalism worldwide nor of innovative projects by some contemporary Pentecostal theologians, historically within the North American context it is a *sine qua non* of Pentecostalism.[1]

The irony of Pentecostalism is that, although it has a heightened charismatic experience, its doctrine of Spirit baptism accentuates the subordination of the Spirit found in the evangelical (including the Wesleyan-Holiness) tradition from which it emerged. Pentecostals often sense deep kinship with evangelicals, but also are aware that their emphasis on charismatic empowerment and speaking in tongues distinguishes them from evangelicals. However, with the focus on charismatic experience, their fundamental similarities can be easily overlooked. The underlying

---

1. Macchia, *Baptized in the Spirit*.

structure of evangelical and Pentecostal soteriology is essentially identical and the Pentecostal doctrine of Spirit baptism acutely indicates this similarity.

D. Lyle Dabney compares Pentecostals trying to formulate their unique theological identity in terms of the foreign categories of evangelical theology to David clambering about in Saul's armor.[2] In order to regain theological mobility and to give the Pentecostal experience a suitable theological expression, Pentecostals must conceive the work of the Spirit in a way that transcends the limited framework of their traditional pneumatology, which primarily sees this work within the narrow confines of a specific dimension of Christian spirituality. Pentecostal theology can realize this by allowing pneumatology proper to inform its vision of grace and embracing a comprehensive pneumatological vision of redemption. This is not an effort to leave behind charismatic empowerment and gifts, but rather one to move Pentecostal pneumatology beyond its traditional compartmentalization and develop a more expansive Pentecostal theology of grace. To accomplish this, first, the essay demonstrates the theological background and source of the subordination of the Spirit in Pentecostal theology. Second, it presents a Pentecostal theology of grace that unifies the doctrine of grace from the perspective of pneumatology. It accomplishes this by beginning with the Holy Spirit's identity in the Trinity and then tracing the Spirit's work in the economy of redemption in relationship to that identity.

The Subordination of the Spirit in Pentecostal Theology

Heir to Protestant Scholasticism, the evangelical understanding of salvation reflects two dialectical structures or paradigms.[3] These are 1) the objective-subjective and 2) the achiever-applier paradigms. "Structure"

2. Dabney, "Saul's Armor," 115–17.

3. In the post-Reformation era of the late sixteenth and seventeenth centuries, the Protestant movements developed clear institutional and theological boundaries. This era and its theology are known as Protestant Scholasticism. Important Protestant scholastic theologians are Theodore Beza, William Ames, Francis Turretin, and Peter van Mastricht. The theology of this period is labeled *scholastic* because Protestants utilized the intellectual tools of medieval scholasticism to build Protestant theological systems. The utilization of scholastic methodology to systematize and articulate the theological insights of early Protestant reform movements produced Protestant Scholasticism (see Muller, *Post-Reformation*, 1:13–18, for a concise description of Protestant scholasticism).

or "paradigm" refers to the primary ways a theological system relates the works of Christ and the Spirit and articulates the content and nature of their works. In order to illustrate the affinity between evangelical and Pentecostal theology, the following first describes the paradigms in evangelical theology and then shows their presence and influence in Pentecostalism.

The Objective-Subjective Paradigm in Evangelical Theology

The evangelical doctrines of justification and sanctification reflect the objective-subjective paradigm.[4] Justification is the objective and extrinsic aspect of salvation. It is objective in two senses. It refers to the work of Christ on the cross and the imputed righteousness of Christ. Consequently, justification is not something that occurs *in* the believer. For example, John Calvin described justification in the following terms: "[J]ustified by faith is he who, excluded from the righteousness of works, grasps the righteousness of Christ through faith and clothed in it, appears in God's sight not as a sinner but as a righteous man.... Covered by the righteousness of Christ ... they should be accounted righteous outside themselves."[5] Justification teaches that Christ's work is for us (*pro nobis*), but outside of us (*extra nos*).

The governing metaphor of justification is the heavenly arraignment. Sinful humans stand guilty before a holy God and divine law and cannot make recompense for their infractions. Jesus Christ fulfills the precepts of God's law and suffers punishment in the place of the inadequate humans and thereby assuages the wrathful deity. The essence of salvation is to express faith in the surrogacy of Christ and thereby to receive the pardon of sin and the conferral of Christ's righteousness before the divine tribunal. Due to its penal emphasis, justification is primarily a forensic, Christocentric, and crucicentric doctrine. Moreover, the Spirit is absent from the work that provides justification. The Spirit plays only an instru-

---

4. For examples of this paradigm in the evangelical Protestant tradition, see Luther, *Luther's Works*, 25:245, 257, 334, 336, 340, 370; Calvin, *Institutes*, 3.11.2 (1:726–27), 3.11.11 (1:739–41), 3.11.23 (1:753), 3.14.21 (1:788); Turretin, *Institutes*, 16.6.1–3 (2:666–67), 15.1.5–7 (2:502–3), 17.1.10 (2:691), 16.2.9–10 (2:640); Wesley, *Works*, 1:453–58, 462 ("The Lord Our Righteousness") and 2:157–58 ("The Scripture Way of Salvation"); and Hodge, *Systematic Theology*, 3:137–41, 145, 213–16.

5. Calvin, *Institutes*, 3.11.2 and 3.11.11 (1:726–27; 1:740–41).

mental role in the application of justification by drawing the person to faith in conjunction with the written and/or declared Word of God.

Sanctification is the subjective or intrinsic transformation of the believer. The Spirit is the primary agent of sanctification. While Protestant theology maintains that justification and sanctification are not *separated*, nevertheless it affirms that they must be kept *distinct*. If justification and sanctification are not distinguished, then justification may be identified with or based on the process of sanctification, which is for most Protestants to undermine salvation by grace through faith. The result is that sanctification is not the primary datum of soteriology. A person does not look to their progress in sanctification for assurance of salvation, but to the righteousness of Christ—justification. Sanctification is not denied nor intentionally minimized, but since the crux of salvation is forensic justification, sanctification necessarily plays a secondary role. The intention is to preserve the gratuitous nature of salvation; nevertheless the outcome is the subordination of sanctification to justification.

The subordination of sanctification to justification produces a similar result in the relation between pneumatology and Christology. Since sanctification is the primary soteriological work of the Holy Spirit, the Spirit's work, by default, is functionally subordinate to the work of Christ.[6] Salvation ultimately rests on justification, the work of Christ, and not sanctification, the work of the Spirit. To be sure, the Spirit's work is necessary to prompt the faith that receives justification and the sanctifying work of the Spirit begins at the moment of conversion, but these works are never the ground or constitutive essence of redemption.[7] The Protestant goal, to affirm that redemption is free to believers, is correct. But the result is that the evangelical understanding of salvation tends to elevate Christology over pneumatology and extrinsic/imputed righteousness over personal transformation.

---

6. Badcock suggests that the Reformation doctrine of justification "results in a certain displacement of the Spirit from the center of the scheme of salvation" (*Light of Truth*, 97). Rusch also remarks that Protestant Orthodoxy tends to objectify soteriology and subordinate pneumatology ("Theology of the Holy Spirit," 25).

7. Althaus, *Martin Luther*, 240–45. Examples of contemporary evangelicals who represent this traditional view are Demarest, *Cross and Salvation*, 358–78; Erickson, *Christian Theology*, 3:969; and Grudem, *Systematic Theology*, 724, 727.

The Achiever-Applier Paradigm in Evangelical Theology

A second way evangelical theology subordinates pneumatology is in the achiever-applier paradigm.[8] The achiever-applier paradigm maintains that Christ achieves or accomplishes redemption and that the Spirit applies the benefits of his redemption. The provision and fundamental nature of salvation falls entirely under the category of Christology. The work that accomplishes salvation is Christ's life of obedience and his suffering on the cross, which correlates with Protestantism's hallmark understanding of justification by faith. Salvation principally consists in receiving forgiveness of sins and Christ's imputed righteousness.

The Spirit applies the benefits of Christ's work. Since Christ achieves salvation through his life, obedience, and vicarious death, the only thing left for the Spirit to do is to distribute the benefits of the redemption procured by Christ. In order to facilitate the application of redemption, the Spirit enlightens the mind, softens the heart, and inspires the faith necessary to receive the benefits of Christ. Secondarily, if albeit inevitably, the Spirit initiates and sustains the person's sanctification. The primary work of the Spirit is, therefore, portrayed in instrumental and not constitutional terms. That which saves is something Christ accomplished and the Spirit functions only to make that redemption available to the believer.

The argument that sanctification is not of the essence of redemption and that it is subordinate to justification does not mean that Protestants and evangelicals do not affirm its importance. Nevertheless, they tend to say that sanctification is not part of the fundamental nature of salvation, which is to be declared righteous before God's holy presence based on the penal death of Christ. To be saved is primarily to have faith in Christ's death as a payment for human transgression and not to be sanctified by the Spirit.[9] Traditional Protestant and evangelical theology sees this as its chief distinctive vis-à-vis the Catholic theology of grace, and insists on

---

8. For examples of this paradigm in Protestant and evangelical theology, see Calvin, *Institutes* 3.1.1 (1:537); Turretin, *Institutes*, 14.14.4 (2:465); Erickson, *Christian Theology*, 3:945, 968; Demarest, *Cross and Salvation*, 44–45; and Letham, *Work of Christ*, 81.

9. This line of reasoning is present in key progenitors of the three traditions that shape contemporary evangelical theology such as Martin Luther, John Calvin, and Charles Wesley: see Luther, *Luther's Works*, 25:245, 257, 334, 336, 340, 370; Calvin, *Institutes*, 3.11.2 (1:727), 3.11.11 (1:738–41), 3.11.23 (1:753); and Wesley, *Works*, 1:455–58 ("The Lord Our Righteousness") and 2:157–58 ("The Scripture Way of Salvation"). Hodge, *Systematic Theology*, 3:215–16, perennially popular among traditional evangelicals, gives this theology its classic Protestant scholastic expression.

this point in order to preserve the notion of justification by grace through faith.[10]

The Ordo Salutis in Evangelical Theology

The subordination of pneumatology to Christology comes to a third paradigmatic expression in the *ordo salutis* (order of redemption).[11] The *ordo salutis* is a method of explaining the logical, and to some extent, the temporal sequence of the various biblical facets of human redemption, such as election, calling, regeneration, faith, justification, adoption, sanctification, perseverance, and glorification.[12] The elements of the *ordo salutis* correspond to the objective-subjective paradigm. The objective aspects are justification and adoption. The subjective aspects are regeneration, faith, perseverance, and glorification, which comprehensively comprise sanctification.

Although the elements of the *ordo salutis* have a linear relationship (calling, faith, regeneration, justification, and sanctification), a hierarchical one also characterizes them. The hierarchy of the *ordo salutis* and

---

10. For example, see *Formula of Concord*, Article 3, in Tappert, *Book of Concord*, 472–75; Calvin, *Institutes*, 3.11.6, 11 (1:732, 738–41); Turretin, *Institutes*, 16.2.9–10, 16.2.19–21, 17.1.9–14 (2:640–41, 644–45, 690–91).

11. For the development of the *ordo salutis* from the Reformation era through Protestant scholasticism, see McGrath, *Iustitia Dei*, 219–40.

12. The above is a Reformed *ordo salutis*. For examples, see Murray, *Redemption*, 87. For traditional and contemporary examples, see Turretin, *Institutes*, 15.1—17.2 (2:501–702); Ames, *Marrow of Theology*, 153–74; Owen, *Works*, 5:28–32; Hodge, *Systematic Theology*, 2:639–82; 3:253–58; and Erickson, *Christian Theology*, 3:929–1002. Wesley arranged the elements of redemption as prevenient grace, repentance prior to justification, justification, new birth/regeneration, repentance after justification and the gradual process of sanctification, and entire sanctification. For background on the Wesleyan *ordo salutis*, see Lindström, *Wesley and Sanctification*, 113–20. The status of the *ordo salutis* in Wesley's theology is disputed. Randy Maddox prefers *via salutis* rather than *ordo salutis*. Maddox believes that Reformed scholasticism created the *ordo salutis* and that it is incompatible with Wesley's pastoral concern in the soteriological process (see Maddox, *Responsible Grace*, 157–58). In contrast, Kenneth Collins, while using the *via salutis* to describe Wesley's doctrine of salvation, nevertheless maintains that the *ordo salutis* underscores an essential aspect of Wesley's soteriology; namely, that the process of salvation contains perceptible stages of growth and advancement (see Collins, *Scripture Way*, 185–90). J. Kenneth Grider, a Wesleyan-Holiness theologian, has the following order of redemption: prevenient grace and repentance, justification, regeneration, initial sanctification, reconciliation, adoption, and entire sanctification (see Grider, *Wesleyan-Holiness*, 350–420).

attribution of certain of its aspects to Christ and the Spirit reflect the assumptions of the objective-subjective and achiever-applier paradigms. Although perhaps unintended, these paradigms and their consequence for the assignment of different works to Christ and the Spirit in the order of redemption reflect a twofold tendency toward subordination within the evangelical doctrine of salvation. On the one hand, evangelical theology subordinates the inner transformation of the believer or sanctification to the imputed righteousness of Christ or justification. On the other hand, it gives primacy to the work of Christ relative to that of the Spirit.

The Presence of the Paradigms in Pentecostalism

Evangelical theology provides the conceptual structure for Pentecostal theology. Although the language of the paradigms may not be central in Pentecostal preaching, they provide the framework for the Pentecostal way of relating the work of Christ and the Spirit. A survey of Pentecostal theology corroborates their influence. Below I cite Larry Hart's recent *Truth Aflame* for illustrative purposes, but additional documentary evidence from other important Pentecostal systematic theologies is in the notes. Although Hart's text is not a classical Pentecostal account in all respects, its purpose is to provide a current Pentecostal introduction to systematic theology, and reflects the traditional categories of the paradigms and their consequences for pneumatology.

First, Pentecostal theology follows the tendency of evangelicalism to define salvation in terms of the christocentric objective and pneumatological subjective paradigm. Larry Hart affirms that in the gospel, "God provides a twofold remedy with both an objective and a subjective pole: (1) the cross of Christ and (2) the Spirit of Christ." He calls the former justification and describes it as a forensic transaction in which Christ's death pays the debt of sin and provides the basis for God to acquit the guilty and declare Christians righteous. The subjective pole is the Spirit's transformation of the moral and spiritual condition of believers.[13]

---

13. Hart, *Truth Aflame*, 343, 354, 362, 390–91. Myer Pearlman, the early Assemblies of God theologian, stated, "the outward aspect of grace is provided by the atoning work of Christ; the inward aspect is the work of the Holy Spirit" (Pearlman, *Knowing the Doctrines*, 222). Also, see Gause, *Living in the Spirit*, 50 and Higgins, Dusing, and Tallman, *Introduction to Theology*, 119.

Second, Pentecostal theology casts the work of Christ and the Spirit in terms of the achiever-applier paradigm. Hart states, "we will explore the *application* of Christ's redemptive work, portrayed in the Scriptures as the particular domain of the Holy Spirit . . . [and] the Spirit alone can communicate to us the saving benefits of Christ's death."[14] On the one hand, this statement contains an obvious truth: Christ's work on the cross provides redemption. Yet at the same time, the language and theory behind it imply that the Spirit does not contribute to the benefits of redemption, but only to their distribution. Thus, the result is the reduction of the Spirit to the instrument or agent of applying the redemptive benefits otherwise earned by Christ.

In terms of the *ordo salutis*, late nineteenth-century Reformed and Wesleyan theologians identified Spirit baptism as a post-conversion aspect of the *ordo salutis*. They separated Spirit baptism from conversion and described it as a second or subsequent work of grace.[15] Once dislodged from conversion, three models of Spirit baptism emerged in nineteenth century Holiness and revivalist theologies. Holiness theologians united Wesleyan perfectionism and Pentecostal power under Spirit baptism.[16] In contrast to the Wesleyan-Holiness teaching that Spirit baptism is for the eradication of sin, Reformed revivalists emphasized empowerment for ministry as the primary purpose of Spirit baptism.[17] Finally, "Third Blessing" proponents argued that the believer should receive three works

14. Hart, *Truth Aflame*, 372, 363. For additional examples, see Gause, *Living in the Spirit*, 12, 20, 49; Higgins, Dusing, and Tallman, *Introduction to Theology*, 108; Jenney, "Holy Spirit," 397, 400, 417; Pearlman, *Knowing the Doctrines*, 286; Pruitt, *Fundamentals*, 205; Williams, *Systematic Theology*, 2:233; 3:33; and Williams, *Renewal Theology*, 2:4.

15. In dialogue with John Wesley, John Fletcher argued that Spirit baptism is a post-conversion experience that initiates entire sanctification (Knight, "John Fletcher's Influence," 26–27 and Dayton, *Theological Roots*, 48–54). Wesley maintained the concurrence of Spirit baptism with conversion. However, in time, Fletcher's view became dominant in the Wesleyan-Holiness traditions. For discussions on this issue, see Dieter, "Development," 68; Faupel, *Everlasting Gospel*, 79, 90; and Reasoner, "American Holiness," 133, 143.

16. Phoebe Palmer is an example of including perfection and power under Spirit baptism (see Faupel, *Everlasting Gospel*, 84–85).

17. Torrey, "Baptism," 12–16. For the Reformed evangelical background of Pentecostal theology, see Blumhofer, "The 'Overcoming' Life: A Study in the Reformed Evangelical Contribution to Pentecostalism" and "The 'Overcoming Life': A Study in the Reformed Evangelical Origins of Pentecostalism"; and Wessels, "Spirit Baptism."

of grace: conversion, entire sanctification, and Spirit baptism for empowered ministry.[18] The important point is that Spirit baptism became one discrete aspect of the *ordo salutis*. The primary work of the Spirit, therefore, became a sub-category of the broader topic of sanctification or subjective application of redemption.

Pentecostal theology generally adopts an Arminian/Wesleyan structure of the *ordo salutis*, but a Reformed revivalist view on the nature and purpose of Spirit baptism.[19] This means it linked Spirit baptism with empowerment for ministry in contrast to entire sanctification. Aside from initial evidence, the Pentecostal doctrine of Spirit Baptism is virtually indistinguishable from the Reformed revivalist teaching.[20] From the perspective of historical theology, the identification of tongues as the necessary concomitant to Spirit baptism is the unique permutation of Pentecostal theology to the doctrine of Spirit baptism popular in nineteenth-century revivalism. The result is that pneumatology features prominently in only one aspect of the order of redemption—Spirit baptism. While perceived to be at work in other facets of the order of redemption, the Spirit is generally neglected under these elements and only becomes prominent in Spirit baptism. Thus, Pentecostal theology mirrors the structural relationships between Christ and the Spirit embedded in the evangelical theological tradition.

The Influence of the Paradigms in the Pentecostal Doctrine of Spirit Baptism

The objective-subjective, achiever-applier paradigms, and the impact these have on the order of redemption provide the theological grammar for the Pentecostal doctrine of Spirit baptism. Pentecostals distinguish Spirit baptism from justification and conversion or salvation. One is

---

18. See Dayton, "Doctrine," 121 and Faupel, *Everlasting Gospel*, 87–90. For a contemporary account of this theology, see Pruitt, *Fundamentals*.

19. For Pentecostal organizations of the *ordo salutis*, see Arrington, *Christian Doctrine*, 2:20–21, 200–252; Higgins, Dusing, and Tallman, *Introduction to Theology*, 109–20; Pearlman, *Knowing the Doctrines*, 222–67; Pecota, "Saving Work;" and Wyckoff, "Baptism," 431, 446, 449.

20. For example, compare Torrey, "Baptism," 12, and the Assemblies of God position paper on Spirit baptism, General Council of the Assemblies of God, "Baptism in the Holy Spirit," 3.

saved by Christ at the cross and baptized in the Spirit at Pentecost.[21] As illustrated by the discussion of the broader evangelical tradition, the distinction between the proper works of Christ and the Spirit is not unique to Pentecostals. However, Pentecostal theology not only sees the Spirit's primary work in terms of the subjective category of redemption, it radicalizes the subjective nature of the Spirit's work by locating the Spirit's primary work in a post-conversion experience of empowerment for ministry. Whereas evangelical theology dislodges the Spirit's chief role from the objective work of Christ or salvation proper and places the Spirit's work under the broad subjective category of sanctification and application of redemption, Pentecostalism reduces it to an optional experience within the subjective category of grace. Spirit baptism becomes just one (optional) benefit within the *ordo salutis* that the Spirit applies to the believer. The result is that Pentecostal *theology* intensifies the subordination of the Spirit already present within the evangelical tradition.

The Pentecostal hermeneutical strategy of understanding the relationship between Lukan and Pauline pneumatology facilitates the compartmentalization of the Spirit to one aspect of the *ordo salutis*. William W. Menzies and Robert P. Menzies argue that the "Pentecostal gift . . . provides for witness, not justification before God or personal cleansing."[22] Thus, the defining feature of Pentecostalism has nothing to say about salvation itself or even sanctification, but rather relates to a narrowly conceived role of charismatic empowered witness. Gordon Anderson's suggestion is also a superlative case in point. In what Anderson calls the "Chuck Swindoll argument," he deals with the fact that a multitude of evangelical leaders, who have not had the experience of Spirit baptism, nevertheless have tremendously successful ministries. In an attempt to show that the Pentecostal doctrine of Spirit baptism does not entail spiritual elitism, Spirit baptism becomes just one of nine dimensions of Christian experience. Moreover, although Anderson affirms that Spirit baptism gives the believer more power for ministry, he admits that it is not ultimately necessary.[23] In light of the above critique, a clarification is in order. The issue is not whether or not Pentecostals emphasize the Holy

---

21. For example, see Dye, "Are Pentecostals Pentecostal?" 64–66.
22. Menzies and Menzies, *Spirit and Power*, 115.
23. Anderson, "Baptism in the Holy Spirit."

Spirit. They clearly do so in their lives and ministries. The question is: does their *theology* do justice to their *experience* of the Spirit?

A Pentecostal Theology of Grace

Pentecostals have tried to give their *experience* of the Spirit's work *theological preeminence* in the doctrine of Spirit baptism. However, the articulation of this doctrine through the inherited categories of the objective-subjective and achiever-applier paradigms reduces this work to an ancillary option. The solution is to see the Spirit at work in every dimension of the economy of redemption, both in respect to the incarnation and grace. As Pentecostal theology seeks to develop its distinct voice, it should undertake the task in an ecumenical and conversational spirit with evangelicalism and other Christian traditions. Indeed the day of Pentecost was an ecumenical event and contemporary Pentecostal theology can be enriched by listening to testimonies of the Spirit's work both from within and from without their tradition. With this in mind, the present proposal seeks to articulate a Pentecostal theology of grace in dialogue with the Roman Catholic David M. Coffey and evangelical Protestant Jonathan Edwards. Moreover, it seeks to put forward a comprehensive vision of the Spirit's work through an integration of Christology and pneumatology from the perspective of a fundamental trinitarianism.

Pneumatology and Trinitarian Identity

A Pentecostal concept of grace derives from pneumatology proper and is not only interested in pneumatizing soteriological motifs traditionally dominated by christological and moral emphases. As such, it begins with the Spirit's identity in the Trinity. Traditional Pentecostal approaches that focus on Spirit baptism and that detail the contribution of pneumatology to the conventional loci of systematic theology reflect a different methodology.[24] That is, they begin with the work of the Spirit in the economy of redemption. Their procedure mirrors christological thinking that begins "from below" instead of "from above," and trinitarian theology that begins with the economic rather than the immanent Trinity. The scholas-

---

24. Classical Pentecostals Menzies and Menzies, *Spirit and Power*, are an example of the former and Charismatic Baptist Clark H. Pinnock, *Flame of Love*, is illustrative of the latter.

tic terms for these different routes of theological reflection are the *ordo inventionis* and *ordo doctrinae*. Each direction is appropriate because of the unity of being and act in God. In other words, God's activity or what God does (economy) reveals who God is (ontology). This principle is the foundation, for example, of Karl Rahner's famous dictum "The 'economic' Trinity is the 'immanent' Trinity and the 'immanent' Trinity is the 'economic' Trinity."[25] Modern theology's preference to begin from below or with the economic Trinity reflects the epistemological and methodological concerns of modernism. However, in a certain respect, the ontological or immanent Trinity has logical and theological precedence because it shapes divine activity and thereby the content of revelation and redemption. Without discounting the importance and value of Pentecostal theologies that begin with the work of the Spirit, a Pentecostal theology of grace based on the identity of the Spirit can supplement them. Indeed, from a theological perspective, the Spirit's trinitarian identity or pneumatology proper informs the Spirit's role in grace.

The identity of the Holy Spirit assumed here derives from a version of the Augustinian mutual love model influenced by the insights of Jonathan Edwards and David Coffey.[26] A social vision of love is central to the mutual love model. The interpersonal movements involved in the concept of self-communication capture the social nature of love. Love, understood as self-communication, involves two elements: transcendent objectification and assimilation. First, love, as a transcendent act, goes forth beyond the self to another person/s in a concrete way (John 3:16 and 1 John 4:9). Second, the act of going forth is to draw or assimilate the other(s) into the ambit of the personal existence of the one who initially goes forth in love (John 17:20–26).

The trinitarian God reflects the self-communicative structure of love. God the Father eternally brings forth the divine person of the Son. The Son, therefore, subsists as the *transcendent objectification* of the Father's eternal act of self-communication (although the subsistence of the Son is immanent to the divine nature). The self-communication of

---

25. Rahner, *Trinity*, 22.

26. For Edwards' trinitarian theology, see Studebaker, "Jonathan Edwards' Augustinian Trinitarianism"; "Integrating Pneumatology"; and "Jonathan Edwards' Pneumatological Concept." The key texts for Coffey's theology, in chronological order, are *Grace*; "'Incarnation'"; "Proper Mission"; "Holy Spirit"; "Theandric Nature"; *Deus Trinitas*; "Spirit Christology"; and *Did You Receive the Holy Spirit?*.

God in the Son is necessary for the possibility of love in God because love requires an object of affection. The Son subsists by the Father's act of self-communication because of the unity of being and act in God. Since being and act are inseparable in God, the Son is a subsistence of the fullness (i.e., *homoousios*) of the divine being, and, therefore, a distinct divine person. The assimilation of the Father and the Son occurs in the subsistence of the Holy Spirit as their mutual love. The subsistence of the Holy Spirit as the love of communion that flows from the Father for the Son and from the Son for the Father completes the immanent circulation of love or self-communication because the Spirit unites the Father and the Son.

Stated in more personal terms, the Spirit is the divine person who constitutes the loving union of the trinitarian God. The Spirit is not an impersonal unifying power, but the divine person (a subsistence of the fullness of the divine nature) whose personal identity and action assimilates the Father and the Son into interpersonal communion. The Spirit's personal identity is the basic ontological datum that grounds all statements regarding the personal work of the Spirit.

Having established a fundamental trinitarianism and pneumatology, the next step is to build on its foundation a Pentecostal theology of grace. The transition to grace moves the focus from the Spirit's immanent identity to the Spirit's economic activity. Moreover, within the economy of redemption, the Spirit's role in the incarnation precedes grace. This means that the Spirit's function in the incarnation informs the Spirit's work in grace. With this in mind, the goal is twofold: 1) to develop a Spirit Christology that is paradigmatic for a pneumatological concept of grace and 2) to accomplish this coordination from the perspective of pneumatology.

Spirit Christology

The incarnation mirrors the trinitarian structure of the self-communication of God.[27] The eternal objectification and assimilation of the self-communication of God in the Son finds its fullest economic parallel in the incarnation of the Son in Jesus Christ. When the Father's love for humanity is objectified in the economy it brings Jesus' humanity into existence and into union with the Son. The creation of his humanity is necessary; otherwise, the objectification of the Father's love in creation

---

27. Coffey, *Deus Trinitas*, 60–65.

would not transpire. The union of Jesus' humanity with the Son takes place because all expressions of the Father's love have the Son as their final end and, therefore, bring the object (in this case Jesus' human nature) into union with the Son. Furthermore, the Father's love directed *ad extra* that achieves the incarnation is the Holy Spirit.[28] Stated in summary, the incarnation is an event in which the Father bestows love on humanity by communicating the Holy Spirit and through that communication of the Spirit achieves the creation and radical union of the Son with the humanity of Jesus Christ.

The incarnate Son completes the economic self-communication of God by answering the Father's love with a commensurate love. As Jesus develops, he returns love to the Father and is thereby bound in love with the Father. His love reaches its zenith on the cross. He cries, "Father, into your hands I commit my spirit" (Luke 23:46) and thus expresses his utter devotion to the Father. Jesus' love for the Father is the "incarnate" love of the Son because it comes to manifestation in and through the human capacities of Jesus. David Coffey clarifies that Christ's answering love to the Father is the "incarnation" of the Holy Spirit. Since the Son's love for the Father in the immanent Trinity is the Holy Spirit, his love for the Father in the incarnation is the Holy Spirit. But, it is an "incarnated" love because it is the Son's love for the Father expressed through Christ's humanity.[29] The important point for pneumatology is that in Christ the Holy Spirit is the *mutual love* of the Father and the Son. The Spirit is the love of the Father who unites the humanity of Jesus with the Son and the Son's love that unites Jesus with the Father.[30] Thus, the Spirit's role in the incarnation corresponds with the Spirit's trinitarian identity.

Pneumatological Concept of Grace

The development of the pneumatological concept of grace depends on its coordination with Spirit Christology. Christ paradigmatically expresses

---

28. Since the Father's love for the Son is the Holy Spirit and that which unites the Father to the Son, the Father's love directed toward Jesus' humanity is the same Spirit and terminates in the Son and thereby brings Jesus' humanity into personal union with the Son.

29. Coffey, "'Incarnation,'" 472–80.

30. For a fuller development of Spirit christology, see Studebaker, "Integrating Pneumatology."

what it means to be human and, what is, from the perspective of sinful humanity, redeemed humanity. To be saved is to become in some sense what Christ was. However, Jesus was the Christ through the activity of the Spirit. Thus, grace has an orientation to Christology and pneumatology because they mutually condition one another. In place of the bifurcation of Christology and pneumatology reflected in the paradigms already discussed, a Pentecostal theology of grace seeks to integrate them.

Grace and the Self-Communication of the Trinitarian God

The pneumatological concept of grace has two dimensions that correspond to the economic self-communication of God fully realized in Christ. The first aspect of the Spirit as grace correlates with the transcendent self-communication of God. In the initial movement of grace, the Father loves the human person, and in doing so communicates the Holy Spirit to the person. The result of the first dimension of the self-communication of God is that the Spirit is present with each human person from the moment of the beginning of their existence, calling them to fellowship with the Son and the Father. Although not all respond to the Spirit's call, many do, and come to faith in Christ.

When human persons yield to the Spirit as the Father's love (i.e., the first dimension of grace), they come into union with the Son through the same Spirit who united Jesus' humanity to the Son, and thereby participate in the assimilative dimension of the self-communication of God, or the Spirit as mutual love. Grace involves receiving the Father's love, which constitutes one a child of God, and then participating in the return of love to the Father whereby believers become, along with the Son, children of God who love the Father.[31] Moreover, grace is pneumatological because the Spirit constitutes the redemptive relationship between the human person and Christ and the Father. Grace is the participation of human persons in the economic self-communication of the trinitarian God, realized in Jesus Christ. Grace is pneumatological because the Spirit is the divine person who inducts human persons into the fellowship of the Son and the Father.

---

31. Coffey, *Did You Receive the Holy Spirit?*, 110–11.

Grace and the Incarnation

The Spirit's activities in incarnation and grace are formally identical, but not strictly equivalent. In the incarnation, the Spirit is the Father's love poured out on humanity, which achieves the hypostatic union of Jesus' humanity with the divine Son. In grace, the Spirit is the divine love who draws human persons into union with the Son and the Father. Thus, in the former the Spirit unites the concrete humanity of Jesus with the divine person of the Son, and in the latter unites human persons with the Son and the Father. The Son is the term of both acts of union.[32] Recognizing a correlation between grace and the incarnation does not entail identity between the two redemptive experiences. Human persons do not become incarnations of the Son, for that would obliterate their human personal identity. Whereas Christ is the union of human *nature* with the person of the Son, redemption brings human *persons* into union with the Son.

At this point, it is necessary to discuss the difference between human nature and person. On one level, there is no difference, as human nature is essentially a capacity for personal identity or subjectivity. On another level, we can draw a distinction between a specific person and the capacity for personhood. Yet, this is always done at the level of abstraction because the capacity for personhood always exists in an individuated person. Moreover, although speaking of capacity gives the impression of being abstract, this is not the case in the incarnation. In the incarnation, the Son comes into union not with an abstract human capacity for personhood, but with the concrete capacity of Jesus. Jesus' personal identity is never a purely unthematized one or an abstract capacity, but always that of the divine Son coming to expression in and through Jesus' capacities for human personhood. The union of the incarnation produces a unified personal identity—i.e., a hypostatic union. The Son exists in and through the personal capacities of Jesus Christ's humanity and his humanity exists in and through the person of the divine Son.

In a similar although not univocal way, grace brings forth a unity of persons, namely, the person of the believer and Christ. The believer possesses a distinct personal identity that comes into fellowship with the Son. Christians are not incarnations of the Son, for that occurred only once in Jesus Christ. However, the Christian is a child of God. As Christ was the

---

32. Coffey, "Proper Mission," 227–39; *Deus Trinitas*, 60–65; *Grace*, 147–55; "Spirit Christology," 326–28; and "'Incarnation."

specific humanity of Jesus brought into union with the divine Son, so the Christian is a human person brought into union with the divine Son. In both instances, the Spirit is the divine person who draws humanity in the incarnation and human persons in grace into relationship with the Son and thereby also with the Father.

Pneumatological Grace and a Relational Redemption

The pneumatological concept of grace is relational because it posits the person of the Spirit as the essential nature of grace. Catholic theologian David Coffey points out that the Holy Spirit unites believers to God in a "mediated immediacy." Believers experience a *mediated* relation to the Father and the Son and an *immediate* relation to the Holy Spirit.[33] Through the Spirit they are drawn into communion with the Father and the Son. The believer's relation with the Spirit is immediate and with the Father and the Son mediate, precisely because of its personal nature. This means that believers have a mediated relationship with the Father and the Son because they are brought into relationship with them through their immediate relation with the Holy Spirit. Yet at the same time, and by virtue of the unity of the divine essence, they have an immediate relation to the divine persons.

The obvious dialectic of this pattern is unavoidable because theology must affirm both the irreducible reality of the three persons and the indivisible nature of the divine essence. The same dialectic is present in the immanent Trinity. The divine persons have immediate union with one another because of the unicity of the divine essence, but at the same time, the Spirit subsists as the mutual love that mediates or unites the Father and the Son.[34] Despite the insuperable dialectic, the mediatory role of the Spirit helps to pinpoint why the Spirit is grace. Since the Spirit is the divine person who draws the believer into the ambit of trinitarian fellowship, the Spirit is grace. Grace is the experience of possessing the Spirit and of being possessed by the Spirit and thereby assimilated to the fellowship of the Father and the Son.[35]

The recognition of the Spirit's mediating role is what makes grace pneumatological, and yet it also entails relationship with the Son and the

---

33. Coffey, *Did You Receive the Holy Spirit?*, 74–75, 87–88.
34. Coffey, *Did You Receive the Holy Spirit?*, 102.
35. Coffey, *Did You Receive the Holy Spirit?*, 104.

Father. Given the trinitarian nature of redemption, why define grace as pneumatological when redemption is thoroughly trinitarian? Why not call it a trinitarian concept of grace? The reason is that grace is specifically the divine person who brings the human person into redemption. Although the Father and the Son are essential, the Spirit is the point of entry. Redemption is the process in which the Spirit draws human persons into union with the trinitarian God. The Spirit is the divine person communicated to human persons and through whom they have their initial and primary relationship with the Father and the Son. The Holy Spirit is the divine love who unites the divine persons and thus is also the divine person who unites human persons with the Father and the Son.[36] Since redemption consists in union with the trinitarian God, and the Spirit acts to realize that union between God and believers, the Spirit is properly referred to as grace; thus, we have a pneumatological concept of grace. Salvation begins when the Spirit brings the person into relationship with the Father and the Son. The divine and human society produced through the initiative of the Spirit of grace reflects the structure of the Trinity. As mutual love constitutes the social life of the Father and the Son, so also it characterizes the relationship between individual believers and God and of the saints collectively with each other and the trinitarian God.

The Yield of a Pentecostal Theology of Grace

With the theology of grace outlined, we can highlight several ways that it moves beyond the traditional assumptions of grace in Pentecostal theology. First, the Pentecostal theology of grace integrates Christology and pneumatology. This is in contrast to the tendency of traditional evangelical and Pentecostal theology to divide salvation into discrete christological and pneumatological dimensions, corresponding respectively to justification and sanctification, and intensified in the doctrine of Spirit baptism. On the basis of the Spirit's identity in the Trinity, and the correlation between the immanent identity and economic activity, the Spirit plays a constitutive role in incarnation and grace. What this means is that the work of the Spirit is formative and substantive for the reality of both the incarnation and grace. Moreover, the Spirit's work in both is symmetrical and, therefore, incarnation and grace are corresponding realities (although the uniqueness of the incarnation must be maintained). The

---

36. Edwards, *Ethical Writings*, 8:377–86.

Pentecostal theology of grace proposed here, which integrates Christology and pneumatology, is of another sort than the traditional paradigm that trades on the essential difference between Christ's work for us and the Spirit's work in us. Indeed, if one accepts the integration of Christology and pneumatology, then the traditional isolation of christological and pneumatological dimensions of redemption breaks down.

The Pentecostal theology of grace also achieves a comprehensive account of the Spirit's work in the economy of redemption, in place of traditional Pentecostal theology's compartmental perspective. In contrast to the Pentecostal practice of locating the primary work of the Spirit in one dimension of grace, the gift of the Spirit becomes the essence of grace. Rather than being merely an optional benefit of redemption, the gift of the Spirit is the very substance of redemption.

Finally, the personal nature of the Pentecostal theology of grace replaces the judicial paradigm with a relational one. It continues to affirm salvation by grace through faith, but recasts this in relational categories. Salvation is by grace through faith because the liberation of humanity from sin for new life occurs only through the loving and personal presence of the Spirit who draws believers into the fellowship of the trinitarian God. Salvation is a work of the Spirit that recapitulates in the believer the union of humanity achieved through the Spirit in the incarnation. Just as the Holy Spirit provided the foundation and horizon of Jesus' life through union with the Son, so the Spirit opens up a similar possibility of transformed life in union with the Son for the believer.

Conclusion

Pentecostalism is paradoxical. On the hand, it has, over the past century, facilitated a global renewal of the explicit experience of the Holy Spirit and charismatic manifestations. On the other hand, its defining doctrine of Spirit baptism radically subordinates the theological importance of the Spirit. In other words, its theology of the Holy Spirit has not kept pace with its experience of the Spirit. The source of Pentecostalism's anemic pneumatology lies in its tendency to adopt the soteriological paradigms of Protestant Evangelicalism. The theology of the paradigms can be summarized as 1) Christ accomplishes the objective work on the cross that justifies the person and 2) the Spirit subjectively applies redemption, which is understood primarily in terms of sanctification. According to these paradigms, the Holy Spirit operates in the subjective aspects of the order of redemption. Pentecostal theology extends this logic by locating the Spirit's primary work in one dimension of the subjective category—Spirit baptism. Thus, Pentecostals have a pneumatological aspect of redemption, but not a vision of grace comprehensively informed by pneumatology. The solution proposed here turns to the Trinity and articulates a theology of the Spirit as grace from the Spirit's trinitarian identity. This achieves a Pentecostal theology of grace, by conceiving of the gift of the Holy Spirit as the essence of grace rather than as merely one of the gifts of grace.

Bibliography

Althaus, Paul. *The Theology of Martin Luther*. Translated by Robert C. Schultz. Philadelphia: Fortress, 1966.

Ames, William. *The Marrow of Theology*. Translated by John D. Eusden. Boston: Pilgrim, 1968.

Anderson, Gordon L. "Baptism in the Holy Spirit, Initial Evidence, and a New Model." *Paraclete* 27 (1993) 1–10.

Arrington, French L. *Christian Doctrine: A Pentecostal Perspective*. 3 vols. Cleveland, TN: Pathway, 1992–1994.

Badcock, Gary D. *Light of Truth and Fire of Love: A Theology of the Holy Spirit*. Grand Rapids: Eerdmans, 1997.

Blumhofer, Edith L. "The 'Overcoming' Life: A Study in the Reformed Evangelical Contribution to Pentecostalism." *Pneuma* 1 (1979) 7–19.

———. "The 'Overcoming Life': A Study in the Reformed Evangelical Origins of Pentecostalism." Ph.D. diss., Harvard University, 1977.

Calvin, John. *Institutes of the Christian Religion*. Edited by John T. McNeill. Translated by Ford Lewis Battles. 2 vols. Library of Christian Classics 20. Philadelphia: Westminster, 1960.

Coffey, David M. *Deus Trinitas: The Doctrine of the Triune God*. New York: Oxford University Press, 1999.

———. "Did You Receive the Holy Spirit When You Believed?" *Some Basic Questions for Pneumatology*. The Père Marquette Lecture in Theology. Milwaukee: Marquette University Press, 2005.

———. *Grace: The Gift of the Holy Spirit*. Faith and Culture 2. Sydney, Australia: Catholic Institute of Sydney, 1979.

———. "The Holy Spirit as the Mutual Love of the Father and the Son." *Theological Studies* 51 (1990) 193–229.

———. "The 'Incarnation' of the Holy Spirit." *Theological Studies* 45 (1984) 466–80.

———. "A Proper Mission of the Holy Spirit." *Theological Studies* 47 (1986) 227–50.

———. "Spirit Christology and the Trinity." In *Advents of the Spirit: An Introduction to Pneumatology*, edited by Bradford E. Hinze and D. Lyle Dabney, 315–38. Marquette Studies in Theology 30. Milwaukee: Marquette University Press, 2001.

———. "The Theandric Nature of Christ." *Theological Studies* 60 (1999) 405–31.

Collins, Kenneth J. *The Scripture Way of Salvation: The Heart of John Wesley's Theology*. Nashville: Abingdon, 1997.

Dabney, D. Lyle. "Saul's Armor: The Problem and Promise of Pentecostal Theology Today." *Pneuma* 23 (2001) 115–46.

Dayton, Donald W. "The Doctrine of the Baptism of the Holy Spirit: Its Emergence and Significance." *Wesleyan Theological Journal* 13 (1978) 114–26.

———. *Theological Roots of Pentecostalism*. Grand Rapids: Francis Asbury, 1987.

Demarest, Bruce. *The Cross and Salvation: The Doctrine of Salvation*. Foundations of Evangelical Theology 1. Wheaton: Crossway, 1997.

Dieter, Melvin E. "The Development of 19th Century Holiness Theology." *Wesleyan Theological Journal* 20 (1985) 61–77.

Dye, Colin. "Are Pentecostals Pentecostal?: A Revisit to the Doctrine of Pentecost." *The Journal of the European Pentecostal Theological Association* 19 (1999) 56–80.

Edwards, Jonathan. *The Works of Jonathan Edwards*. Vol. 8. *Ethical Writings*, edited by Paul Ramsey. New Haven: Yale University Press, 1989.

Erickson, Millard J. *Christian Theology*. 3 vols. Grand Rapids: Baker, 1983–1985.

Faupel, D. William. *The Everlasting Gospel: The Significance of Eschatology in the Development of Pentecostal Thought*. Journal of Pentecostal Theology Supplement Series 10. Sheffield: Sheffield Academic Press, 1996.

Gause, R. Hollis. *Living in the Spirit: The Way of Salvation*. Cleveland, TN: Pathway, 1980.

General Council of the Assemblies of God. "The Baptism in the Holy Spirit: The Initial Experience and Continuing Evidences of the Spirit-Filled Life." Position paper adopted by the General Presbytery of the General Council of the Assemblies of God, August 11, 2000 (also found at http://www.ag.org/top/Beliefs/Position_Papers/pp_4185_spirit-filled_life.cfm).

Grider, J. Kenneth. *A Wesleyan-Holiness Theology*. Kansas City: Beacon Hill, 1994.

Grudem, Wayne. *Systematic Theology: An Introduction to Biblical Doctrine*. Grand Rapids: Zondervan, 1994.

Hart, Larry D. *Truth Aflame: Theology for the Church in Renewal*. Rev. ed. Grand Rapids: Zondervan, 2005.

Higgins, John R., Michael L. Dusing, and Frank D. Tallman. *An Introduction to Theology: A Classical Pentecostal Perspective*. Dubuque, IA: Kendall/Hunt, 1994.

Hodge, Charles. *Systematic Theology*. 3 vols. 1871. Reprint, Grand Rapids: Eerdmans, 1970.

Horton, Stanley M., ed. *Systematic Theology: A Pentecostal Perspective*. Rev. ed. Springfield, MO: Logion, 1995.

Jenney, Timothy P. "The Holy Spirit and Sanctification." In *Systematic Theology: A Pentecostal Perspective*, edited by Stanley M. Horton, 397–421. Rev. ed. Springfield, MO: Logion, 1995.

Knight, John A. "John Fletcher's Influence on the Development of Wesleyan Theology in America." *Wesleyan Theological Journal* 13 (1978) 13–33.

Letham, Robert. *The Work of Christ.* Contours of Christian Theology. Downers Grove, IL: InterVarsity Press, 1993.

Lindström, Harald. *Wesley and Sanctification: A Study in the Doctrine of Salvation.* Translated by H. S. Harvey. 1946. Reprint, Grand Rapids: Francis Asbury, 1980.

Luther, Martin. *Luther's Works.* Edited by Hilton C. Oswald. Translated by Walter G. Tillmanns and Jacob A. O. Preus. Vol. 25, *Lectures on Romans: Glosses and Scholia.* Saint Louis: Concordia, 1972.

Macchia, Frank D. *Baptized in the Spirit: A Global Pentecostal Theology.* Grand Rapids: Zondervan, 2006.

Maddox, Randy L. *Responsible Grace: John Wesley's Practical Theology.* Nashville: Kingswood Books, 1994.

McGrath, Alister E. *Iustitia Dei: A History of the Christian Doctrine of Justification.* 2d ed. Cambridge: Cambridge University Press, 1998.

Menzies, William W. and Robert P. Menzies. *Spirit and Power: Foundations of Pentecostal Experience.* Grand Rapids: Zondervan, 2000.

Muller, Richard A. *Post-Reformation Reformed Dogmatics.* Vol. 1, *Prolegomena to Theology.* Grand Rapids: Baker, 1987.

Murray, John. *Redemption: Accomplished and Applied.* 1955. Reprint, Carlisle, PA: Banner of Truth and Trust, 1979.

Owen, John. *The Works of John Owen.* Edited by Thomas Russell. Vol. 5, *Two Short Catechisms.* London: Richard Baynes, 1826.

Pearlman, Myer. *Knowing the Doctrines of the Bible.* Rev. ed. Springfield, MO: Gospel Publishing House, 1981.

Pecota, Daniel B. "The Saving Work of Christ." In *Systematic Theology: A Pentecostal Perspective*, edited by Stanley M. Horton, 354–72. Rev. ed. Springfield, MO: Logion, 1995.

Pinnock, Clark H. *Flame of Love: A Theology of the Holy Spirit.* Downers Grove, IL: InterVarsity Press, 1996.

Pruitt, Raymond M. *Fundamentals of the Faith.* Cleveland, TN: White Wing, 1995.

Rahner, Karl. *The Trinity.* Translated by Joseph Donceel. Introduction by Catherine Mowry LaCugna. 1970. Reprint, New York: Crossroad, 1998.

Reasoner, Victor P. "The American Holiness Movement's Paradigm Shift concerning Pentecost." *Wesleyan Theological Journal* 31 (1996) 132–46.

Rusch, William G. "The Theology of the Holy Spirit and the Pentecostal Churches in the Ecumenical Movement." *Pneuma* 9 (1987) 17–30.

Studebaker, Steven M. "Integrating Pneumatology and Christology: A Trinitarian Modification of Clark H. Pinnock's Spirit Christology." *Pneuma* 28 (2006) 5–20.

———. "Jonathn Edwards' Pneumatological Concept of Grace and Dispositional Soteriology: Resources for an Evangelical Inclusivism." *Pro Ecclesia* 14 (2005) 324–39.

———. "Jonathan Edwards' Social Augustinian Trinitarianism: An Alternative to a Recent Trend." *Scottish Journal of Theology* 56 (2003) 268–85.

Tappert, Theodore G., trans. and ed. *The Book of Concord: The Confessions of the Evangelical Lutheran Church*. Philadelphia: Mühlenberg Press, 1959.

Torrey, R. A. "The Baptism with the Holy Spirit." In *Late Nineteenth Century Revivalist Teachings on the Holy Spirit*, edited by Donald W. Dayton, 9–20. The Higher Christian Life. New York: Garland, 1985.

Turretin, Francis. *Institutes of Elenctic Theology*. Edited by James T. Dennison, Jr. Translated by George M. Giger. 3 vols. Phillipsburg, NJ: Presbyterian and Reformed, 1992–1997.

Wesley, John. *The Works of John Wesley*. Edited by Albert C. Outler. Vol. 1, *Sermons 1, 1–33*. Vol. 2, *Sermons 2, 34–70*. Nashville: Abingdon, 1984–1985.

Wessels, Roland. "The Spirit Baptism, Nineteenth Century Roots." *Pneuma* 14 (1992) 127–57.

Williams, E. S. *Systematic Theology*. 3 vols. Springfield, MO: Gospel Publishing House, 1953.

Williams, J. R. *Renewal Theology: Salvation, the Holy Spirit, and Christian Living*. 3 vols. Grand Rapids: Academie Books, 1991.

Wyckoff, John W. "The Baptism in the Holy Spirit." In *Systematic Theology: A Pentecostal Perspective*, edited by Stanley M. Horton, 423–55. Rev. ed. Springfield, MO: Logion, 1995.

4

This Spirit Is God: A Pentecostal Perspective on the Doctrine of the Divine Attributes

Andrew K. Gabriel

Introduction

> What do we understand by the word "God"? What comes spontaneously to mind when we hear this term? Most likely the answer will be: *Father*. Or perhaps even more emphatically: the *Super Father*, who transcends the world and to whom we pray. What is sure, however, is that the word "God" does not lead us *in the first place to think of the Holy Spirit*. This discloses a quite fundamental deficiency of our conscious faith and of our piety.[1]

This quote expresses the background of and reason for the journey on which I would like to go with this essay. As in classical theism, Pentecostals have tended to neglect the triune nature of God in their understanding of God's attributes. While theologians have begun to integrate christological implications into their revisions of classical theism, they have regularly ignored the Holy Spirit when modifying the classical doctrine of God. In an effort to be more adequately trinitarian, this essay offers a Pentecostal perspective on the doctrine of God by advocating for and exploring the potential of a pneumatological approach to the doctrine of the divine attributes. I will argue that considering the work of the Spirit leads to a new appreciation and perspective regarding God's immanence. I begin

---

1. Mühlen, "Holy Spirit as Person," 11.

by noting the lack of trinitarian reflection with respect to the doctrine of God's attributes within the Christian tradition, including Pentecostalism, and then suggest that the traditional Pentecostal approach to the biblical text inhibits this reflection. I then assess the current state of pneumatology in relation to the doctrine of God. From there, I will proceed by outlining the grounds for a pneumatological approach and then propose trajectories on which it seems that a pneumatological approach leads us. This pneumatological approach works out the implications that the same Spirit Pentecostals experience in worship and devotion, this Spirit is God. We will see that although the Holy Spirit has historically been neglected in forming the doctrine of the divine attributes, the Spirit is integral to our understanding of who God is, especially in understanding God as immanent.

A Lack of Trinitarian Reflection on the Doctrine of God

Many contemporary theologians have observed that in classical theology the doctrine of the divine attributes was ruled by philosophical theology.[2] Granted, we may admit with Veli-Matti Kärkkäinen that "in reality, the term 'classical theism' is a scholarly construction existing only in the minds of theologians, a generic concept drafted in hindsight to point out some dominant features in the development of the doctrine of God among Christian theologians." Nevertheless, in his recent historical survey of the doctrine of God, Kärkkäinen does concur that historically "much of the plurality of the biblical dynamic view of God was lost."[3]

In classical theology, the two main ways of discussing God's attributes were through philosophical negation (negative theology) and analogical predication, to the neglect of the divine trinitarian economy. That is, one would either focus on what God is "not" to somehow give a picture of what God is like, or one would make God into a super-human by predicating of God the greatest of human attributes (e.g., strongest, wisest). In all of this, however, the fact that God is three divine persons was generally neglected, and the God of the biblical narrative was made to fit into these philosophical categories. With respect to the theology of the divine attributes, Colin Gunton observes that the pattern has been an "ignoring of particular divine actions, with the exception of the most

2. Johnson, *She Who Is*, 19–21.
3. Kärkkäinen, *Doctrine of God*, 121.

general appeal to dogmatic Christology."[4] Gunton's latter statement regarding Christology marks, nevertheless, an important step toward a trinitarian doctrine of God. That which is probably the most familiar example in contemporary theology can be found in Jürgen Moltmann's *The Crucified God*. Here Moltmann provides a christological critique of the classical doctrine of the impassibility of God. In the classical tradition, Aquinas wrote that "a relation of God to creatures, is not a reality in God, but in the creature."[5] For Aquinas, God is immutable (not subject to change) since what is perfect (here, God) cannot be subject to change.[6] In contrast, based upon the incarnation of the Son of God in Jesus Christ and his suffering on the cross, Moltmann asserts that God does suffer an "active suffering, the suffering of love, in which one voluntarily opens himself to the possibility of being affected by another."[7] By following Moltmann's lead of finding the immanent Trinity truly present in the economic Trinity, I would suggest that pneumatology must also be taken as an avenue into the doctrine of God.[8]

Although Pentecostals have attempted to be more biblical than philosophical in their approach to the doctrine of God, a select survey of Pentecostal presentations of the doctrine of God reveals that, as with classical theism, Pentecostals have neglected the trinitarian nature of God.[9] Like classical theists, Pentecostals do affirm that God is triune,[10] but have not adequately integrated this confession into their doctrine of God's attributes.

Though published in 1993, well after the revival of trinitarian theology, William Menzies and Stanley Horton's *Bible Doctrines: A Pentecostal Perspective*, exhibits absolutely no trinitarian reflection in the few pages

---

4. Gunton, *Act and Being*, 15.
5. Aquinas, *Summa Theologiae*, 1.6.2.
6. Aquinas, *Summa Theologiae*, 1.9.1.
7. Moltmann, *Crucified God*, 230.
8. I have made this proposal in Gabriel, "Beyond the Cross," forthcoming.
9. Witness the fact that Pentecostals tend to write about "Bible Doctrine" (as some titles below attest) rather than dogmatics or systematic theology, and that a number of Pentecostal books on doctrine are written by those who are primarily biblical scholars rather than systematic theologians, e.g., Arrington, *Christian Doctrine*. Arrington has his Ph.D. in biblical languages and Pauline studies and is Professor Emeritus of New Testament Greek and Exegesis at Church of God Theological Seminary.
10. Though what this means is a matter of disagreement between classical and oneness Pentecostals.

it devotes to discussing the attributes of God.[11] The situation is similar in early Pentecostal theology. Consider, for example, Myer Pearlman's classic text *Knowing the Doctrines of the Bible* (1937). In his section on the attributes of God, the Trinity is only mentioned in his discussion of God as one (which is not generally considered an attribute of God) and Christ is mentioned once as an example of God's righteousness; as one filled with the Spirit, he is one who judges with righteousness (Isa 11:3).[12] The Holy Spirit receives no attention.

John Higgins, Michael Dusing, and Frank Tallman's Pentecostal introduction to theology well displays the Pentecostal tendency toward a biblical theology rather than a dogmatic theology. That is, like other Pentecostals, they do not reflect upon what the dogma of the Trinity might mean for their doctrine of God, but rather are concerned with how "the attributes of God depicted for us in the Scripture give one an accurate and dependable picture of who God is."[13] The authors discuss the term "God" as found in Scripture, without any reference to implications that the divinity of Jesus Christ or the Holy Spirit have for this doctrine. For example, Christ is mentioned only to say that God knew before creation that he would die, that God's holiness, which "was enshrined in the moral law given in the Scriptures," is "demonstrated by Jesus Christ," that God's justice necessitated the death of Christ for the salvation of humanity, and that God's love motivated "His sending Christ to die in our place."[14] The Holy Spirit is mentioned as one who works in us to emulate God's moral attributes.[15] The few references to Christ and the Spirit that do occur, however, have *nothing to do with the fact that they themselves are divine persons, that is, that they are God.*

A similar state of affairs is found in the discussion of the attributes of God within Guy P. Duffield and Nathaniel M. Van Cleave's, *Foundations of Pentecostal Theology*. They do, however, speak to a limited extent of Christ with respect to the divine attributes, noting that since "Jesus Christ is the same yesterday and today and forever" (Heb 13:8), then all of the divine attributes are invariable for all time. We may note, however, that this is more of a concern with a proof-text from Scripture than a

11. Menzies and Horton, *Bible Doctrines*, 50–53.
12. Pearlman, *Knowing the Doctrines of the Bible*, 60 and 64.
13. Higgins, Dusing, and Tallman, *Introduction to Theology*, 21.
14. Higgins, Dusing, and Tallman, *Introduction to Theology*, 24, 26, and 27.
15. Higgins, Dusing, and Tallman, *Introduction to Theology*, 26, 29.

The Spirit Is God

dogmatic theological argument (though the interpretation does presuppose the doctrine of the incarnation).[16] The Holy Spirit does get a limited reference, in that, when discussing the omnipresence of God, Duffield and Van Cleave note that God is present in his Church in a special way through the Holy Spirit.[17] Other than this, Christ and the Holy Spirit are mentioned not because they are divine persons, but only as examples of "God's" divine agency. That is, they are mentioned because God acts to accomplish something through them. Their divinity, however, is inconsequential to the argument, since the point is that "God" is holy or righteous (etc.) by acting upon them, not that Jesus Christ or the Holy Spirit, as divine themselves, are exhibiting these divine attributes. For example, God's love is said to be displayed by sending the Holy Spirit as the Comforter.[18] In this example, the divinity of the Holy Spirit is inconsequential for understanding God's attribute of love. A survey of additional Pentecostal (and non-Pentecostal) systematic theologies would reveal similar results.

The fact is that, in general, Pentecostals have not been forced to think about the doctrine of the divine attributes (as they have been forced, for example, to think about the issue of Spirit baptism). Thus, the lack of development in this area of theology is not surprising. Pentecostal systematic theologies—and some would question if we may properly use the designation "Pentecostal" here—have generally been written for an audience of lay people or as introductory text books for students in theology, and they are often written exclusively for Pentecostals.[19] As a result, most theologians would agree with David Bundy's observation that "it is clear

---

16. Duffield and Van Cleave, *Foundations of Pentecostal Theology*, 69. Following this argument, they note also (p. 70) that Christ's love is unchanging, according to Rom 8:38–39.

17. Duffield and Van Cleave, *Foundations of Pentecostal Theology*, 70.

18. Duffield and Van Cleave, *Foundations of Pentecostal Theology*, 78. Further examples: the resurrection of Christ is mentioned as a display of God's power (p. 72), but this concerns the act of God (the Father it appears) on Christ, not an implication from Christology itself. The same may be said for the discussion of God's righteousness in justifying sinners by means of Christ (p. 77). The Holy Spirit's sanctifying activity is mentioned in the discussion on God's holiness (p. 75), but again, the authors are not attempting to draw a pneumatological implication for the doctrine of God, but are simply noting that the Holy Spirit aids us to be holy as God is holy (noting 1 Pet 1:15–16).

19. For a general discussion (i.e., not specifically with reference to the doctrine of God) and reference to additional Pentecostal systematic theologies (including numerous non-English language works) see Bundy, "Systematic Theology in Pentecostalism," 89–107.

that the genre of [Pentecostal] systematic theology is still in its earliest phase."[20] Terry Cross specifically affirms this with respect to the doctrine of God, suggesting that "Pentecostals have been deficient in crafting a doctrine of God."[21]

Recently, however, some Pentecostals have given more attention to the doctrine of God by reflecting upon the theology of Open Theism, which (of most significance to Arminian Pentecostals) posits that God does not know the future exhaustively, though God does know all that can possibly be known. Pentecostal reflection on Open Theism, however, is also done largely without any explicit consideration of God's triune nature.[22] One significant exception can be found in Terry Cross's response to Clark Pinnock's call for Pentecostals to reflect on the relationality of God.[23] Cross follows Isaak Dorner's christological exposition of the doctrine of divine immutability, arguing that God does not change ethically, but that God changes ontologically, particularly as the Son of God is incarnated in human form.[24] However, again we see that this trinitarian reflection on the doctrine of God is specifically from a christological point of view. A pneumatological approach to the doctrine of God remains unexplored by Pentecostals. And, as we have seen, Pentecostals have been more concerned with being biblical than being trinitarian in this doctrine. This leads us to our next point.

---

20. Bundy, "Systematic Theology in Pentecostalism," 101. Cf. Pinnock, "Divine Relationality," 3, who writes "There is not at present a full-blown Pentecostal systematic theology, although work is underway on it."

21. Cross, "Rich Feast of Theology," 46. With respect to Pentecostal theology in general, see p. 28.

22. Some Pentecostals have rejected Open Theism, others have embraced it. Negative responses to Open Theism include: Railey, "Open Theism" and Lee, "'Openness of God.'" Positive responses to Open Theism include Thompson, "Does God Have a Future?" and Archer, "Open Theism View." An inconclusive response is found in Ellington, "Who Shall Lead Them Out?" And making neutral observations see, Studebaker, "Mode of Divine Knowledge." Studebaker is not evaluating the legitimacy of Open Theism, but simply argues that it stands in continuity with the Arminian tradition.

23. Pinnock, "Divine Relationality," 3–26 (p. 20 makes it clear that Pinnock is commending Open Theism to Pentecostals, though this is not his primary concern, since he affirms that "a relational theist need not accept it").

24. In the same volume as the above article, see Cross, "Rich Feast of Theology," 42–43. Cross makes it clear on p. 44 that he accepts some of Pinnock's proposals, but does not embrace Open Theism.

"Biblical" versus Trinitarian Theology

Although the focus on Scripture is to be applauded in many respects, the Pentecostal drive for a "biblical" theology has in fact inhibited pneumatological developments regarding the doctrine of God. By "biblical" I mean founded on Scripture, with frequent citation of Scripture and largely attempting to use terms found in Scripture (not the academic discipline of biblical theology).[25] The problem for biblically minded Pentecostals (and Evangelicals along with them) is that their method of approaching Scripture inhibits a truly trinitarian doctrine of God, and a pneumatological doctrine of God, as I wish to state it here. I do not mean that Pentecostals are not trinitarian (I have affirmed that above). I mean that, though trinitarian in confession, much of Pentecostal theology is not "trinitarian theology," if "trinitarian theology" is defined as the doctrine of the Trinity in general and how this doctrine affects and shapes other theologies—one can be a "trinitarian" (which more or less means "Christian" these days), without doing trinitarian theology.[26] Indeed, inasmuch as Pentecostals make dogmatic appeals to Christology in treating the doctrine of God, they too do trinitarian theology. However, as we have seen, such dogmatic appeals are not typical. My point is that while trinitarian theology is (most often) biblical, not all "biblical" theology is necessarily trinitarian.

The Bible does not contain an explicit doctrine of the Trinity (even the word "Trinity" is not found in the Bible). To do trinitarian theology, one must, to quote the title of a recent I. Howard Marshall book, go "beyond the Bible."[27] When looking to formulate the doctrine of God, Pentecostal theologians who focus primarily on the biblical witness focus on statements which speak of "God" or "the Lord" to see how God is portrayed. The "problem," if we may call it that, is that in the biblical witness, "God" may refer to God in general, but it most frequently refers to what trinitarian theology specifies as God the Father. In Johannine literature

---

25. Terry Cross speaks of "biblical theology" in a similar manner with respect to Rodman Williams' systematic theology. Cross writes, "I would contend that Williams's work is really a biblical theology, not a systematic theology. . . . A biblical agenda is important as a foundation, but a systematic theology from a Pentecostal-charismatic perspective must do more" ("Theology of the Word and the Spirit," 118, 122, cf. 127).

26. Sanders, "Trinity Talk," 264 and Schwöbel, "Renaissance of Trinitarian Theology," 1.

27. Marshall, *Beyond the Bible*.

we do find the tendency to speak of the three divine "persons" as Father, Son/Jesus, and Spirit. This terminology is largely limited to the Johannine corpus however. By contrast, Pauline literature tends to describe this threefold relationship as God, Jesus/Lord, and Spirit, although Paul does seem to exhibit trinitarian presuppositions.[28] Accordingly, in an attempt to remain faithful to the biblical text, theologians engaging in the doctrine of the Trinity will speak of God's threefold relationship as Father, Son, and Spirit, as well as God, Jesus, and Spirit. The confusion comes because the term "God" is used in trinitarian theology to refer to the divine life in general as well as to the divine person of the Father. Accordingly, Veli-Matti Kärkkäinen describes the doctrine of God as focusing "on interpretations of what in trinitarian language is called Father."[29] And he does this even though one of the themes that flows throughout his book is how theologians have historically represented God as triune in their theologies.[30] To restate the problem, using biblical terms, one may speak of "God" as God the Father in particular. A trinitarian doctrine of God however, at least since the contemporary revival of trinitarian theology post-Barth, must include the consideration that God is in fact *three* divine persons; namely, God is the Father, the Son, and (and this is the point I with to push here) the Holy Spirit. Such a trinitarian doctrine of God should remain consistent, nevertheless, with the presentation of "the Lord" or "God" in general found in the Bible, since the doctrine of the Trinity itself is said to flow from and be consistent with the thought of the biblical authors.

Pneumatology and the Doctrine of God

As stated previously, contemporary theology has, on the whole, seen a revival of trinitarian theology, and with it, pneumatology. Writing what may be regarded as a landmark in contemporary pneumatology, Hendrikus Berkhof remarked in 1964, "The efforts of many theologians are needed to fill what is still more or less a vacuum in the dogmatics of the contemporary churches."[31] He complained that there was little written on the Spirit in European languages other than English, and that even

28. Gabriel, "Pauline Pneumatology," 347–62, and Fee, *God's Empowering Presence*.
29. Kärkkäinen, *Doctrine of God*, 7.
30. Similarly, Spittler, *God the Father*, includes a chapter on God as Trinity.
31. Berkhof, *Doctrine of the Holy Spirit*, 11.

The Spirit Is God

here it was primarily limited to devotional or semi-theological works.[32] We may add to this that the Western Church has a history of suppressing the Spirit at times.[33] People, especially those with ecclesiastical power, can sometimes be uncomfortable with movements of the Spirit. Such suppression may be found from the condemnations of Montanism in the second century, to certain responses to the Spirit in contemporary Pentecostalism and the Charismatic movement.[34] This is not to suggest that theologians never wrote or spoke about the Holy Spirit.

Especially since Berkhof's work, many theologians have taken note of the neglect of the Spirit in theology, and works on the doctrine of the Holy Spirit have become legion. With the rise of world Pentecostalism, ecumenical discussions (which, in conversation with Eastern Orthodoxy have brought the *filioque* discussion to the fore), and certain cultural changes, interest in pneumatology is on the rise.[35] In 1985, Kilian McDonnell still felt justified to speak of the Spirit as the "Cinderella" of theology, but now (as of 2003) he agrees that the situation has changed.[36] Now the shy Holy Spirit is said to be found wherever there is life.[37] As the Holy Spirit has been found to be at work throughout the world, one can even claim that theologians have, to some extent, found the face of the Spirit (in contrast to Walter Kasper who refers to the Holy Spirit as "faceless"[38]). Leonardo Boff, for example, claims that, inasmuch as the Spirit is found in the midst of liberation, "the Spirit *takes on a thousand faces.* . . . Its divine face is that of transfigured or humiliated humanity."[39] What is essential however, is to note that, as McDonnell correctly remarks,

---

32. Berkhof, *Doctrine of the Holy Spirit*, 10.

33. Pinnock, *Flame of Love*, 11. Compare the remarks by Johnson in *She Who Is*, 128–31.

34. Tabbernee, "Real Paraclete," 97–116.

35. Pinnock, "Recovery of the Holy Spirit," 5, and Hinze and Dabney, "Introduction," 17–22.

36. McDonnell, "Trinitarian Theology," 191–93. The idea of the Spirit as the "Cinderella" of theology comes from Sirks, "Cinderella of Theology," 77–89. For McDonnell's remarks published in 2003 see *Other Hand of God*, 2.

37. Moltmann, *Spirit of Life*. Cf. the title of Bruner and Hordern, *Shy Member of the Trinity*.

38. Kasper, *God of Jesus Christ*, 223.

39. Boff, *Trinity and Society*, 209.

> The issue is not pneumatological nose counting (how many times the Spirit is mentioned). The issue is the integrity of the theological vision. One can have a superabundance of references to the Spirit and still have a serious pneumatological deficit because Pneumatology has not been integrated into the theological vision in a way that is appropriate.[40]

A pneumatological deficit remains in the doctrine of the divine attributes.

Beyond simply the writing of pneumatologies, we have also recently seen the advent of what is often referred to as a theology of the third article (given the place of the confession of the Spirit in the creeds) or pneumatological theology. In contrast to pneumatology, which is primarily concerned with the person of the Holy Spirit and his work in the world, pneumatological theology is theology that focuses on understanding and exploring how pneumatology affects, supplements, and might reform other doctrines. Theologians engaged in such theology often remind readers (I suspect in large part because they aim to convince those who have followed Barth's christological focus) that near the end of his life, Karl Barth himself called for just such a theological project. He anticipated:

> the possibility of a theology of the third article, a theology where the Holy Spirit would dominate and be decisive. Everything that one believes, reflects, and says about God the Father and God the Son in understanding the first and second articles would be demonstrated and clarified basically through God the Holy Spirit.... I give only indications of what I occasionally dream of regarding the future of theology.[41]

The realization of Barth's dream is still in its developing stages. As recently as 1991, Moltmann observed, "if we look critically at the actual results of [contemporary pneumatology], we are bound to conclude that in sober

---

40. McDonnell, "Response to Bernd Jochen Hilberath," 295. Zizioulas concedes that Eastern Orthodoxy certainly does not have all of the answers to this Western problem (see *Being as Communion*, 126).

41. Barth, "Nachwort," 311, as translated in McDonnell, *Other Hand of God*, 209. Also translated in Barth, *Theology of Schleiermacher*, 278. Cf. Busch, *Karl Barth*, 494.

fact, although light has been thrown on a whole number of individual aspects, a new paradigm in pneumatology has not yet emerged."[42]

One landmark work since that time is Clark Pinnock's *Flame of Love*, which, though a pneumatology (as the subtitle *A Theology of the Holy Spirit* suggests) is in large part a work in pneumatological theology. Pinnock's *Flame of Love* may be considered a work in pneumatology inasmuch as his reflections do end up forming a constructive vision of the Spirit.[43] Nevertheless, the main focus of the book is examining how the doctrine of the Spirit makes contributions to the doctrines of the Church, salvation, Christ, and so forth—seeing how "the Spirit challenges theology at numerous points."[44] Unlike theologians who follow him in engaging in pneumatological theology, Pinnock does have a chapter that offers a discussion on the doctrine of God in which he examines the place of the Spirit in the life of the Trinity. Pinnock's discussion, however, is more concerned with how a social doctrine of the Trinity shapes our understanding of the Spirit and helps to establish the distinct personhood of the Spirit rather than being concerned with how our understanding of the Spirit shapes our understanding of God. Accordingly, Terry Cross, commenting on *Flame of Love*, observes, "The doctrine of God offers us a basis for understanding the Spirit in the 'liveliness of the Trinity' within 'loving relationality.'"[45] This is primarily an instance of the social Trinity shaping our understanding of the Spirit rather than of the understanding of the Spirit shaping our understanding of who God is.

Pneumatological theology also appears to be the emerging paradigm for Pentecostal theology. As Steven Studebaker has indicated in his contribution to this collection of essays, historically, Pentecostal theology

---

42. Moltmann, *Spirit of Life*, 1. Moltmann's previous writings *The Church in the Power of the Spirit*, *God in Creation*, and *The Way of Jesus Christ*, may themselves be seen as efforts to work out this paradigm.

43. Pinnock invites his readers to view the Spirit as "the bond of love in the triune relationality, as the ecstasy of sheer life overflowing into a significant creation, as the power of creation and new creation, as the power of incarnation and atonement, as the power of new community and union with God, and as the power drawing the whole world into the truth of Jesus" (*Flame of Love*, 247).

44. Pinnock, *Flame of Love*, 11. Perhaps we can say that contemporary pneumatology has realized that the Spirit belongs everywhere. That is, pneumatology becomes pneumatological theology.

45. Cross, "Pinnock's *Flame of Love*," 10, with quotes from Pinnock, *Flame of Love*, 21. Nevertheless, Pinnock's pneumatology does contribute to his view of God's personal relationality, as we shall see below.

has often focused on the issues of Spirit baptism, speaking in tongues, and spiritual gifts. That is, the focus has been on interpreting certain experiences of the Spirit. More recently however, as even this collection of essays indicates, Pentecostals have moved beyond the task of discussing their traditional distinctive beliefs (though they still discuss them) and are exploring what their understanding of and experience of the Spirit implies for the whole of their theology. Among these works, one notes the recent writings of Veli-Matti Kärkkäinen, Amos Yong, and Frank Macchia.[46] These authors have focused on soteriology, ecclesiology, ecumenism, and theologies of creation, religions, and mission, but not on the doctrine of God's attributes. Pentecostals have certainly shown concern for the doctrine of God, but on account of the historical split between Oneness Pentecostals and their counterparts, the discussion has been primarily focused on the doctrine of the Trinity and has taken place outside of the paradigm of pneumatological theology.[47]

The Spirit, of course, is not the concern of Pentecostals alone. Roman Catholic Denis Edwards and Wesleyan D. Lyle Dabney are among those who have written on some of the same issues from a pneumatological perspective.[48] While the contribution of all of these authors has been helpful in a number of areas, none has specifically attempted to do what might be referred to as pneumatological theology proper. That is, these authors have not offered a sustained discussion of how pneumatology affects our understanding of God (theology proper), particularly the attributes of God. The same may be said of general pneumatologies. Although containing some insights concerning the doctrine of God, sometimes even explicitly acknowledged, these insights remain isolated in pneumatology, not being integrated into the doctrine of God.

As stated above, a pneumatological approach to the doctrine of the divine attributes has been largely ignored by the wider field of trinitar-

---

46. Kärkkäinen, *Toward a Pneumatological Theology*; Yong, *Spirit Poured Out*; and Macchia, *Baptized in the Spirit*. As well, see the numerous articles by various authors in *Pneuma* and the *Journal of Pentecostal Theology*. Most, if not all, of these theologians would affirm that Pinnock's writings have had a significant influence on their thought.

47. E.g., Amos Yong, "Oneness and Trinity: Identity, Plurality, and World Theology," chapter 5 in *Spirit Poured Out*, 203–34.

48. Edwards, *Breath of Life*. D. Lyle Dabney's writings include a series of lectures Dabney delivered in Canberra, Australia, which are published in Preece and Pickard, *Starting with the Spirit*. See also Dabney, "Otherwise Engaged in the Spirit," 154–62, and "Why Should the Last Be First?" 240–61.

ian theology as well. We have seen that, with the revival of trinitarian theology, the Son of God has been considered by merging christological considerations into the doctrine of God, but the Spirit has not. When the Holy Spirit is discussed among theologians of the Trinity, discussion generally focuses on speculating on the procession of the Holy Spirit within the immanent Trinity and whether or not the *filioque* is legitimate.[49] Related to this, is the concern among trinitarian theologians to affirm the full personhood of the Spirit and to affirm that the Spirit is more than (if at all) the bond of love between the Father and the Son.[50] There are a few trinitarian theologians who are beginning to integrate the Spirit more explicitly into their doctrines of God.[51] Yet overall, it may be said that within the doctrine of God, discussion of the Spirit has focused on affirming the Spirit's activity in relation to both the Father and the Son, but has neglected to consider what the Spirit's actions imply for the doctrine of the divine attributes.

Apologetic for a Pneumatological Theology of the Divine Attributes

Before exploring the potential areas of consideration for a pneumatological theology proper, I wish first to explain in more detail why this approach is necessary. The first and most obvious reason is that the Holy Spirit is indeed God. And if this is the case, then the attributes of the Spirit should be considered when one seeks to understand who God is. While it is true that there are no Spirit-specific attributes, it is also surely true that we can learn something of God's attributes by looking at the Spirit. With Elizabeth Johnson I affirm that "Forgetting the Spirit is not ignoring a faceless, shadowy, third hypostasis but the mystery of God vivifying the world, closer to us than we are to ourselves, drawing near and passing by in liberating compassion."[52] The doctrine of God should not be divorced from the doctrine of the Holy Spirit. Pentecostals do profoundly realize that the Spirit they experience in their worship and devotion is God, but Pentecostals have not adequately worked out the implications of this truth.

49. E.g., Moltmann, *Trinity and the Kingdom*, 178–87.
50. E.g., Moltmann, *Spirit of Life*, 268–309.
51. E.g., Gunton, *Act and Being*, and Shults, *Doctrine of God*.
52. Johnson, *Creator Spirit*, 20.

Second, integrating pneumatology into the doctrine of God is an effort to be more thoroughly trinitarian. That is, if one only approaches the doctrine of God from the perspective of Christology, one is limited in consideration of God's acts in history. The classical trinitarian confession is that God is *three—tri*une. Whether one uses the term "persons" or "modes" or "ways" of existing or being, the point is that God is a plurality of three and not two. Nevertheless, much of trinitarian doctrine is done as though God were only two persons.

Writing with concern for the doctrine of the Trinity and the integrity of the doctrine of God, Karl Rahner lamented the separation between the dogmatic treatises "On the One God" and those "On the Triune God."[53] Typical of trinitarian theology after Rahner, John Thompson interprets this christologically: "In other words, Christology and the Trinity were virtually divorced."[54] Note that Thompson seems not to even consider pneumatology's lack of influence on the doctrine of God. Similarly to Thompson, we may say *pneumatology* and the Trinity were virtually divorced.

It should be clear, then, that in looking to formulate a pneumatological doctrine of God, I am not suggesting that we neglect the other divine persons, but rather that we supplement the current discussion with a pneumatological approach in an effort to be fully trinitarian. And, as Ralph Del Colle aptly remarks, "to be more thoroughly trinitarian is to be more thoroughly pneumatological."[55] At the same time, McDonnell has a point when he writes, "to do pneumatology is to do Trinity"; after all, the Spirit is always in relation to the Father and the Son. That is, the Spirit is never "alone" since the Trinity is a tri-unity.[56] When reflecting on the Spirit one necessarily finds his relations to the Father and Christ. This is true from the perspective of the *perichoresis* (eternal mutual indwelling) of the divine persons, as well as the fact that the Spirit is not a spirit in general, but precisely the Spirit of God and of Christ.

While the revival of trinitarian theology and pneumatological theology has found influence across all of the theological disciplines, it seems to have moved too quickly past the most fundamental one. Even as the

---

53. Rahner, *The Trinity*, 16.
54. Thompson, *Modern Trinitarian Perspectives*, 22.
55. Del Colle, "Response to Jürgen Moltmann and David Coffey," 339.
56. McDonnell, *Other Hand of God*, 1.

The Spirit Is God 83

revival of pneumatology was in its infancy, Heribert Mühlen recognized "the narrowness of the traditional teaching on God." Mühlen observed that the doctrine of the Holy Spirit "is almost inevitably seen as a pious addition, an edifying ornament, but never as the [or even "a"] most basic proposition of the teaching on God."[57] Though a few decades have passed, this remains true. McDonnell remarks, "The revival of trinitarian doctrine and renewed theological interest in the Holy Spirit have not so far converged in any significant way."[58] This convergence should occur, however, as it will lead to a more thoroughly trinitarian doctrine of God.

This leads us to the third point, which is the *perichoresis* of Christian doctrine. Although theologians often attempt to separate doctrines into distinct theological topics, it is easy to see that each of the theological doctrines inform one another. We have seen how this is the case in pneumatological theology. The same has been observed of trinitarian theology.[59] Just as the doctrine of the Holy Spirit and the doctrine of God as Trinity affect other doctrines, so also the doctrine of the Holy Spirit has promise for addressing the doctrine of God. Granted, the doctrine of the Holy Spirit and the doctrine of God may legitimately be treated as two topics in a theological scheme. However, what is important is that one does not forget that they affect each other. Likewise, McDonnell and Catherine LaCugna "affirm the *perichoresis* (mutual inter-dependence) between doctrines, in particular between Christology, pneumatology, and trinitarian doctrine. Each doctrine gains in richness by being developed in concert with each of the others."[60]

A fourth reason for adopting a pneumatological approach to the doctrine of the divine attributes is that this approach will necessarily

57. Mühlen, "Holy Spirit as Person," 12, 13. Writing around the same time, Pittenger recognized that his doctrine of God was lacking due to its deficient place for the Spirit (*Holy Spirit*, 15).

58. McDonnell, *Other Hand of God*, 2.

59. For instance, Sanders notes, "The more pervasive Trinity talk becomes, the more it spreads out from its home base in the doctrine of God proper and infiltrates other doctrinal loci" ("Trinity Talk," 266). Sanders lists examples of specific works on creation, anthropology, ecclesiology, and soteriology.

60. LaCugna and McDonnell, "Returning from 'The Far Country,'" 192. Elsewhere LaCugna writes, "Today the trinitarian project is to update archaic dogmatic language and to restore trinitarian theology to its original christological context, re-establishing the '*perichoresis*' (mutual inter-dependence) between the doctrine of God, christology and pneumatology" (LaCugna, "Current Trends in Trinitarian Theology," 141).

overcome the historical reliance on philosophical theology. This was one of Karl Rahner's concerns when he penned his axiom, "The 'economic' Trinity is the 'immanent' Trinity and the 'immanent' Trinity is the 'economic' Trinity."[61] Focusing on the Spirit to approach the doctrine of God should correct the tendency to turn to abstract attributes, because a turn to the Spirit should automatically bring us back to God's action in the world.[62] Here we see the immanent Trinity present in the economy of salvation. The Spirit is God reaching out with one of his "two hands" (as Irenaeus put it) to act in history. God is not confined to his self-sufficient divine life but reaches out beyond it as the Spirit. Furthermore, with the Spirit, unlike with Christ, we are not inhibited in our theological reflections by the union of two natures, divine and human. That is, with the Spirit we do not have to discern or defend what may be properly spoken of as affecting the divine nature. Here, God is simply acting in an unmediated way. Perhaps we should say that the Spirit himself is the mediation of God's acts in history. In this manner, McDonnell writes, "there is a habit of mind which sees the Spirit as the place of mediation whereby God touches the church and the world and sets them on the road back to God."[63] This "mediation" role is, in trinitarian terms, true with respect to the relationship of God the Father and the Son to the world. Nevertheless, since we affirm that the Spirit too is God, we may say that the Spirit is the "place" where God is acting immediately in the world.

Fifth, a pneumatological theology of the divine attributes will make explicit what is often sensed to be true in Christian experience. That is, theology has to catch up to what experience is telling us. Mühlen notes, "It is true, of course, that the *experience* of the living God has always been deeper and broader than the traditional *teaching* about God."[64] The truth is that most of the Christian experience of God can be attributed to the Spirit. As Johnson notes, "Whenever people speak in a generic way of 'God,' of their experience of God or of God's doing something in

---

61. Rahner, *The Trinity*, 22.

62. I say "should" because, in contrast to my assertion, Gunton (*Act and Being*, 106) presents a pneumatological doctrine of divine freedom, but his focus is solely on the Spirit in the immanent Trinity.

63. McDonnell, *Other Hand of God*, 8. Cf. Pinnock who writes, "Spirit mediates the presence of God in creation and enables the creature to participate in God. The creature, distinct from the Father in the Son, is united to God by the Spirit" (*Flame of Love*, 60).

64. Mühlen, "Holy Spirit as Person," 14.

the world, more often than not they are referring to the Spirit, if a triune prism be introduced."[65] In this manner, Paul spoke of someone entering a place where the spiritual gifts were being practiced. That person is said to exclaim, "God is really among you!" (1 Cor 14:25). Mühlen wrote that he foresaw that the experience of God the Spirit would lead to a change: "God will be approached not in the first place as the Creator-God who dwells blissfully *on high* in isolation, but equally as the Holy Spirit who dwells *in us* and who reigns in our hearts."[66] This change, I would suggest, is already happening. Theologians now apply the idea of the *kenosis* of God not only to the Son of God and his incarnation, but also to God in general as God creates a world in which there is room for creaturely freedom.[67]

Pneumatological Insights for a Doctrine of God

Finally we have reached the goal of this study. What difference does it make for the doctrine of the divine attributes if we consider the Spirit? It seems that this may be summarized in the idea of immanence. That is to say, by considering the Spirit one gains a greater appreciation for and emphasis on the immanence of God. Before seeing how this is the case, let us first consider what is meant by immanence.

Immanence must be defined together with its counterpart, transcendence. These ideas present spatial images. They depict God as being either above and beyond the world, or close to the world. Though transcendence is a spatial image, in theological terms it does not refer simply to space, but primarily to the Creator/creation distinction. That is, God is "beyond" the world inasmuch as he is other than it. Shirley Guthrie explains, "God's transcendence, then, means that he is 'wholly other,' beyond all human knowledge and all human moral and religious capacities, '*above* us, *above* space and time, and *above* all concepts and opinions and potentialities.'"[68] God's transcendence is especially seen as we contrast the attributes of God with those of creation. Theologians speak of God's infinity, eternity, immensity, omnipresence, aseity, simplicity, immutabil-

---

65. Johnson, *Creator Spirit*, 42.
66. Mühlen, "Holy Spirit as Person," 31 (emphasis original).
67. E.g., Denis Edwards, *Breath of Life*, 107–10; essays in Polkinghorne, ed., *Work of Love*; and Pinnock, "God's Vulnerable Strength."
68. Guthrie, "Nearness and Distance," 33, who quotes Barth, *Knowledge of God*, 28.

ity, and impassibility. These are all expressions of God's transcendence.[69] Immanence may, to a limited extent, be considered the opposite of transcendence, however, it is important to note that God is able to be immanent to creation precisely because he is transcendent from it.[70]

Immanence also pertains to God's interaction with the world, often with respect to the providence of God. Those who discuss God's immanence are often responding to deism, which sees God as the Creator but nothing more. For example, Borden Bowne defines immanence with respect to providence: "we mean that God is the omnipresent ground of all finite existence and activity. The world . . . continually depends upon and is ever upheld by the ever-living, ever-present, ever-working God."[71] This again is a reminder that transcendence and immanence are not opposites. If God did not transcend creation, God could not be immanent to creation.

Inasmuch as the attributes which express God's transcendence have historically been most prominent in doctrines of God, it appears that God's immanence has been neglected. This may be exemplified in Colin Gunton's observation that the historical tradition is overwhelmed by negative theology when it comes to God. He remarks that "negative theology has in effect driven out the positive, so that the God who makes himself known in Scripture has been turned into one who cannot be known as he is."[72] We seem most comfortable talking about what God is not, thinking that this somehow best expresses the transcendence of God. The truth, however, is that even negative theology falls short of describing God. As Guthrie recognizes, terms like in-finite, time-less, un-changing, and un-limited are nevertheless,

> still definitions of God in terms of man, since they think of God as what *man* is not. . . . If God is really transcendent, he cannot be grasped by *any* human language, biblical or philosophical, "liberal" or "conservative," pious or secular. To fall back on the classical negative language, we have said, will not do to describe his

---

69. These topics are among those discussed in chapter 4, "Transcendence and Immanence," of Bloesch, *God the Almighty*.

70. Though not unbiblical or non-trinitarian notions, most discussions concerning transcendence and immanence take the approach of philosophical theology. E.g., Robertson, *Loss and Recovery* and Farley, *Transcendence of God*.

71. Bowne, *Immanence of God*, 3, cf. v.

72. Gunton, *Act and Being*, 17.

transcendence (and thus to confirm the very point we are making), God is unknown and unknowable, undefinable, incomprehensible, incomparable.[73]

Such radical remarks might appear to imply that we can know nothing of God at all. On the contrary, God can even transcend his transcendence and reveal himself for who he is.[74] This takes place as God is immanent to creation. In the end, what transcendence tells us is that philosophical descriptions of God are not adequate and that all language, whether negative or positive, in some sense falls short in describing God. On the other hand, given that God has revealed himself, all language can convey truth about who God is. Recognizing this we can turn to God's immanence in creation to state in positive terms who God is.

By suggesting that a consideration of the Spirit leads one to emphasize the immanence of God, I do not mean to suggest that the Spirit is not transcendent. I have already said that God's transcendence presupposes God's immanence. This is true also of the Spirit as a divine person. Clark Pinnock points out that "most essentially Spirit is transcendent and divine, not mere flesh; it is the energy of life itself."[75] Too often though, transcendence is taken to refer to more than just the Creator/creation distinction. God is also seen to be unaffected by the material world and what happens in it.[76] A renewed emphasis on the Spirit in the doctrine of God overcomes this understanding of transcendence.

The Spirit is "God with us" today. The Spirit is often the one thought of as elusive, but we may say of the Father that he "lives in unapproachable light" and that "no one has seen or can see" him (1 Tim 4:16). Similarly, Mühlen remarks, God appeared in bodily form, "yet, he is no longer with us in the form of this particular man either; he has gone away. What has remained is that Spirit within us, of which it is said that he has been sent into our hearts (Gal 4:6)."[77] In fact, there is nowhere to flee from the presence of God the Spirit (Ps 139:7). As Pinnock expresses it, "Most wonderfully, the Spirit is God's face turned toward us and God's presence

---

73. Guthrie, "Nearness and Distance," 35, 36.
74. Guthrie, "Nearness and Distance," 37, cf. 39.
75. Pinnock, *Flame of Love*, 14.
76. Johnson, *Creator Spirit*, 17.
77. Mühlen, "Holy Spirit as Person," 20.

abiding with us, the agency by which God reaches out and draws near, the power that creates and heals."[78]

McDonnell most eloquently expresses the immanence of God in the Spirit.[79] He refers to the Spirit as the touch of God and to the Spirit's contact function. In the Christ event the Spirit touches Jesus as he effects the incarnation, anoints Jesus at his baptism, and empowers him for ministry. Beyond this, Christ sends the Spirit from the Father and the Spirit comes and empowers the Church. The Spirit also leads us to the Son, and to return praise to the Father. The Spirit was the touch of God upon Christ, and similarly, upon the Church. McDonnell writes, "without the Spirit, God remains a private self, an isolated glory, an island apart. In this sense the Spirit is sovereign and all inclusive, the universal horizon, the exclusive point where we touch God and God touches us from within."[80] Though McDonnell's discussion focuses on ecclesial life, Molly Marshall extends this to the cosmological level as well: "The Spirit is the point of contact between the life of God and the world that is yet coming to be. Described as 'divine nearness,' the Spirit makes possible the universal contact between God and history, between God and all creation."[81]

The immanence of God in the Spirit may be seen as we consider a number of the divine attributes from a pneumatological perspective. First, we see the immanence of God in the Holy Spirit as we consider the doctrine of God's omnipotence. Molly Marshall is among the few who explicitly recognize that "pneumatology carries considerable promise for addressing . . . the character of God" and she sees this particularly with respect to divine power and agency.[82] Marshall suggests that in the Spirit we see God sharing his power. Thus, in the world processes, agency can not be fully ascribed to God.[83] In the Spirit we see that God's omnipotence is omnipotence of love. By the Spirit we are invited to participate in the life of God. This perichoretic life is not all-determined by God,

---

78. Pinnock, *Flame of Love*, 14.

79. See esp. ch. 10, "God Beyond the Self of God," and ch. 12, "The Spirit is the Touch of God," in McDonnell, *Other Hand of God*. Cf. Pinnock who speaks of the Spirit as God "touching people" (*Flame of Love*, 188).

80. McDonnell, *Other Hand of God*, 119.

81. Marshall, *Joining the Dance*, 13.

82. Marshall, *Joining the Dance*, 4.

83. Marshall, *Joining the Dance*, 12.

The Spirit Is God

but one which is a dance with mutual contributors.[84] Marshall recognizes there are biblical examples where the Spirit does "forcefully take over one's personality" but this does not appear to be normative of the Spirit's actions.[85] Presumably, when Paul writes that "the fruit of the Spirit is love, joy, peace, patience, kindness, goodness, faithfulness, gentleness and self-control" (Gal 5:22–23), we can be sure that God does not cause such "fruit" as, hatred, misery, disorder, uneasiness, impatience, malice or unfaithfulness. Rather, these are characteristics of those who are not dancing with the Spirit, or, in Paul's words, those who do not "keep in step with the Spirit" (Gal 5:25).

Similar insights may be gleaned from liberation theologians. José Comblin states decisively, "The activities of the Spirit are different from the actions produced without the Spirit."[86] Through the Hebrew Scriptures, the Spirit "inaugurated its liberative action" as the Spirit came upon judges (e.g., Judg 13:25) and kings (1 Sam 10:10).[87] Today, the Spirit is said to be found where communities are made to recognize their plight, move toward speech and action, and experience life and liberation. If the Holy Spirit works to liberate people, the Spirit must be liberating people from something that was not caused by God. As Mark 3:25 notes, "If a house is divided against itself, that house cannot stand." God's power is at work in the Spirit to liberate people, not to set them in bondage. The Spirit is immanent to creation, acting as partner in a dance, not as a transcendent primary cause of events for which creaturely agents are only secondary causes. Sometimes God's creatures do not join the dance, but it is not characteristic of the Spirit to force us to.

This leads to a second perspective concerning the immanence of God in the Spirit, which is the relationality of God. Divine relationality is seen in the Spirit's empowering and sanctifying of believers and in the Spirit's activity of gifting people and creating communion. In the Spirit, God draws close to the world in mutual relation with it. On account of this Clark Pinnock remarks, "God is not a featureless monad, isolated

---

84. Marshall, *Joining the Dance*, 158–59.
85. Marshall, *Joining the Dance*, 13.
86. Comblin, "The Holy Spirit," 148.
87. Comblin, "The Holy Spirit," 147. Cf. Boff who writes, "The Spirit's third mission is to *liberate* from the oppressions brought into being by our sinful state" (*Trinity and Society*, 194).

and motionless, but a dynamic event of loving actions and personal relationality."[88]

We do not arrive at an understanding of the personhood of the Holy Spirit by first looking at the doctrine of the Trinity, which teaches us that God is relational and personal. Rather, we reach the doctrine of the Trinity by examining how the divine persons exist in the economy of salvation. Looking at the Spirit tells us that God is a relational God. The Spirit empowers believers to witness to God's salvation, sanctifies believers to live a life of witness and love, gifts people that the church may be built up, and creates communion and fellowship among believers. The Spirit brings people together, gathering the Church and making them one with God. Rather than thinking of the Spirit somewhat statically as the "bond of love,"[89] I prefer to think of the Spirit as the one who bonds in love. Along these lines, Pinnock posits, "The Spirit calls us to participate in the relationship of intimacy between the Father and the Son and to be caught up in the dance already begun."[90] The Spirit draws us into the relationship as he enables us to say "Abba, Father" (Rom 8:15 and Gal 4:6).

Third, the Spirit displays God's holiness as he is immanent to us. John Webster has argued convincingly that the biblical portrayal of divine holiness concerns much more than God's transcendence. "Holy" often conveys images of God as utterly beyond us spatially and morally. Webster, in contrast, describes God's holiness as "pure majesty in relation."[91] He emphasizes that holiness is relational in character. God is not holy because he is removed from creation, but rather is holy as he is immanent to it. God is holy in relation to his people—the Redeemer is the "holy one of Israel" (e.g., Isa 47:4). God is holy as he takes up the cause of his people and draws them into fellowship with himself. As the Holy One, God calls us to holiness and overcomes sin through the reconciling work of the Son as well as the sanctifying work of the Spirit. Webster writes, "God the Holy Spirit is the one who completes this work of making holy,

---

88. Pinnock, *Flame of Love*, 42.

89. Though it may not have been the intention of this theology, Denis Edwards observes that at the "popular level, the idea of the Spirit as the mutual love between Father and Son has been misunderstood and reified, resulting in an inadequate view of the Spirit of God as something impersonal that exists between the other two trinitarian persons" (*Breath of Life*, 149–50).

90. Pinnock, *Flame of Love*, 46.

91. Webster, *Holiness*, 41.

The Spirit Is God

perfecting the creature by binding the creature's life into that of Christ and so realizing *in* the creature what has been achieved *for* the creature. The Spirit's holiness is thus known in his work of sanctifying."[92] In light of Studebaker's proposal in this book, we may add that the Spirit is holy in his regenerating work (i.e., not just in applying the work of Christ). It is no accident that the Spirit is called the "Holy" Spirit, for the Spirit is immanent to us being holy as he makes us holy.

Closely related to God's holiness is our fourth consideration, God's faithfulness. This is otherwise discussed as divine immutability or divine constancy. God's faithfulness is seen in the Spirit's perfecting work in the whole of creation. Salvation is not just for humanity but for the whole of creation. "*All* things" have been reconciled to God through Christ (Col 1:20), and the Spirit brings this into reality as he perfects or completes this work. This idea goes back to the Cappadocian theologians. Creation, Gregory of Nyssa writes, "began with the Father, advanced through the Son, and is completed in the Holy Spirit."[93] Gunton, a contemporary theologian, describes this perfecting work of the Spirit as "pulling things forward to that for which God has made them."[94] The Spirit is the Giver of Life, who faithfully liberates creation from its groaning.

Remaining within the realm of theology of nature, we reach our last perspective of how a pneumatological approach to the divine attributes presents God as immanent. This concerns divine passibility—the suffering of God in creation. A number of theologians have proposed a form of trinitarian panentheism where creation is not outside of God, but rather dwelling inside of God, and where the Spirit is said to dwell within all of creation. This builds on the idea that God is "over all, and through all and in all" (Eph 4:6).[95]

Some have gone to the extreme of presenting the Spirit's relationship with the natural world using incarnational terms. Mark Wallace, for example, speaks of the "Spirit as the enfleshment of God's sustaining

---

92. Webster, *Holiness*, 52 and cf. 48. Cf. Gunton who writes, "It is this connection with perfecting that above all characterizes the holiness of the Spirit" (*Act and Being*, 188).

93. Gregory of Nyssa, "On the Holy Spirit," 320.

94. Gunton, *Act and Being*, 78.

95. Though Eph 4:6 is found in the context of a discussion regarding Church unity, Gordon Fee notes the universal implications of v. 6. Regarding vv. 4–6, Fee writes that "Paul can conclude only with the 'one God' who is the ground and source of everything" (*God's Empowering Presence*, 704).

power in the biosphere" and the "Spirit who enfleshes divine presence in nature."[96] This then means that as creation suffers from human assault, so does God, who dwells in creation by the Holy Spirit. Such versions of panentheism appear to violate the Creator/creation distinction and neglect the truth that, although immanent, the Holy Spirit, too, is transcendent.[97]

Denis Edwards' explication of panentheism and the Creator Spirit is more helpful. Edwards presents a carefully qualified concept of panentheism which "understands God as wholly other to creatures, and, precisely as such, as radically interior to them," "understands the spatial image of all-things-in God as an appropriate but limited analogy," and "conceives of the Creator as enabling creatures to have their own proper autonomy and integrity."[98] Employing this concept of panentheism, Edwards sees the Spirit immanent to creation suffering with the suffering of creation. "It is a divine pain that springs from infinite compassion."[99] We might add that the Spirit suffers as he grieves (cf. Eph 4:30) in response to those creaturely actions which frustrate the Spirit's perfecting action in creation.[100]

I am not suggesting that the Spirit presents God as being at the total mercy of creation, suffering with no means of escape. Trinitarian panentheism presents the Spirit as immanent to creation by God's choice.[101] God freely created and freely chooses to sustain creation by the Spirit's power. God chooses to remain in creation where he is vulnerable to its suffering. This is similar to God's suffering on the cross, which Moltmann insisted is an instance of "*active* suffering, the suffering of love, in which one voluntarily opens himself to the possibility of being affected by another."[102]

To conclude this section, it is evident that a new appreciation and perspective regarding the immanence of God is found when one approaches the doctrine of the divine attributes from a pneumatological

---

96. Wallace, "Wounded Spirit," 59, 62.

97. Gabriel, "Theology of Nature," 202–4.

98. Edwards, *Breath of Life*, 140–41.

99. Edwards, *Breath of Life*, 113.

100. Gabriel, "Theology of Nature," 205–7.

101. Cf. Bloesch who writes, "God's immanence is an act of his freedom, not a quality of his being. Just as he freely relates to his creation, so he is also free to withdraw from his creation" (*God the Almighty*, 99).

102. Moltmann, *Crucified God*, 230 (emphasis added).

perspective. We have seen this illustrated by considering five attributes of God: omnipotence, relationality, holiness, faithfulness, and passibility.

Conclusion

We may conclude that "the Spirit is not a pit stop along the trinitarian highway," but is integral to the Christian doctrine of God.[103] We began this exploration noting how both classical theism and Pentecostal theology have neglected the trinitarian nature of God with respect to the doctrine of the divine attributes. Unlike classical theists who were driven philosophically, Pentecostals have primarily been more biblically oriented, concerned with presenting (in their view) what the Scriptures teach about "God." Their approach to the biblical texts, however, has inhibited trinitarian reflection in this area of doctrine. Following these observations, I argue that it is necessary for the Christian doctrine of God to include significant influence from pneumatology. While Pentecostals have been more concerned with a theology of the experience of the Spirit, this new approach will develop their recognition that this Spirit is God. Moreover, this pneumatological influence on the doctrine of God will make it more trinitarian, will facilitate the necessary turn to the economic Trinity, and will be more coherent with the experience of God to which many Christians already testify. Finally, I propose that integrating the Spirit into the doctrine of God produces an increased emphasis on the immanence of God. In fact, in some instances, attributes that have traditionally been understood as transcendent attributes of God are presented from the perspective of the Spirit as immanent attributes of God. We have seen that, as the Holy Spirit, God is not all-controlling, but a relational God, who, as holy, is faithful to humanity, even to the point of allowing himself to suffer in creation. The Holy Spirit, as the touch of God, is God as immanent.

In the year 2000 Clark Pinnock wrote, "It is time for Pentecostals to realize that they have a distinctive doctrine of God implicit in their faith and that they need to make it explicit—not just for purely academic purposes but for revival too, because Christianity is only as dynamic as its understanding of God."[104] My hope is that this essay has taken a step in this direction.

103. McDonnell, *Other Hand of God*, 112.
104. Pinnock, "Divine Relationality," 6.

Bibliography

Aquinas, Thomas. *Summa Theologiæ*. New York: Benziger Brothers, 1947.

Archer, Kenneth J. "Open Theism View: 'Prayer Changes Things.'" *Pneuma Review* 5 (2002) 32–53.

Arrington, French L. *Christian Doctrine: A Pentecostal Perspective*. 3 vols. Cleveland, TN: Pathway, 1992–1994.

Barth, Karl. *The Knowledge of God and the Service of God*. Translated by J. L. M. Haire and Ian Henderson. London: Hodder & Stoughton, 1938.

———. "Nachwort." In *Schleiermacher-Auswahl*. Edited by Heinz Bolli. Munich: Siebenstern-Taschenbuch, 1968.

———. *The Theology of Schleiermacher*. Edited by Dietrich Ritschl. Translated by George Hunsinger. Grand Rapids: Eerdmans, 1982.

Berkhof, Hendrikus. *The Doctrine of the Holy Spirit: The Annie Kinkead Warfield Lectures, 1963–1964*. Richmond, VA: John Knox, 1964.

Bloesch, Donald G. *God the Almighty: Power, Wisdom, Holiness, Love*. Downers Grove, IL: InterVarsity Press, 1995.

Boff, Leonardo. *Trinity and Society*. Translated by Paul Burns. Maryknoll, NY: Orbis, 1988.

Bowne, Borden P. *The Immanence of God*. Boston: Houghton, Mifflin & Co., 1905.

Bruner, Frederick Dale and William E. Hordern. *The Holy Spirit: Shy Member of the Trinity*. Minneapolis: Augsburg, 1984.

Bundy, David. "The Genre of Systematic Theology in Pentecostalism." *Pneuma* 15 (1993) 89–107.

Busch, Eberhard. *Karl Barth: His Life from Letters and Autobiographical Texts*. Translated by John Bowden. Philadelphia: Fortress, 1976.

Comblin, José. "The Holy Spirit." In *Systematic Theology: Perspectives from Liberation Theology*, edited by Jon Sobrino and Ignacio Ellacuria, 146–64. Maryknoll, NY: Orbis, 1996.

Cross, Terry L. "A Critical Review of Clark Pinnock's *Flame of Love: A Theology of the Holy Spirit*." *Journal of Pentecostal Theology* 6 (1998) 3–29.

———. "The Rich Feast of Theology: Can Pentecostals Bring the Main Course or Only the Relish?" *Journal of Pentecostal Theology* 16 (2000) 27–47.

———. "Toward a Theology of the Word and the Spirit: A Review of J. Rodman Williams's *Renewal Theology*." *Journal of Pentecostal Theology* 3 (1993) 113–35.

Dabney, D. Lyle. "Otherwise Engaged in the Spirit: A First Theology for a Twenty-First Century." In *The Future of Theology: Essays in Honor of Jürgen Moltmann*, edited by Miroslav Volf, Carmen Krieg, and Thomas Kucharz, 154–62. Grand Rapids: Eerdmans, 1996.

———. "Why Should the Last Be First? The Priority of Pneumatology in Recent Theological Discussion." In *Advents of the Spirit: An Introduction to Pneumatology*, edited by Bradford E. Hinze and D. Lyle Dabney, 240–61. Marquette Studies in Theology 30. Milwaukee: Marquette University Press, 2001.

Del Colle, Ralph. "A Response to Jürgen Moltmann and David Coffey." In *Advents of the Spirit: An Introduction to Pneumatology*, edited by Bradford E. Hinze and D. Lyle Dabney, 337–44. Marquette Studies in Theology 30. Milwaukee: Marquette University Press, 2001.

Duffield, Guy P. and Nathaniel M. Van Cleave. *Foundations of Pentecostal Theology*. Los Angeles: L.I.F.E. Bible College, 1983.

Edwards, Denis. *Breath of Life: A Theology of the Creator Spirit*. Maryknoll, NY: Orbis, 2004.

Ellington, Scott A. "Who Shall Lead Them Out?: An Exploration of God's Openness in Exodus 32.7–14." *Journal of Pentecostal Theology* 14 (2005) 41–60.

Farley, Edward. *The Transcendence of God: A Study in Contemporary Philosophical Theology*. Philadelphia: Westminster, 1958.

Fee, Gordon D. *God's Empowering Presence: The Holy Spirit in the Letters of Paul*. Peabody, MA: Hendrickson, 1994.

Gabriel, Andrew K. "Beyond the Cross: Moltmann's Crucified God, Rahner's Rule, and Implications for the Doctrine of God." *Didaskalia* 19 (forthcoming).

―――. "Pauline Pneumatology and the Question of Trinitarian Presuppositions." In *Paul and his Theology*, edited by Stanley E. Porter, 347–62. Pauline Studies 3. Leiden: Brill, 2006.

―――. "Pneumatological Perspectives for a Theology of Nature: The Holy Spirit in Relation to Ecology and Technology." *Journal of Pentecostal Theology* 15 (2007) 195–212.

Gregory of Nyssa. "On the Holy Spirit: Against the Followers of Macedonius." In vol. 5, *Nicene and Post-Nicene Fathers: Series II*, edited by Philip Schaff and Henry Wace, 315–25. Peabody, MA: Hendrickson, 1994.

Gunton, Colin E. *Act and Being: Towards a Theology of the Divine Attributes*. Grand Rapids: Eerdmans, 2002.

Guthrie, Shirley C., Jr. "The Nearness and Distance of God." In *Transcendence and Mystery*, edited by Earl D. C. Brewer, 32–45. New York: IDOC, 1975.

Higgins, John R., Michael L. Dusing, and Frank D. Tallman. *An Introduction to Theology: A Classical Pentecostal Perspective*. 2d ed. Dubuque, IA: Kendall/Hung, 1994.

Hinze, Bradford E. and D. Lyle Dabney, ed. *Advents of the Spirit: An Introduction to the Current Study of Pneumatology*. Marquette Studies in Theology 30. Milwaukee: Marquette University Press, 2001.

―――. "Introduction." In *Advents of the Spirit: An Introduction to Pneumatology*, edited by Bradford E. Hinze and D. Lyle Dabney, 1–34. Marquette Studies in Theology 30. Milwaukee: Marquette University Press, 2001.

Johnson, Elizabeth A. *She Who Is: The Mystery of God in Feminist Theological Discourse*. New York: Crossroad, 1992.

―――. *Women, Earth, and Creator Spirit*. New York: Paulist, 1993.

Kärkkäinen, Veli-Matti. *The Doctrine of God: A Global Introduction: A Biblical, Historical, and Contemporary Survey*. Grand Rapids: Baker Academic, 2004.

———. *Toward a Pneumatological Theology: Pentecostal and Ecumenical Perspectives on Ecclesiology, Soteriology, and Theology of Mission*. Edited by Amos Yong. Lanham, MD: University Press of America, 2002.

Kasper, Walter. *The God of Jesus Christ*. Translated by Matthew O'Connell. London: SCM, 1983.

LaCugna, Catherine M. "Current Trends in Trinitarian Theology." *Religious Studies Review* 13 (1987) 141–47.

LaCugna, Catherine M. and Kilian McDonnell. "Returning from 'The Far Country': Theses for a Contemporary Trinitarian Theology." *Scottish Journal of Theology* 41 (1988) 191–215.

Lee, Edgar R. "The 'Openness of God' from a Pentecostal Perspective." *Enrichment Journal* 7 (2002) 134–37. Online http://enrichmentjournal.ag.org/200204/200204_134_openness_of_god.cfm.

Macchia, Frank D. *Baptized in the Spirit: A Global Pentecostal Theology*. Grand Rapids: Zondervan, 2006.

Marshall, I. Howard. *Beyond the Bible: Moving from Scripture to Theology*. Acadia Studies in Bible and Theology. Grand Rapids: Baker Academic, 2004.

Marshall, Molly T. *Joining the Dance: A Theology of the Holy Spirit*. Valley Forge, PA: Judson, 2003.

McDonnell, Kilian. *The Other Hand of God: The Holy Spirit as the Universal Touch and Goal*. Collegeville, MN: Liturgical Press, 2003.

———. "A Response to Bernd Jochen Hilberath." In *Advents of the Spirit: An Introduction to Pneumatology*, edited by Bradford E. Hinze and D. Lyle Dabney, 293–99. Marquette Studies in Theology 30. Milwaukee: Marquette University Press, 2001.

———. "A Trinitarian Theology of the Holy Spirit?" *Theological Studies* 46 (1985) 191–227.

Menzies, William W. and Stanley M. Horton. *Bible Doctrines: A Pentecostal Perspective*. Springfield, MO: Logion, 1993.

Moltmann, Jürgen. *The Church in the Power of the Spirit: A Contribution to Messianic Ecclesiology*. Translated by Margaret Kohl. London: SCM, 1977.

———. *The Crucified God: The Cross of Christ as the Foundation and Criticism of Christian Theology*. Translated by. R. A. Wilson and John Bowden. London: SCM, 1974.

———. *God in Creation*: An Ecological Doctrine of Creation, translated by Margaret Kohl, The Gifford Lectures 1984-1985. London: SCM, 1985.

———. *The Spirit of Life: A Universal Affirmation*. Translated by Margaret Kohl. Minneapolis: Fortress, 1992.

———. *The Trinity and the Kingdom: The Doctrine of God*. Translated by Margaret Kohl. San Francisco: Harper & Row, 1981.

———. *The Way of Jesus Christ: Christology in Messianic Dimensions*. Translated by Margaret Kohl. San Francisco: Harper, 1990.

Mühlen, Heribert. "The Holy Spirit as Person." In *The Holy Spirit and Power: The Catholic Charismatic Renewal*, edited by Kilian McDonnell, 11–33. Garden City, NY: Doubleday, 1975.

Pearlman, Myer. *Knowing the Doctrines of the Bible*. Springfield, MO: Gospel Publishing House, 1937.

Pinnock, Clark H. "Divine Relationality: A Pentecostal Contribution to the Doctrine of God." *Journal of Pentecostal Theology* 16 (2000) 3–26.

———. *Flame of Love: A Theology of the Holy Spirit*. Downers Grove, IL: InterVarsity Press, 1996.

———. "God's Vulnerable Strength: Omnipotence as Love." In *Strength in Weakness*, edited by Michael Parsons and David Cohen. Eugene, OR: Wipf and Stock, forthcoming.

———. "The Recovery of the Holy Spirit in Evangelical Theology." *Journal of Pentecostal Theology* 13 (2004) 3–18.

Pittenger, Norman. *The Holy Spirit*. Philadelphia: United Church Press, 1974.

Polkinghorne, John, ed. *The Work of Love: Creation as Kenosis*. Grand Rapids: Eerdmans, 2001.

Preece, Gordon and Stephen Pickard, ed. *Starting with the Spirit: The Task of Theology Today II*. Adelaide, Australia: Australian Theological Forum Press, 2001.

Rahner, Karl. *The Trinity*. Translated by Joseph Donceel. New York: Herder & Herder, 1970.

Railey, James H. "Open Theism: An Arminian-Pentecostal Response." Assemblies of God Theological Seminary. Bible and Theology Department Lecture Series, September 24, 2003. Online http://www.agts.edu/faculty/faculty_publications/articles/railey_open-theism.pdf.

Robertson, John C., Jr. *The Loss and Recovery of Transcendence: The Will to Power and the Light of Heaven*. Princeton Theological Monograph Series 39. Allison Park, PA: Pickwick, 1995.

Sanders, Fred. "Trinity Talk, Again." *Dialog* 44 (2005) 264–72.

Schwöbel, Christoph. "Introduction: The Renaissance of Trinitarian Theology: Reasons, Problems and Tasks." In *Trinitarian Theology Today: Essays on Divine Being and Act*, edited by Christoph Schwöbel, 1–30. Edinburgh: T&T Clark, 1995.

Shults, F. LeRon. *Reforming the Doctrine of God*. Grand Rapids: Eerdmans, 2005.

Sirks, G. J. "The Cinderella of Theology: The Doctrine of the Holy Spirit." *Harvard Theological Review* 50 (1957) 77–89.

Spittler, Russell P. *God the Father*. Springfield, MO: Gospel Publishing House, 1976.

Studebaker, Steven M. "The Mode of Divine Knowledge in Reformation Arminianism and Open Theism." *Journal of the Evangelical Theological Society* 47 (2004) 469–80.

Tabbernee, William. "'Will the Real Paraclete Please Speak Forth!': The Catholic-Montanist Conflict Over Pneumatology." In *Advents of the Spirit: An Introduction to Pneumatology*, edited by Bradford E. Hinze and D. Lyle Dabney, 97–116. Marquette Studies in Theology 30. Milwaukee: Marquette University Press, 2001.

Thompson, John. *Modern Trinitarian Perspectives*. New York: Oxford University Press, 1994.

Thompson, Matthew K. "Does God Have a Future?: A Pentecostal Response to Christopher Hall's and John Sanders' Recent Book." *Pneuma* 26 (2004) 130–37.

Wallace, Mark I. "The Wounded Spirit as the Basis for Hope in an Age of Radical Ecology." In *Christianity and Ecology: Seeking the Well-Being of Earth and Humans*, edited by Dieter T. Hessel and Rosemary Radford Ruether, 51–82. Cambridge, MA: Harvard University Press, 2000.

Webster, John. *Holiness*. Grand Rapids: Eerdmans, 2003.

Yong, Amos. *The Spirit Poured Out on All Flesh: World Pentecostalism and the Possibility of Global Theology*. Grand Rapids: Baker Academic, 2005.

Zizioulas, John D. *Being as Communion: Studies in Personhood and the Church*. Crestwood, NY: St. Vladimir's Seminary Press, 1985.

PART II

Defining Issues in Pentecostal Biblical Studies:
Classical and Emergent

5

The Charismatic Theology of St. Luke Revisited[1]
(Special Emphasis upon Being Baptized in the Holy Spirit)

Roger Stronstad

To begin on a personal note, I came to learn about the Holy Spirit in stages. First, I grew up in a Pentecostal pastor's home in small town British Columbia. By the time I was a teenager I had learned anecdotally that there were Christians in other churches who did not have the same beliefs or experiences about the Holy Spirit that we did. More surprisingly, some of them were actually hostile toward the twentieth-century Pentecostal Movement. Second, after I graduated from high school and enrolled in a Pentecostal Bible college, I was academically exposed to the issues that divided Pentecostals and other Protestants concerning the doctrine of the Holy Spirit. Third, graduation from Bible college led briefly to pastoral ministry, again in small town British Columbia, and then two years later I enrolled in a fledgling trans-denominational graduate school located in Vancouver, British Columbia, namely, Regent College. At Regent I was introduced to the full scholarly discussion about the Holy Spirit then taking place, particularly as it was presented in two recently published books, now classics on the subject. These were *A Theology of the Holy Spirit*, by Frederick Dale Bruner and *Baptism in the Holy Spirit*, by James D. G. Dunn. Less scholarly, but perhaps equally, if not more, influential at

---

1. Stronstad, *Charismatic Theology*.

the popular level was John R. W. Stott's booklet, *The Baptism and Fullness of the Holy Spirit*.

I learned much from this literature, even though I found that, because of my Pentecostal heritage, I disagreed with some of what I was reading. But I also saw two things that I found puzzling. First, this literature informed its readers that Pentecostals taught things that I as a Pentecostal did not believe or teach, and second, they said that Luke's data about the Holy Spirit, particularly in the book of Acts, was to be interpreted by Paul's teaching about the Holy Spirit in his epistles. Though this hermeneutical approach to the doctrine of the Holy Spirit in Acts was persuasively articulated, it ran contrary to my own approach to interpreting Acts. And so, in the hermeneutics of non-Pentecostal evangelical Protestantism I found the motive and the subject for my master's thesis, which bore the mundane title *The Holy Spirit in Luke–Acts*. A lightly revised version was published ten years later by Hendrickson Publishers, under the title *The Charismatic Theology of St. Luke*.[2]

A Miscellany of Observations and Presuppositions

A miscellany of observations informed and/or shaped my approach to the study of Luke's doctrine of the Holy Spirit. These include the canonical disruption of Luke–Acts, the integrity and unique status of Luke as a historian and theologian, the independence of Luke vis-à-vis Paul, and Luke's assumption that Spirit baptism follows salvation. The following section develops these in detail.

The Canonical Divide

This is the first of my observations. The "canonical divide" is the fact that, though Luke's Gospel, and its sequel, the Acts of the Apostles, are two parts/volumes of one book, in the canonical shape of the New Testament they are divided by the Gospel of John. No other book in the entire canon of Scripture is treated in this fashion. One result of the canonical divide is that Luke and Acts came to be treated as two different literary genres,

---

2. Subsequently, I also published a collection of essays on the Holy Spirit (*Spirit, Scripture, and Theology*) and a specialized study on the Holy Spirit (*Prophethood of All Believers*). In addition, I have published two booklets: *Signs on the Earth Beneath* and *Baptized and Filled*.

namely Gospel and Acts. A second, perhaps inevitable, result of the canonical divide was that interpreters sometimes thought they found different theological perspectives in each genre. Thus, for example, Luke's most characteristic term, "filled with the Holy Spirit," was given a different meaning when it was found in Luke's Gospel than when it was in Luke's Acts of the Apostles.[3] Based on a close reading of the Gospel and the Acts, and supported by Henry J. Cadbury's earlier seminal study of Luke's writings (where he identified Luke's book as Luke–Acts),[4] I argued that Luke's two-volume book was characterized by theological homogeneity. Thus, for example, it would not do to assert, as some scholars were doing, that Jesus' experiences of the Spirit were irrelevant for understanding the disciples' experiences of the Holy Spirit reported in Acts, beginning with the outpouring of the Holy Spirit on the disciples on the day of Pentecost.

Luke: Historian, Theologian, and Teacher

Luke identifies his two-volume book as historical narrative (Greek: *diēgēsis* [Luke 1:1], and *logos* [Acts 1:1]). This identification puts him in the context of earlier historiography, both secular and sacred. No one who has turned from Luke–Acts to the sacred histories of the Hebrew Bible, to later histories such as 1 Maccabees, to the histories of Luke's contemporary, Josephus, or to the histories of the Greco-Roman culture from Herodotus onwards, will mistake Luke–Acts for anything other than what Luke has claimed for it. In addition, no one who turns from Luke–Acts to these centuries-long historiographical traditions will mistake Luke for anything other than the equal of his predecessors, and in some cases their superior. But Luke–Acts is more than just a fine example of ancient historical writing, and Luke is more than a mere historian.

In addition to being an exemplary historian, Luke is also a theologian. As a Christian who writes the history of Jesus, his disciples, and their converts, he cannot really be otherwise. My studies in the historical literature of the Hebrew Bible taught me this. In addition, I. Howard Marshall's book, *Luke: Historian and Theologian*, confirmed my conviction that Luke wrote his two part narrative about the origin and spread of Christianity as an intentional theologian. Soon a scholarly consensus about Luke's theological intentionality emerged. About a decade ago the book *Witness to*

---

3. Cf. Hull, *Holy Spirit in the Acts*, 68–69 and Delling, "πίμπλημι," 130.
4. Cadbury, *Making of Luke–Acts*.

the Gospel: The Theology of Acts, edited by I. Howard Marshall and David Peterson, illustrated that something like a scholarly consensus about the theological significance of Luke's historical narratives had arrived. All of a sudden my monograph, *The Charismatic Theology of St. Luke*, initially greeted with some reservation, became more mainstream. But Luke is more than a theologian who writes narrative theology.

Luke is also, self-consciously, a teacher. He writes with didactic aims. In his prologue, Luke explains to Theophilus (and to every reader of Luke–Acts) about his catechetical or instructional intention: "it seemed fitting for me . . . to write . . . so that you may know the exact truth about the things which you have been taught" (*catēchēthēs*, Luke 1:4). So, although Theophilus has been taught (instructed about all that Jesus has done and taught), Luke, nevertheless, writes his narrative account to instruct him more fully and more accurately. In this regard Theophilus seems to be like the catechumen Apollos, who, Luke says, was instructed in the way of the Lord, but nevertheless was given more accurate teaching by Priscilla and Aquila (Acts 18:25–26). Luke does not tell his readers by what catechetical methodologies Apollos was instructed by Priscilla and Aquila, but all those who read his narratives can observe the many different teaching strategies by which he teaches history and theology to the catechumen Theophilus. These include, but are not limited to: 1) the use of Hebrew Bible/Septuagint terminology, 2) echoes of Old Testament typology, 3) reports of charismatic (i.e., Spirit-inspired) exegesis, 4) programmatic narratives, 5) inclusion, 6) promise-fulfillment, 7) parallelism, and 8) sermons and speeches.[5]

Luke's many narratival strategies and instructional techniques mean that Luke, historian and theologian, is a skilled teacher *par excellence.* Indeed, an unprejudiced reading of Luke–Acts shows that he rivals Paul as the greatest theologian and teacher in the primitive church. This observation means that Luke is just as important a teacher as Paul. It also means, for example, that his teaching about being "baptized in the Holy Spirit" is just as important, if not more important, than Paul's teaching about being "baptized in the Holy Spirit" (1 Cor 12:13). Therefore, just as Paul's letters, when properly interpreted, teach twenty-first century Christians, so Luke's two-part narrative, when properly interpreted, also teaches twenty-first century Christians important historical and theo-

---

5. Stronstad, "Baptized and Filled," 5–21.

logical lessons, not least of which is his distinctive doctrine about being baptized in the Holy Spirit.

Luke was Independent of Paul

The third of my presuppositions was that Luke's theological emphasis concerning the Holy Spirit is independent of and different from Paul's. Now, even in the 1970s, this was a commonplace idea in the biblical theological movement. Unfortunately, this insight had not been accepted by those interpreters of Acts who were influenced by Reformed hermeneutics and theology. Thus, for example, Stott insisted as a matter of principle that all seven references to the baptism in the Holy Spirit must not only mean the same thing, but must mean what Paul meant by the term (1 Cor 12:13).[6] Also, examples of the reception of the Holy Spirit in Acts must be interpreted by Paul's perspectives, such as those articulated in Rom 8:9.[7] By looking at Luke's narratives about the Holy Spirit through Paul's glasses, interpreters such as Stott and Dunn muzzled Luke and silenced his distinctive message about the Holy Spirit in the contemporary Church. In this way, a certain school of interpreters has created a Pauline canon within the larger canon of the New Testament. Surprisingly, despite strong criticism of his approach to interpreting Luke's narratives about the Holy Spirit, Dunn persists in making Paul's writings the canonical standard.[8] However, by adopting the presuppositions of the biblical theological movement, my interpretation of Luke's narratives about the Holy Spirit gave a radically different description of Luke's theology about the Holy Spirit. The contrast with the aforementioned interpreters is stark. Interpreting Luke as a theologian who not only writes independently of Paul but who also has different perspectives than Paul does result in the observation that Luke reports a vocational/charismatic activity of the Holy Spirit—both for Jesus in the Gospel and the disciples and their converts in Acts. In contrast, to interpret Luke as though he were Paul leads to a soteriological/initiation-conversion interpretation of the Holy Spirit in Luke's narratives. However, the latter approach is methodologically illegitimate.

---

6. Stott, *Baptism and Fullness*, 23.
7. Dunn, *Baptism in the Holy Spirit*, 55.
8. Dunn, "Baptism in the Spirit."

The "Right Standing before God" Prerequisite

In Luke–Acts all who receive the Holy Spirit have first gained the essential spiritual prerequisite, namely, they are already saved. In every example that Luke reports, from Elizabeth and Zacharias (Luke 1:41, 67) to the Ephesian Twelve (Acts 19:6), all are in right standing before God *before* they receive the Holy Spirit. Luke uses a variety of terms to identify this prerequisite. For example, Elizabeth and Zacharias are "righteous" and the Ephesian Twelve are "believers" (Luke 1:6 and Acts 19:2). But whatever the term, in each case Luke always identifies a person's right standing before God before he reports their subsequent reception of the Holy Spirit.

Not only does Luke identify people's spiritual pre-qualifications before he reports that they receive the Holy Spirit, he also reports Peter's statement about this pattern of Christian experience in his Pentecost sermon (Acts 2:37–38). To the question asked by the Pentecost pilgrims, "Brethren what shall we do?" Peter replies, "Repent, and let each one of you be baptized in the name of Jesus Christ for the forgiveness of sins; and you shall receive the gift of the Holy Spirit." Thus, according to Peter, the gift of the Holy Spirit (which, in context, must be being "baptized in the Holy Spirit," which Jesus announced his disciples would shortly receive [Acts 1:4–5]), can only be received by those who have first repented of their sins and, therefore, have come into right standing before God, and have their sins forgiven. Simply put, repentance/forgiveness is the essential spiritual prerequisite for being "baptized in the Holy Spirit." In other words, being "baptized in the Holy Spirit" in Luke–Acts cannot be a soteriological experience. Rather, it is that charismatic experience that the disciples received on the day of Pentecost (Acts 2:14–21).

These observations about Luke's data are commonly dismissed out of hand by many interpreters within the Evangelical tradition. This is because they interpret Peter's statement reported in Acts 2:38 according to Paul's theology (1 Cor 12:13), rather than according to Luke's theology. For example, in his book *The Holy Spirit*, Donald G. Bloesch writes: "If our text (i.e., Acts 2:38–39) is taken in isolation, it is possible to infer that a charismatic endowment by the Spirit follows faith and repentance."[9] Although he makes the correct inference about the meaning of Acts 2:38–39 he spoils it all by insisting: "Repentance and baptism are not

---

9. Bloesch, *Holy Spirit*, 309.

the conditions for receiving the gift of the Holy Spirit (cf. Acts 2:37–38). Repentance, faith, and the baptism of the Spirit happen concurrently in the Christian experience."[10] Therefore, to demonstrate that Luke's theology about Spirit baptism is different from that espoused by many contemporary interpreters, we will look first at Luke's general principle from his initial examples of the "right standing before God" prerequisite, then we will look at the spiritual prerequisites of those whom he reports to be "baptized in the Holy Spirit," namely, the disciples on the day of Pentecost and the household of Cornelius (Acts 2 and 10).

General Examples: The Gospel of Luke

Luke's examples start at the beginning of his first account, the so-called Gospel of Luke. Immediately after concluding his Prologue (Luke 1:1–4) Luke introduces his catechumen, Theophilus, to an aged priestly couple, a certain Zacharias and Elizabeth (Luke 1:5–80). Luke reports that "they were both righteous in the sight of God, walking blamelessly in all . . . the requirements of the Lord" (Luke 1:6). The fact that Luke says they "walked blamelessly" implies that their righteousness was of long-standing. Then Luke advances his narrative to six months later, reporting that Elizabeth was "filled with the Holy Spirit" (Luke 1:41). Three months after that, her husband, Zacharias, "was (also) filled with the Holy Spirit and prophesied" (Luke 1:67). And it was the same for another elderly resident of Jerusalem, a certain Simeon (Luke 2:25–35). Luke reports that he was righteous and devout, looking for "the consolation of Israel." This implies that his righteousness too was long-standing. On that day when Joseph and Mary brought their new-born son to the Temple (Luke 2:22–24), Simeon, who had the Spirit upon him, and who had revelations by the Spirit, was now led by the Spirit to bless this baby who would become God's agent of salvation, both for the Gentiles and for Israel. And so, both for Elizabeth and Zacharias, and for Simeon, there is an obvious gap between their salvation experience, which qualified them as "righteous," and their Spirit-filled prophetic experiences. In their cases, then, their experiences of the Holy Spirit were about prophetic ministry and not about salvation.

---

10. Bloesch, *Holy Spirit*, 298.

General Examples: The Acts of the Apostles

In his "continuation narrative" (Acts), Luke continues to report many other examples where salvation preceded and was the essential prerequisite for the gift of the Spirit. The two most significant examples are Luke's report of the outpouring of the Holy Spirit upon the disciples on the day of Pentecost (Acts 2:1–21), and many years later upon Cornelius and his household (Acts 10:1—11:18). Because of their crucial place in Luke's narrative, these episodes will be discussed more fully in subsequent paragraphs. But, before we get to them, we observe other examples as the narrative of Acts unfolds. For example, in Acts 4:31, Luke reports that the disciples, "were all filled with the Holy Spirit, and *began* to speak the word of God with boldness." Luke identifies these disciples as "their own *companions*," that is, companions of Peter and John (Acts 4:23). These companions are the 5,000 "believers" of Acts 4:4, whose number must have also included many of the 3,000 who were saved on the day of Pentecost (Acts 2:41). In addition, Luke reports Philip's "evangelistic" ministry in Samaria (compare Acts 21:8). Fleeing the outbreak of persecution against the disciples in Jerusalem (Acts 8:1–4) Philip went down to Samaria and proclaimed Christ to them (Acts 8:5). Many Samaritans "believed . . . the good news about the Kingdom of God," that is, "they received the Word of God" (Acts 8:12, 14). In time Peter and John came down to Samaria, and because the Holy Spirit had not yet fallen upon the believing Samaritans, Peter and John prayed that these believers might receive the Holy Spirit, which they did (Acts 8:15–17). Luke also reports a final example of this separation between salvation (believing) and receiving the Holy Spirit. This is the episode about Paul and the twelve Ephesian disciples (Acts 19:1–7). When Paul encountered these disciples at Ephesus he asked, "Having believed, did you receive the Holy Spirit?" The disciples answered, "No." Paul explained to them further about John the Baptist and Jesus, baptized them, and prayed for them. When he laid his hands on them, "the Holy Spirit came on them, and they *began* speaking in tongues and prophesying" (Acts 19:6). As the disciples had earlier done on the day of Pentecost, these disciples in Ephesus received the Holy Spirit of prophecy some time after they believed.

The Charismatic Theology of St. Luke *Revisited*

The Essential Spiritual Prerequisite of the One Hundred and Twenty

Having surveyed Luke's examples of the bestowing of the gift of the Spirit throughout Acts, we must now back up to the Pentecost narrative (Acts 2:1–41). Luke reports that on this first post-Easter feast of Pentecost, the disciples, "were all filled with the Holy Spirit and began to speak with other tongues as the Spirit gave utterance" (Acts 2:4). Luke explicitly identifies this experience to be an eschatological outpouring of the Spirit of prophecy (Acts 2:14–21). But contrary to Luke's clear report, generations of interpreters have insisted, and continue to insist, that the disciples' experience of the Spirit was primarily about salvation (initiation-incorporation, coming to faith), and concede, grudgingly, that secondarily it may be about Christian vocation. But though this interpretation of the outpouring of the Holy Spirit upon the disciples on the day of Pentecost is commonly believed by many Christians, it cannot be correct. What makes it impossible is that Luke has shown in his Gospel many times, and in many different ways, that the disciples were in right standing before God for several years before the day of Pentecost. Consider the evidence. Jesus called men such as Levi to forgiveness (Luke 5:27–32). He called certain disciples of John the Baptist, whose sins had already been forgiven, to become his own disciples (Luke 5:1–11). Twelve of them became his apostles during the time of his public ministry (Luke 6:13).

Having been sent out, the Twelve did the same thematic works that Jesus himself had done, namely, they cast out demons and healed the sick (Luke 9:1–7). And so, they preached the gospel (good news) in words and miraculous deeds (Luke 9:6, 10). Later, the ministry of the Seventy was so like Christ's own ministry that Jesus assured them, "the one who listens to you listens to me; and the one who rejects you rejects me; and he who rejects me rejects the one who sent me" (Luke 10:16). Further, Jesus reminded this group of disciples that their names were recorded in heaven (Luke 10:20). Finally, Jesus shared his last Passover with the apostles, which means that, nothing less than fifty days before Pentecost, they shared in the inaugural redemptive meal of the new covenant. In light of this evidence from throughout the Gospel, I find it absurd to say that the outpouring of the Holy Spirit on the day of Pentecost was about salvation rather than about vocation. This is because (1) the disciples were saved (i.e., believers) long before the day of Pentecost and (2) Luke explicitly identifies the outpouring of the Spirit on the day of Pentecost as being about prophecy (Acts 2:17–18). The gap between the salvation of the disciples and their reception of the Spirit is not an anomaly. In every example we have examined in Luke–Acts this is the invariable pattern.

The Essential Spiritual Prerequisite of Cornelius and his Household

There is one final example of being baptized in the Holy Spirit to be investigated. This is the example of Cornelius, the centurion stationed at Caesarea (Acts 10:1). The Cornelius episode is so strategic in the story of the spread of Christianity that Luke makes it just about the longest single narrative unit in Acts (Acts 10:1—11:18). So important are Cornelius's spiritual qualifications for receiving the Spirit that Luke identifies them three times in the narrative. First, Luke reports Cornelius to be a devout man, a God-fearer, an alms-giver, and a receiver of visions (Acts 10:2–4). Second, Luke reports the description of Cornelius that his messengers give to Peter, namely, that he is righteous, God-fearing, well spoken of throughout the Jewish community, and one who has received directions from an angel (Acts 10:22). Third, Luke reports what Peter learns about Cornelius from these same messengers as they travel together along the way from Joppa to Caesarea. They say that Cornelius already knows about John's baptism, about Jesus of Nazareth, about his being anointed by the Holy Spirit, and about his charismatic ministry (Acts 10:34–38). Further, so important is Peter's visit to Cornelius and Cornelius's subsequent reception of the Holy Spirit that Luke reports it twice (10:1–48 and 11:1–18). Thus, in Luke's estimation, Cornelius has many essential spiritual qualifications, even though these qualifications are not unique to him. They are the same qualifications possessed by others, who have earlier received the Holy Spirit.

The spiritual qualifications of those men and women who received the Holy Spirit before him anticipated Cornelius's qualifications and also give Theophilus and Luke's readership the key to understanding the meaning of his reception of the Spirit. For example, like Zacharias and Elizabeth, Cornelius was righteous. Like Simeon, Cornelius was not only righteous but also had visions, a medium of divine revelation (Num 12:6 and Joel 2:28). Like the centurion of Galilee, he had a high reputation among the Jews and was a man of faith (Luke 7:2–10; Acts 10:22; 11:17). Like Peter and John, he was a man of prayer (Acts 3:1) and, like Barnabas and Matthias, he had the necessary qualifications for apostleship—knowing about (but apparently not having witnessed) John's ministry and Jesus' anointing and ministry. While he was not a disciple of Jesus at that earlier time, Cornelius, as far as Luke's narrative shows, was spiritually more qualified to receive the Spirit than anyone outside of the twelve.[11]

But Cornelius did not receive the Holy Spirit merely as an individual. Among the many people who gathered with Cornelius to await the arrival of Peter were his relatives and close friends who, like Cornelius himself, were also God-fearers (Acts 10:24). At least one of Cornelius's soldiers was, like Cornelius, a devout man (Acts 10:7). Thus, we may presume that many, if not all, of his extended household shared his piety and faith. Along with Cornelius and his household, his close friends gathered with him, "before God" (Acts 10:32).

And so, as Peter talked to them about Jesus, the Holy Spirit fell upon them all, and they spoke with tongues, exalting God (Acts 10:45–46). All of this means that while Peter was still speaking the Holy Spirit fell upon a believing/faith community (Acts 11:17), a community that, as much as any in New Testament times, deserved to be identified as a house church prior to the falling of the Spirit upon them, and after receiving the Spirit they deserved to be identified as a charismatic community.

Summary

Luke's reports of the many men and women who possessed essential spiritual prerequisites prior to their experience of receiving the Holy Spirit are extensive. He begins with the report about Zachariah and Elizabeth and ends with the report about the twelve Ephesian disciples. Not only are his reports extensive and pervasive, they are also explicit and unambiguous. As Luke reports it, the Holy Spirit was only poured out on men and women, on individuals and on groups, who already possessed the appropriate spiritual prerequisites. Clearly then, Luke's data compels his readers to recognize that there is an interval between salvation and receiving the Holy Spirit. Since this is a matter of Luke's explicit data, his readers are compelled to recognize that in Luke–Acts, receiving the Spirit is about

---

11. In her volume, *Diaspora Setting*, Levinskaya discounts Luke's report about the spiritual condition of Cornelius. She concludes: "he (Cornelius) is a centurion in the *Cohorts Italica* which means that he . . . participated in the official cult . . . (he) has to demonstrate publicly his polytheism . . . he is an idolater, participating in offerings to pagan gods" (p. 123). It is difficult to reconcile Levinskaya's description of Cornelius with Luke's description.

Christian vocation or charismatic experience rather than about salvation. In fact, no amount of verbal gymnastics or linguistic slight-of-hand (at which many interpreters excel) can overturn the evidence. To deny that the disciples, Cornelius and his household, or the Ephesian Twelve were communities of faith (i.e., Christian communities) before they received the Holy Spirit is preposterous and absurd.

Baptized in the Holy Spirit

Having demonstrated that Luke consistently reports that everyone in his narrative who received the Holy Spirit had a "right standing" or "salvation" standing as the essential prior condition to receiving the Spirit, it is now necessary to examine the meaning of being baptized in the Holy Spirit. This term appears just seven times in the New Testament, but it has a value all out of proportion to the small number of references to it.

The Biblical Data

Of the seven references in the New Testament to being baptized in the Holy Spirit, one is to be found in Paul's first letter to Corinth. There he writes: "for by one Spirit we were all baptized into one body" (1 Cor 12:13). This is about initiation-incorporation. In addition, each of the four evangelists reported that John the Baptist prophesied that his successor would "baptize in the Holy Spirit and fire" (Matt 3:11–12; Mark 1:7–8; Luke 3:16–17; and John 1:30–34). Further, Luke, and Luke alone, reports that Jesus renewed and applied John the Baptist's prophecy to the soon-approaching day of Pentecost (Acts 1:4–5). Finally, Luke reports that Peter identified Cornelius' reception of the Spirit to be a fulfillment of John the Baptist's prophecy about being baptized in the Holy Spirit (Acts 11:16). This data shows that Matthew, Mark, John, and Paul each have one reference to being baptized in the Holy Spirit. It also shows that Luke has three references to this experience. From these numbers one may infer that being baptized in the Holy Spirit is more important to Luke than it is to any other writer in the New Testament. As a corollary, one may also infer that the meaning of the term in Luke's narrative is the normative meaning. A further corollary is that Paul's use of the term in his letter to the Corinthians does not determine its meaning in Luke–Acts. One final observation is that each of Luke's three references to the term is to be interpreted in the immediate context where the term is used (Luke 3:16–17; Acts 1:5, 2:1–21; Acts 10:44–48; 11:15–17).

Prophecy: John the Baptist's Successor Will Baptize in the Holy Spirit and Fire

The prophet John the Baptist, herald and forerunner to the coming Messiah, prophesied that his successor would baptize in the Holy Spirit and fire (Luke 3:16). Until today, many interpreters continue to debate whether John prophesied about one baptism, in which Spirit and fire had either the same meaning or a complementary meaning, or whether he prophesied two baptisms, that is, one baptism in the Spirit and a distinctly different baptism in fire. Fortunately for the serious interpreter, John himself explained what his prophecy meant. He continued his prophecy, explaining: "And his winnowing fork is in his hand to thoroughly clear his threshing floor, and to gather the wheat into his barn; but he will burn up the chaff with unquenchable fire" (Luke 3:17). John's explanation of his prophecy was, of course, an agricultural or harvest metaphor. This metaphor is about fruitfulness (wheat harvest) and destruction (the chaff is burned). These two polarities in the metaphor parallel the polarities in his prophecy. The wheat harvest parallels the prophecy that his successor would baptize in the Holy Spirit; the burning of the chaff parallels the prophecy that his successor would baptize in fire. Therefore, in the light of John's own explanation, it is clear that John prophesied two baptisms; a baptism in the Holy Spirit upon the penitent (bringing blessing), and a baptism in fire upon the impenitent (being judgment).

John's successor, whom the narrative identifies as Jesus, did not, however, fulfill the two baptisms that John had prophesied for him. In fact, right at the beginning, at his inaugural sermon in Nazareth, Jesus identified a different agenda from the one that John had prophesied for him. He read from the book of the prophet Isaiah:

> The Spirit of the Lord is upon me,
> Because he anointed me to preach the gospel to the poor,
> He has sent me to proclaim release to the captives,
> And recovery of sight to the blind,
> To set free those who are downtrodden,
> To proclaim the favorable year of the Lord (Luke 4:18–19).

Giving the book back to the synagogue official, Jesus declared, "Today this Scripture has been fulfilled in your hearing" (Luke 4:21). Clearly, Jesus proclaimed a different agenda for his ministry than the one that John had earlier prophesied.

The agenda that Jesus fulfilled was radically different in tone from either the tone of John's own ministry, or the tone that he prophesied would characterize the Messiah's ministry. Those tones were about tree-destroying fire and chaff-destroying fire (Luke 3:9, 17). In contrast, from the very beginning, the tone of Jesus' Spirit-anointed ministry was about good news, divine favor, and gracious words (Luke 4:18–21). The obvious contrast between the judgmental tone of John's prophetic ministry and the gracious tone of Jesus' prophetic ministry, and between what John prophesied and what Jesus did, created a crisis for John, and perhaps even disillusionment. Thus, he sent two messengers to Jesus, asking: "Are you the One who is coming, or do we look for someone else?" (Luke 7:19–20). The fact was that Jesus would baptize in the Holy Spirit and fire, but obviously not in the way that John envisioned. Jesus would indeed baptize in chaff-destroying fire, but he would cast this fire of judgment upon the earth in the (implied) distant future (Luke 12:49). Also, he would baptize in the Holy Spirit, but not until after his resurrection and ascension, that is, not until the first post-Easter day of Pentecost.

Prophecy Renewed: Jesus Would Baptize his Disciples in the Holy Spirit

Jesus did not fulfill John's prophecy that his successor would "baptize in the Holy Spirit and fire," until after his death. This did not disqualify John as a true prophet or Jesus as the Lord's Anointed (i.e., Messiah, Christ). Just days before he ascended into heaven, Jesus renewed John's prophecy. Luke reports how, "gathering the disciples together he commanded them . . . to wait for what the Father had promised, 'which,' he said, 'you heard from me; for John baptized with water, but you shall be baptized in the Holy Spirit not many days from now'" (Acts 1:4–5).

This prophecy was fulfilled a few days later in Jerusalem, when, as part of a sudden, dramatic theophany at the house (of God) the disciples, ". . . were all filled with the Holy Spirit and began to speak with other tongues [i.e., foreign languages], as the Spirit was giving them utterance" (Acts 2:2–4). This was a fulfillment of John's prophecy, but not completely. Jesus baptized his disciples with the Holy Spirit (blessing) but he did not baptize them with the judgment of chaff-destroying fire (note the absence of "fire" in Jesus' renewal of John's prophecy, Acts 1:5). But, "what does this mean?" the thronging Pentecost pilgrims wondered, their curiosity aroused by the metaphorical wind and fire and the tongues-speaking. The meaning, especially of the tongues-speaking, appeared self-evident to some in the crowd. Mockingly they concluded, "they are full of sweet wine" (Acts 2:13), i.e., they are drunk. But not everyone mocked. Many marveled, being bewildered, amazed, and greatly perplexed (Acts 2:5–12). Seizing the opportunity created by the three signs of Pentecost, Peter stood forth from the company of disciples to explain. His explanation was a pneuma discourse (i.e., Spirit-inspired speech). Specifically, it was also an example of charismatic exegesis (i.e., Spirit-inspired interpretation). Filled with the Holy Spirit, Peter announced, "this is what was spoken of through the prophet Joel" (Acts 2:16). By appealing to Joel's prophecy Peter made it clear to the bewildered worshippers that this outpouring of the Holy Spirit was about prophetic inspiration. As Joel had prophesied, when God poured out his Spirit in the last days,

> ... sons and daughters shall prophesy.
> And your young men shall see visions.
> And your old men shall dream dreams.
> Even upon my bondslaves, both men and women,
> I will in those days pour forth of my Spirit
> *And they shall prophesy* (Acts 2:17–18).

By juxtaposing the narrative about John's prophecy that Jesus would baptize in the Holy Spirit (Acts 1:4–5) and the Pentecost narrative (2:1–21), Luke makes it plain that the outpouring of the Holy Spirit upon the disciples was their being, "baptized in the Holy Spirit." Further, by reporting Peter's Spirit-inspired exegesis to explain this event, Luke teaches several points. This pouring forth of the Holy Spirit was: 1) the last days/eschatological gift of the Spirit, 2) the gift of prophecy, 3) inclusive in terms of age, gender, and economic status, and 4) attested by signs, not the least of which was speaking in other tongues.

As an event in the unfolding drama of salvation history, the outpouring of the Holy Spirit upon the disciples on the day of Pentecost was a once-for-all, never to be repeated event. But, as Luke's history of the spread of Christianity shows, the experience of being baptized in the

Holy Spirit continued for new disciples such as Cornelius and his household of God-fearers. As Peter announced on the day of Pentecost, the Father's promise, first prophesied by John the Baptist, was for the first generation of disciples, their children, and indeed, for all who are afar off (Acts 2:38). In fact, Peter learned through his encounter with Cornelius that being baptized in the Holy Spirit extended much farther than he could ever have imagined on the day of Pentecost.

Prophecy Fulfilled: A Caesarean House Church was Baptized in the Holy Spirit

Luke's extensive report about the Cornelius episode is not about Cornelius' salvation, that is, his initiation-incorporation. Luke's report does not show Peter evangelizing this Italian centurion. Rather, his report identifies a massive array of Cornelius's existing spiritual qualifications and reveals that he had a totally unexpected knowledge about the complementary ministries of John the Baptist, and, more importantly, of Jesus of Nazareth (see discussion above). Luke's two-volume narrative provides Theophilus with two possible clues about the source of Cornelius's knowledge. Either Cornelius was the unidentified centurion of Luke 7:2–10, or he learned about John and Jesus from Philip the evangelist, who apparently lived in Caesarea from the time of his encounter with the Ethiopian court official (Acts 8:40) until the time of Paul's visit (Acts 21:8).

This introduction to Luke's report about the Holy Spirit falling upon Cornelius and his household has but one purpose. It is to show that Cornelius and his household, by any and every New Testament standard, had become Christian before being baptized in the Holy Spirit. Should there still be any doubt in the reader's mind, Luke reports the outpouring of the Spirit in these words: "the gift of the Holy Spirit has been poured out on the Gentiles also" (Acts 10:45). The words "gift" and "also" direct the attention of Luke's readers back to his Pentecost narrative (Acts 2:1–40). There he reported that Peter promised to all who repented of their sins: "you will receive the gift of the Holy Spirit" (Acts 2:38). Clearly, and no verbal gymnastics, no matter how skilled, can overturn this New Testament fact, the gift of the Holy Spirit, whether to Jews on the day of Pentecost or to Gentiles in Caesarea, was given to those whose sins had been forgiven because they had repented. In Luke's theology about the Holy Spirit, the gift of the Spirit always presupposes a prior repentance.

This observation of Luke's theology about the gift of the Holy Spirit to Cornelius is confirmed by a cluster of descriptions and comparisons to the Pentecost narrative. For example, in both narratives those who received the Holy Spirit spoke in tongues (Acts 2:4 and 10:46). The content of this Spirit-inspired speech was that both the disciples on the day of Pentecost and later Cornelius exalted God (Acts 2:11and 10:46). Further, as reported by Luke, Peter observed that Cornelius and his household received the Holy Spirit (Acts 10:47), and also that God gave to Cornelius the same gift as had earlier been given to the disciples after they had believed (Acts 11:17).

In other words, both Luke's descriptions of what happened and his report about Peter's comparison with the day of Pentecost mean that the gift of the Holy Spirit to Cornelius was the same gift of prophecy that had been poured out upon the disciples earlier. Clearly, everyone who reads Luke's report about Cornelius' reception of the Spirit is fully justified in concluding that 1) like the disciples on the day of Pentecost, Cornelius and his household were baptized in the Holy Spirit and 2) this was the prophetic, vocational gift of the Spirit.

Though Luke's narrative itself justifies these conclusions, Luke spells out this very thing for his readers in his duplicate account (Acts 11:1–18). He does so by reporting Peter's own interpretation of the outpouring of the Spirit upon Cornelius after Peter has returned from Caesarea to Jerusalem. Back in Jerusalem Peter reports to the apostles and the brethren:

> And as I began to speak, the Holy Spirit fell upon them just as *he did* upon us at the beginning. And I remembered the word of the Lord, how he used to say, "John baptized with water, but you shall be baptized with the Holy Spirit." If God therefore gave to them the same gift as *he gave* to us also after believing in the Lord Jesus Christ, who was I that I could stand in God's way? (Acts 11:15–17)

By this evidence Luke compels his readers to observe a pattern: being baptized in the Holy Spirit is signified by the sign of speaking in tongues and, in turn, the sign of speaking in tongues signifies that "being baptized in the Holy Spirit" has taken place (Acts 1:4–5, 2:4; 10:44–48; 11:15–17).

Summary

Through the events associated with the Spirit-baptism of Cornelius and his household, Peter and the Jewish Christian community learned momentous lessons. For example, Peter learned the thrice repeated lesson that God had "cleansed" Cornelius and the community who worshipped with him (Acts 10:10–16). As Peter himself acknowledged, Cornelius and his community of God-fearers, "were welcome to him [God]" (Acts 10:35). This was the message of salvation that Peter would come to announce to Cornelius (Acts 11:14). This was the gospel that it was enough that Cornelius and his household were a righteous, God-fearing community of faith. This was the good news that these Gentiles did not also have to be circumcised to be saved, as some Jewish Christians insisted (Acts 15:1, 5). No, before the Holy Spirit fell upon Cornelius and his household, before they were baptized in the Holy Spirit, before they spoke in tongues, God had already cleansed their hearts by faith (Acts 15:9). Therefore, for the second time (Acts 2, 10) Luke shows that only those who already qualify as believers/believing communities can then be baptized in the Holy Spirit. Once again, this evidence is compelling. Being baptized in the Holy Spirit is not about salvation, but it is about Christian vocation. Ironically, it seems that Peter and the Jewish Christians of his generation grasped this truth much more readily than many Christians in the twentieth and twenty-first centuries.

This exposition of Luke's explicit data about the three "baptism in the Holy Spirit" texts is unambiguous. It is about "blessing" and about being consecrated, set apart for prophetic witness, and mission (Luke 3:16–17; Acts 1:4–5; 11:15–17). In spite of this, many Christians have forced a radically different meaning upon Luke's data. Interpreting Luke's texts according to select Pauline statements, they have capriciously asserted that being "baptized in the Spirit" in Luke–Acts is all about being saved. For example, Walter C. Kaiser, defining "baptized in the Holy Spirit" from within the Evangelical Reformed tradition, writes:

> We believe it is best to go with Paul's inspired statement of purpose in 1 Corinthians 12:13 that this baptism was the initial work of God of incorporating all believers, first at Pentecost, then at Samaria, and again at Caesarea, into one unified body of Christ in the Holy Spirit. Therefore, all who believed, at the time of their conversion, were brought by God in the Holy Spirit to join this

body and to be part of this one body that is called the believing church of Jesus Christ.[12]

However, there is a mediating approach. This mediating approach is forced on interpreters by the fact that, in spite of strong, even vehement opposition to Pentecostalism and its understanding of Spirit-baptism, Pentecostalism will not go away. Rather, it advances from strength to strength. Therefore, non-Pentecostals have been forced, albeit somewhat reluctantly, to recognize that there must be some validity to Pentecostal experience and theology. And interestingly, a growing number of Pentecostals have themselves begun to accommodate their doctrine about being baptized in the Holy Spirit to that of their non-Pentecostal colleagues in the Academy. Thus, both non-Pentecostals and Pentecostals, while each retain their distinctive understanding of what being "baptized in the Spirit" means, have nevertheless sought to meet on mutually agreeable common ground. The following examples illustrate this.

The first example is Donald G. Bloesch. In his book, *The Holy Spirit: Works and Gifts* in the *Christian Foundations* series, he makes a variety of statements about being "baptized in the Holy Spirit." On the one hand, he writes, "Luke and John see the principle work of the Spirit as empowering for mission. Luke's distinctive emphasis is on the charismata . . . for Luke the charismata are given for missionary empowering."[13] But on the other hand, he insists that "the baptism with the Holy Spirit and fire" is about the "new birth."[14] In fact, according to Bloesch, "The disciples were not believers until Pentecost." The experience of Pentecost is the experience of conversion; it is being incorporated into the body of Christ.[15] Thus, according to Bloesch, at one and the same time when on the day of Pentecost the disciples were baptized in the Holy Spirit they were: 1) converted, experienced the new birth, and incorporated into the body of Christ and 2) this same Spirit-baptism means that they were also given the charismata for and empowered for mission.

Frank Macchia is a second example of the growing trend among systematicians to have their cake and eat it too. In *Baptized in the Spirit: A Global Pentecostal Theology*, he seeks to mend the rift between "Spirit

12. Kaiser, "Baptism in the Holy Spirit," 31.
13. Bloesch, *Holy Spirit*, 76.
14. Bloesch, *Holy Spirit*, 16.
15. Bloesch, *Holy Spirit*, 300.

baptism as a soteriological and as a charismatic category."[16] In his chapter, "Spirit Baptism in Trinitarian Perspective," he discusses among other subjects, "Spirit-Baptized Justification," "Spirit-Baptized Sanctification," and "Spirit-Baptized Witness."[17] In a concluding paragraph he writes:

> One enters Spirit-baptized existence at Christian initiation. But the experience of Spirit baptism connected to and following from initiation is meant to bring to conscious participation the justice of the Kingdom, the growth in sanctifying grace, and the charismatic openness to bless others and to glorify God that begins in Christian initiation. These experiences are to be ongoing. We have been baptized in the Spirit, we are being baptized in the Spirit, and we will be baptized in the Spirit.[18]

Thus, Spirit-baptism is not one thing, it is everything—initiation, sanctification, and Christian witness. But more so, "it functions as an outpouring of divine love. This is the final integration of the soteriological and the charismatic. No higher or deeper integration is possible."[19] Macchia's exposition of Spirit baptism is a "feel good" approach to a divisive subject. Every tradition is accommodated and affirmed. And he shows a more excellent way—love. But this is all a confusion of categories. If Spirit baptism is everything, it is nothing.

Afterword

Such then is Luke's theology and teaching about the experience of being "baptized in the Holy Spirit." His teaching depends on John the Baptist's prophecy about being baptized in the Holy Spirit, reported examples of the fulfillment of John's prophecy, and on the charismatic exegesis (Spirit-inspired interpretation) of these reports by participants within the episodes themselves. Rightly interpreted, being baptized in the Holy Spirit is a "crisis" experience of the Spirit experienced by those who are already qualified to receive the Spirit because they have a prior right standing before God. Luke identifies this right standing by using a variety of terms, which include righteous, disciple, and believer. Thus, whether it is long or

---

16. Macchia, *Baptized in the Spirit*, 17.
17. Macchia, *Baptized in the Spirit*, 129–53.
18. Macchia, *Baptized in the Spirit*, 154.
19. Macchia, *Baptized in the Spirit*, 298.

short, there is always an interval or gap between when this right standing is put into effect and when believers are baptized in the Holy Spirit. Therefore, Luke's readers are justified in concluding that, on the one hand, being baptized in the Holy Spirit cannot be about the salvation or initiation-incorporation of sinners and, on the other hand, it is, like Jesus' earlier experience of being Spirit-anointed for ministry, the experience of disciples being Spirit-baptized for ministry. In addition, in the explicit examples of being baptized in the Holy Spirit, the sign of Spirit-baptism is speaking in other tongues (i.e., unlearned foreign languages).

Luke's two-part narrative, of course, has much more to report, and, therefore, to teach about the presence and the activity of the Holy Spirit within the believing communities in Luke–Acts. Densely packed throughout his narratives are reports of a variety of works empowered by the Spirit and a variety of words inspired by the Spirit. But, in particular, it is in the stories of people being baptized in the Holy Spirit that Pentecostals find the biblical basis for their own twentieth/twenty-first century crisis experience of being baptized in the Holy Spirit. Pentecostalism, therefore, is self-consciously a renewal and restoration movement, firmly believing against all its detractors that its experiences of being baptized in the Holy Spirit are the same experiences of Spirit baptism about which Luke wrote in his Acts of the Apostles.

In the first century, people were bewildered, amazed, and perplexed when they witnessed the sign of being baptized in the Holy Spirit. Similarly, Pentecostals and Charismatics themselves, and their neighbors in the Church and in the world should also be amazed. However, because of Luke's teaching about being baptized in the Holy Spirit, they should no longer be perplexed and bewildered. Luke's teaching about being baptized in the Holy Spirit is explicit and unambiguous. Therefore, they should not mock the experience or its attesting sign, as some have in the past and as others continue to do in the present.

Before he ascended into heaven, Jesus told his disciples that in order to witness about him from Jerusalem to the ends of the earth they had to be men and women who were baptized and empowered by the Holy Spirit (Acts 1:5 and 8). Unless or until Jesus withdraws this great task, or until it is completed, he will continue to baptize his disciples in the Holy Spirit. Until he withdraws his commission, his Spirit-baptized, Spirit-empowered disciples of the twenty-first century will continue to speak in other tongues—the supernatural sign of being baptized in the Holy

Spirit—to witness about Jesus to every people, nation, tribe, and tongue. Until Jesus withdraws his commission, or until he comes again, his Spirit-baptized and Spirit-empowered disciples will not keep silent.

Bibliography

Bloesch, Donald G. *The Holy Spirit: Works and Gifts*. Downers Grove, IL: InterVarsity Press, 2000.

Bruner, Frederick Dale. *A Theology of the Holy Spirit*. Grand Rapids: Eerdmans, 1970.

Cadbury, Henry J. *The Making of Luke–Acts*. London: S.P.C.K., 1968.

Delling, Gerhard. "πίμπλημι, ἐμπίμπλημι, πλησμονή." In *Theological Dictionary of the New Testament*, edited by Gerhard Friedrich; translated by Geoffrey W. Bromiley, 6:128–34. Grand Rapids: Eerdmans, 1968.

Dunn, James D. G. *Baptism in the Holy Spirit: A Re-examination of the New Testament Gift of the Spirit in Relation to Pentecostalism Today*. London: SCM, 1970.

———. "Baptism in the Spirit: A Response to Pentecostal Scholarship on Luke–Acts." *Journal of Pentecostal Theology* 1 (1993) 3–27.

Hull, J. H. E. *The Holy Spirit in the Acts of the Apostles*. London: Lutterworth Press, 1967.

Kaiser, Walter C., Jr. "The Baptism in the Holy Spirit as the Promise of the Father: A Reformed Perspective." In *Perspectives on Spirit Baptism: Five Views*, ed. Chad Owen Brand, 15–46. Nashville: Broadman & Holman, 2004.

Levinskaya, Irina A. *The Book of Acts in its Diaspora Setting*. The Book of Acts in its First Century Setting 5. Grand Rapids: Eerdmans, 1996.

Macchia, Frank D. *Baptized in the Spirit: A Global Pentecostal Theology*. Grand Rapids: Zondervan, 2006.

Marshall, I. Howard. *Luke: Historian and Theologian*. Grand Rapids: Zondervan, 1970.

Marshall, I. Howard and David Peterson, ed. *Witness to the Gospel: The Theology of Acts*. Grand Rapids: Eerdmans, 1998.

Stott, John R. W. *The Baptism and Fullness of the Holy Spirit*. London: InterVarsity Press, 1964.

Stronstad, Roger. *Baptized and Filled with the Holy Spirit*. Springfield, MO: Life Publishers International, 2004.

———. "Baptized and Filled with the Holy Spirit." Rev. ed. Unpublished.

———. *The Charismatic Theology of St. Luke*. Peabody, MA: Hendrickson, 1984.

———. *The Prophethood of All Believers: A Study in Luke's Charismatic Theology*. Journal of Pentecostal Theology Supplement Series 16. Sheffield: Sheffield Academic Press, 1999.

———. *Signs on the Earth Beneath: A Commentary on Acts 2:1–21*. Springfield, MO: Life Publishers International, 2003.

———. *Spirit, Scripture, and Theology: A Pentecostal Perspective*. Baguio City, Philippines: APTS Press, 1995.

6

Paul's Experience and a Pauline Theology of the Spirit

Cynthia Long Westfall

Introduction

Is there a significant place for the Pauline epistles in the Pentecostal discussion? Is there a correlation between Paul's pneumatology and Luke–Acts and the Pentecostal distinctives?[1] The Pauline epistles are forged in the context of frontier missions where Paul is trouble-shooting or addressing specific concerns. They are not the reflective theology of the scholar or classroom, but rather circumstantial and occasional. As Gordon Fee says, it is "a 'task theology,' a theologizing that takes place in the marketplace, where belief and the experience of God run head-on into the thought systems, religions and everyday life of people."[2] In addressing relevant issues, Paul's personal spirituality is recorded in his epistles and includes his views on the baptizing and fullness of the Spirit and the manifestations of tongues, prophecy, and visions. If personal experience, missions, and contextualization are hallmarks of the Pentecostal movement, then perhaps Paul provides a precedent for the Pentecostal worldview more than any other biblical writer.

However, I see four issues in Pauline study that prohibit an assimilation of Paul into a more central role in the Pentecostal discussion. First,

---

1. While Pentecostal distinctives are difficult to identify, this study is informed by Allan Anderson's *An Introduction to Pentecostalism*.

2. Fee, *Paul, the Spirit, and the People of God*, 2.

Paul has been the poster child for a rationalistic evangelicalism and fundamentalism, and he has been used to cancel out both the implicit theology of the Lukan narrative and the value and place of experience in the process of doing theology—in this context, the interpreters' construction of Paul's theology trumps history or experience. Second, and related to the first issue, we inherit certain theological frames for Paul. Some are drawn from a rationalistic worldview and tend to treat Paul's writings as flat propositional assertions rather than as task theology. A survey of some of the recent studies of Paul's theology demonstrates to me why the Pentecostal movement may be less interested in interacting with Paul as opposed to Luke.[3] There is a tendency to characterize Paul's pneumatology inaccurately with simplistic summaries.[4] These frames are incredibly powerful strongholds, and we can confuse Paul's complex pneumatology with the alleged theological constructs of his pneumatology in the ongoing conversation.[5] Third, the very nature of Paul's contextualized theology makes it less accessible in the Pentecostal interest at the popular level in finding "common ground in real life situations" because Paul is embedded in a very foreign context.[6] His letters are more difficult to identify with than the narratives that are embedded in more or less the same context. This is compounded by a Pentecostal preference for narrative, which anticipated and is consistent with current post-modern preferences. Fourth, even Pentecostal scholars such as Gordon Fee suggest exegetically-based Pauline correctives to terminology and doctrines of

---

3. James Dunn's *The Theology of Paul the Apostle* lays out Paul's worldview like a systematic theology, contributing to the impression that Paul is rationalistic.

4. While Thomas Schreiner's *Paul: Apostle of God's Glory in Christ* looks promising in terms of the topics he selects, on closer examination his chapter on "Life of Love in the Spirit" turns out to be a discussion of ethics and exhortations.

5. Discussed below, the most commonly assumed theological construct for Paul among both Pentecostals and non-Pentecostals is that Paul's understanding of Spirit baptism is *solely* soteriological, and it is contrasted with Luke's "charismatic" understanding (see, for example, Macchia, *Baptized in the Spirit*, 16). As Macchia notes, virtually all Christian communions accept the category of Spirit baptism and "have interpreted it in a way consistent with their understanding of the church and Christian initiation" (Macchia, *Baptized in the Spirit*, 22).

6. This is at least relevant to Anderson's description of a common Pentecostal approach to the Bible as a "concordistic" approach, which is: "they take the Bible as it is and look for common ground in real life situations" where the Bible becomes a source book for experience (Anderson, *Pentecostalism*, 226–27).

subsequence and consequence that have been near and dear to Classical Pentecostalism.[7]

As we practice New Testament theology, and particularly Pauline theology, the categories we utilize in searching, organizing, and describing the text are crucial. By asking new questions, or viewing the text from a new vantage point, we may uncover additional insight. Categories reveal and hide as well as distort information. What categories could we look at to find the correspondences of Paul's pneumatology with Luke's and Pentecostal theological foundations? In order to propose possible correlations, first Paul's theology and experience of revelation will be examined. Second, Paul's depiction of the role of the Holy Spirit and God's presence will be surveyed. Third, Paul's relationship between the Holy Spirit and service will be established. Fourth, Paul's concern for physical, emotional, and spiritual salvation, sanctification, and healing will be studied. Finally, I will analyze Paul's eschatological orientation of the Holy Spirit's ministry.

Paul and Revelation

One area of Pentecostal distinctives involves revelation. Pentecostals have shown a preference for narrative and oral structures, and included personal experience and the use of dreams and visions as forms of revelation.[8] Paul participates in all of these forms of revelation. He finds a theological and didactic purpose in narrative when he asserts that all Scripture is profitable for teaching, reproof, correction, and training (2 Tim 3:16–17).[9] At the time of Paul's writing, this would be a reference

---

7. For example, while Fee affirms the experience of the Spirit, he questions the exegetical basis for placing the doctrine of the baptism of the Holy Spirit subsequent to regeneration (Fee, "Baptism in the Holy Spirit," 87–99). He also suggests that the Spirit movements tend to emphasize individualistic spirituality that focuses on the individual who experiences the experience. This approach lacks sound exegetical basis or adequate theological reflection (Fee, *Paul, the Spirit, and the People of God*, xv).

8. This relates to Walter Hollenweger's work concerning how theology is conceived among Pentecostals as a less rational form of theological discourse with experiential and oral theologizing (Hollenweger, "Priorities in Pentecostal Research," 9–10).

9. While I recognize that 1 Timothy has been placed in the deutero-Pauline canon by the majority of biblical scholars due to linguistic and stylistic differences (in addition to the criticism of anachronistic church structure), I remain unconvinced of the validity of the linguistic arguments against Pauline authorship in view of more recent research on the effects of register (varieties of language in different relationships, situations, and

to the Hebrew Bible, which consists of a large percentage of narrative material. Furthermore, it is clear from Paul's use of pericopes from the Hebrew Bible, that he values narrative and draws theology from it.[10] For example, he utilizes the narrative about the Exodus and the experiences of the wilderness generation to warn the Corinthians. He insists that the Old Testament narratives "happened as examples for us" (1 Cor 10:11). In summary, the narrative of Christ's life lies behind his work, he associates the church with the narrative of Israel and describes the Gentiles as grafted into Israel (Rom 11:17–21).[11]

Paul's personal experience was an essential component in his understanding of revelation. Paul's dramatic conversion and call literally turned his life around from valuing his status in Judaism and persecuting the church. His encounter with Jesus on the Damascus road was the basis of everything he did subsequently (Phil 3:4–11; 1 Tim 1:15–16).[12] He only refers to the story of his conversion briefly in his epistles, but it appears to be shared information with the readers (1 Cor 15:8). He appeals to having seen Jesus (1 Cor 9:1; Gal 1:15) and claims to have received his gospel, as well as his status as an apostle, directly from Jesus Christ (Gal 1:12; Eph 3:2–6). Paul places a great deal of stock in his personal experience, and of course, so does Luke: he repeats Paul's conversion story three times (Acts 9; 22:3–16; 26:9–18). Paul's experience of his call, and the events in his ministry, work together with his study and interpretation of the Hebrew Bible to validate his ministry and his gospel to the Gentiles, which is particularly made clear in Luke's account of the Jerusalem Council in Acts 15.

---

contexts) on the language of an author (see, for example, Leckie-Tarry, *Language and Context*; for the application of these categories to Hellenistic Greek, see Porter, "Dialect and Register in the Greek of the New Testament Theory," 190–208, and Porter, "Register in the Greek of the New Testament: Application with Reference to Mark's Gospel," 209–29. In any case, the high view of Scripture is consistent with Pauline thought, and places 1Timothy in the Pauline circle.

10. As Frank Matera indicates, "Paul's Christ story . . . was intimately related to the story of Israel, a story he reinterpreted in light of what God had done in Christ" (Matera, *New Testament Christology*, 93).

11. For a full discussion of how Paul's theology was grounded in the stories of the Hebrew Bible, see Witherington, *Paul's Narrative Thought World*.

12. For discussions on the impact of the Damascus experience, see Longenecker, *The Road from Damascus*.

In fact, the primary thrust of Luke's argument in Acts validates, supports, and defends Paul, his actions in ministry, and his theology/gospel.[13]

In terms of utilizing oral structures in revelation, Paul participates in and consciously preserves the Christian oral tradition and teaches his churches and ministry team to do the same (cf. 2 Tim 2:2).[14] It is interesting that Paul uses similar language to the later terminology of rabbinic Judaism for the reception and transmission of the stories (1 Cor 11:2, 23; 15:1, 3; 1 Thess 2:13; 4:1; 2 Thess 3:6).[15] The kinds of stories that Paul explicitly refers to in his epistles include pericopes such as the Last Supper, Jesus' sayings, hymns, and creeds. However, it is important to note that for the most part, Paul's letters were written before the Gospels were written, and his letters reflect and assume the preservation and transmission of the larger body of information about Jesus that the Gospels utilized and edited.

Paul presents the Spirit as the primary agent in God's revelation, which is continual and experiential. He prays that the Father will give the Ephesians the Spirit of wisdom and revelation so that they might better know the Father (Eph 1:17). The Spirit comprehends the depths of God and reveals him, his thoughts, and spiritual truths (1 Cor 2:6–15). Paul's use of visions and dreams for guidance and information is recorded in Acts and confirmed in his epistles. Besides Paul's encounter on the Damascus road, Luke records at least five of Paul's visions: In a trance in the Temple he was warned by the Lord to leave Jerusalem immediately, and the Lord also revealed that he was sending him to the Gentiles (Acts 22:17–21); in a dream, a Macedonian begged Paul to come to Macedonia and help them (Acts 16:9–10); in a vision, God encouraged Paul to speak in Corinth with a promise of protection (Acts 18:9–10); after he stood before the Sanhedrin, the Lord appeared to him and said he would testify in Rome (23:11); finally, an angel came to him during a severe storm at sea, and promised he would be tried before Caesar, and no lives would be lost at sea (Acts 27:23). In his epistles, Paul speaks of receiving his gospel by direct revelation from Jesus Christ (Gal 1:11–12), of attending the Jerusalem Council because of a revelation (Gal 2:2), of being caught up into heaven and hearing things he could not repeat (1 Cor 12:1–4),

---

13. Porter and Westfall, "Mission in Acts."
14. See footnote 9.
15. Witherington, *The Christology of Jesus*, 12.

and of receiving a direct revelation about his "thorn in the flesh" (2 Cor 12:7–10). One may say that Luke focuses on the phenomenon of direct revelation more than Paul, nevertheless Paul is the one depicted as having the experiences, if one maintains that Luke's account in Acts is historically reliable. Luke is merely the narrator and at best an observer and interpreter of Paul's experience.

By both Luke's account and his own words, Paul's understanding of revelation has strong correspondences to the Pentecostal distinctives. He appreciates and utilizes narrative from the Old Testament, Christ's life, and his own life. He actively participates in and preserves oral traditions. Finally, it is clear that he values revelation and guidance in dreams and visions and the New Testament records more experiences of these phenomena for Paul than for other characters in the New Testament.

The Holy Spirit and God's Presence

The experience of the Holy Spirit is vital as the indication of God's presence in the Pentecostal movement. Paul also believes that the believers' access to both the Father and Christ comes through the Spirit.[16] He utilizes a number of metaphors to describe God's presence among his people: the body of Christ, God's temple, the family of God, and the kingdom of God. He discusses the role of the filling of the Spirit in worship and draws connections between the exercise of the spiritual gift of prophecy and the dramatic manifestation of God's presence. Paul recognizes the connection between God's presence and the experience of the Holy Spirit.

Paul states that our mutual access to the Father is through Jesus Christ and in the Spirit (Eph 2:18). This is closely related to Paul's description of the Holy Spirit's relationship with the believer in Rom 8:12–27. Conversely, the Spirit is also the conduit of the power that allows us access to Christ, which Paul depicts as heavily experiential. The Father strengthens us with power through the Spirit in our inner being so that Christ dwells in our hearts and allows us to grasp and experience the totality of his love and "to be filled to the measure of all the fullness of God" (Eph 3:14–19).

---

16. Fee observes that the word πνεῦμα (*pneuma* = spirit) occurs in the Pauline corpus 145 times, and the vast majority of occurrences refer to the Holy Spirit (Fee, *God's Empowering Presence*, 14).

Paul's favorite metaphor for the church is the body of Christ, where there is both unity and diversity in the Spirit (e.g., 1 Cor 12-14). But Paul expands his metaphors for this symbiotic unity of believers beyond body imagery, and particularly speaks of the church as God's temple that is indwelt by the Spirit (1 Cor 3:16-17; 2 Cor 6:16; Eph 2:22).[17] Paul also utilizes the metaphor of the family, where the Spirit places believers in the family and bears witness to their family membership (Rom 8:14-17; Gal 4:4-6; Eph 2:19). Furthermore, Paul speaks of the kingdom of God, which is righteousness, peace, and joy in the Holy Spirit—because anyone who serves Christ in this way is pleasing to God and approved by people (Rom 14:17). Relationships within the church are summarized by the phrases "the fellowship of the Holy Spirit" and "the unity of the Spirit" (2 Cor 13:14; Eph 4:4).

The filling of the Holy Spirit involves the experience of God's presence. Frank Macchia notes that, according to both Luke and Paul, the experience of being filled by the Spirit is a kind of "God intoxication" (Acts 2:13; Eph 5:18).[18] We worship "in the Spirit of God" (Phil 3:3). Paul states that "God has poured out his love into our hearts by the Holy Spirit" (Rom 5:5), which alludes to the pouring out of the Sprit prophesied in Joel. While some Pentecostals relate this to sanctification, contextually it is more of an expression of God's love for us (Rom 5:8). However, the love of God poured out in our hearts compels us to love, just as God's forgiveness compels us to forgive. The filling of the Holy Spirit is expressed in worship (Eph 5:18-20) that works out practically in transformed relationships (Eph 5:21—6:9).[19] Our personal effort is needed to keep the unity of the Spirit in our relationships, actions, and attitudes toward one another through the experiential bond of peace, because there is one body and one Spirit, one hope, one Lord, one faith, one baptism, and "one God and Father of all, who is over all and through all and in all" (Eph 4:1-6).

---

17. As Fee says, "the Spirit is the fulfillment of Jewish hopes of the return of the divine presence" (Fee, *Paul, the Spirit, and the People of God*, viii).

18. Macchia expands: "I do not refer here to a drunken state but rather a consciousness wholly taken up with God so that one feels especially inspired to give of oneself to others in whatever gifting God has created within" (Macchia, *Baptized in the Spirit*, 14).

19. In Ephesians, the transformation of relationships is consistent with reconciliation to God that tears down dividing walls and builds a temple (Eph 2:11-22). This is consistent with Amos Yong's description of social salvation that consists of racial, class, and gender reconciliation (Yong, *The Spirit Poured Out on All Flesh*, 93-95).

While the Spirit's gifts are further described in the context of service or mutual edification in 1 Cor 12, as the argument is further developed in 1 Cor 14, the gifts and edification are placed in the context of the church gathering. While the devaluation of untranslated tongues in the worship service may address some Pentecostal practices negatively, the positive description and priority of the practice of prophecy is a quintessential reflection of Pentecostal distinctives. It culminates in any unbeliever who is present being convinced by all that he is a sinner. He is judged by all, and the secrets in his heart are laid bare, so that he falls down and worships God, exclaiming, "God is really among you!" (1 Cor 14:24–25). The picture of the order of worship drawn from 1 Cor 14 supports a spontaneous liturgy characterized by egalitarian-style direct revelation, where spiritualities can take on the characteristics of the host culture in an unlimited potential of expressions that are nevertheless not disorderly, but rather consistent and coherent with the cultural context.

The Holy Spirit and Service

The anointing and empowering of God's people for service is considered an essential phenomenon among Pentecostal distinctives.[20] The connection between being filled by the Spirit and service is transparent in Acts, but Paul's discussion of the Spirit's empowering for service is also extensive and specific in his section on spiritual gifts in 1 Cor 12–14. He also discusses gifts and service in Eph 4:7–15 and Rom 12:4–8.[21]

20. Roger Stronstad defines "charismatic" as "God's gift of His Spirit to His servants, either individually or collectively, to anoint, empower, or inspire them for divine service. . . . Therefore, this charismatic activity is necessarily an experiential phenomenon." In differentiating Paul's pneumatology from Luke's, Stronstad states that Luke exclusively relates the Spirit to service as opposed to salvation or sanctification (Stronstad, *St. Luke*, 12 and 13). While an explicit link with service can be debated in the cases of the mini-Pentecosts of the Samaritan conversions, Cornelius's household, and the disciples in Ephesus, Luke's depiction of the relationship of the Spirit to service is consistent with Paul's, because Paul also teaches that the Holy Spirit is essentially related to service and experience. In response to Stronstad, one might say that Paul's theology is more detailed in defining the Spirit's relationship to service, and more extensive and explicit than Luke's in the areas of salvation and sanctification.

21. However, in parallel but shorter passages concerning the "gifts" in Rom 12:4–8 and Eph 4:7–13, the Spirit's activity in the giving of the gifts is omitted. Rather, Christ is depicted as giving the gifts in Ephesians, and the giver is not specified in Romans. Paul also selects and fashions theological information for his purposes in his "task theology" of addressing the needs of the moment, and comparison shows that he is not exhaustive

Paul asserts that every believer is given a manifestation (φανέρωσις, *phanerōsis*) of the Spirit, connected with gifts, service, and working (1 Cor 12:7–8). Specifically, these gifts are given for service for the common good. Among those gifts are manifestations of tongues and prophecy, which Luke also associates with the baptism of the Holy Spirit. However, Paul expands the possibilities of manifestations that the Spirit gives to believers. With his terminology, Paul depicts the Spirit's empowering of believers for service in explicitly experiential ways. The Pauline terminology concerning the Spirit's baptizing is different but complementary to that of Luke.[22] The differences can be accounted for by Paul's use of more metaphors (gifts and the body parts), as well as a context of "task theology," where Paul is facing specific problems in Corinth. Paul's use of the term "baptized by one Spirit" occurs in the context of how the diversity of gifts and service relate to the unity of God's people. The Spirit's action places believers into one body, which is the metaphor he is using in the broader argument concerning their diversity in service and worship couched by their mutual need for each other (1 Cor 12:13).[23] The focus on service within the church is consistent with Luke's depiction of baptism with the Holy Spirit for empowerment to witness, and the filling of the Spirit as equipping for service, even the mundane management of the distribution of food in a sensitive context (Acts 6:1–7).

Paul's personal experience of the gifts of the Spirit in his calling and ministry is most clearly displayed in his apostleship (Rom 1:1; 1 Cor 1:1; Eph 1:1; 1 Tim 1:1).[24] However, he also claims to have the gift of tongues when he says, "I thank God that I speak in tongues more than all of you" (1 Cor 14:18). According to his example, a person's manifestation

in any of his discussions of the Spirit.

22. In Acts, those baptized by water and the Spirit are "added to their number" (Acts 2:41), showing a close relationship between baptism, the Spirit's baptizing, and conversion.

23. Gordon Fee writes, "The question Paul answers in 1 Corinthians 12:13 is not how people become believers—although that is obviously involved—but how the many of them, composed of Jew and Gentile, slave and free, make up the one body of Christ. Paul's answer: all alike were immersed in the same reality, Spirit, and all alike were caused to drink to the fill of the same reality, Spirit, so as to form one body in Christ" (Fee, *Paul, the Spirit, and the People of God*, 66–67).

24. In Paul's letter openings, he utilizes the language of calling ("called to be an apostle"), which shows a correlation between the experience of one's calling to a specific ministry and the Spirit's distribution of the gifts.

of the Spirit may include more than one gift. However, there is no gift that everyone manifests. This ensures that the body is not imbalanced in its service, and creates interdependency among the members (1 Cor 12:14–26).[25]

The Holy Spirit in Missions and Conversion

The Pentecostal movement is described as a missionary movement characterized by the priority of global evangelism.[26] In Acts and the Pauline epistles, the story of Paul's calling, the narrative framework of his epistles, and the rest of the content, epitomize global evangelism. Paul is the quintessential example of charismatic witness as his message is authenticated by signs and wonders. In addition, Paul devotes some attention to describing and interpreting the phenomena of the reception of the Holy Spirit, which he has experienced, participated in, and witnessed first hand.

Paul's personal empowering/gifting and appointment for witness to the Gentiles as an apostle is one of the primary focuses of Luke's narrative in Acts, since it is repeated three times.[27] When he identifies himself as an apostle, Paul is cognizant of the Spirit's activity in his own evangelistic ministry because of the expressed role of the Spirit in bestowing the gifts, including the gift of apostle, in his theology. If one would agree that the ministry of the Spirit in Acts is power to witness, Paul's remembrances of his mission to the Corinthians are consistent with the Lucan pattern of signs, wonders, and miracles (Acts 2:22 and 8:13) and in a broad sense with Luke's depiction of Paul as one whose evangelistic ministry is inarguably confirmed by apostolic signs, wonders, and miracles (Acts 15:12). Paul reflects Luke's assessment (or vice versa) when he reminds the Corinthians and the Thessalonians that his message and preaching to them "were not with wise and persuasive words, but with a demonstration of the Spirit's power" (1 Cor 2:4; 1 Thess 1:5).[28] If anything, Paul de-

---

25. The grammar in 1 Cor 12:30 makes it clear that, though all the Corinthians have been baptized by the Spirit (1 Cor 12:13), not all of them speak in tongues. In a negative question, the particle μή expects a "no" answer, so that μὴ πάντες γλώσσαις λαλοῦσιν; (*mēpantes glōssais lalousin?*) could be translated "all do not speak in tongues, do they?"

26. Anderson, *Pentecostalism*, 171.

27. Porter and Westfall, "Mission in Acts."

28. Of course, Paul's epistles predate Luke's writing, so technically, Luke would reflect Paul's writing. From the standpoint of the contemporary reader, Luke provides the nar-

picts his evangelistic ministry in Corinth as more charismatic than Luke's depiction (Acts 18). Luke focuses on Paul's priority of preaching by first testifying to the Jews, followed by evangelizing and teaching the Gentiles, choosing not to mention Paul's demonstration of the Spirit's power of signs and miracles (Acts 18:5, 11).[29] However, Luke does record that Paul had a vision in Corinth, when the Lord told him to keep on speaking and not to be silent, highlighting the Spirit's guidance and participation in his preaching (Acts 18:9–11). Paul states his own priorities even more strongly in Rom 15:18–19 concerning the grace God gave him to be a minister of Christ Jesus to the Gentiles: "I will not venture to speak of anything except what Christ has accomplished through me in leading the Gentiles to obey God by what I have said and done—by the power of signs and miracles, through the power of the Spirit."[30]

While Luke describes conversion experiences, including key episodes from Paul's ministry, Paul is writing to believers/saints who, according to him, have been baptized by the Spirit (1 Cor 12:13)[31]—a term associated

---

rative framework through which we understand the Pauline epistles.

29. The NIV says that Paul "devoted himself exclusively to preaching, testifying to the Jews" (Acts 18:5).

30. Amos Yong points out that the biblical ministry that "accomplished signs and wonders, cast out demons, healed the sick, and engaged in power encounters" has the most in common with the current Pentecostal explosion (Yong, *The Spirit Poured Out on All Flesh*, 19). He finds parallels with Phillip's ministry in Samaria rather than the ongoing pattern of Paul's ministry. However, it is arguable that in Acts, the culmination of Philip's and Peter's ministries is Paul's ministry.

31. French Arrington represents one Pentecostal interpretation of 1 Cor 12:13 when he maintains that 1 Cor 12:13 is "conversion baptism" where the Holy Spirit is the agent who incorporates the believer into the body of Christ, which is distinct from Spirit baptism where Jesus is the agent and the Spirit is the element (Arrington, *Encountering the Holy Spirit*, 92). However, the prepositional phrase in 1 Cor 12:13 uses the same preposition as the Gospels and Acts, where Jesus is the specified agent: ἐν ἑνὶ πνεύματι ἡμεῖς πάντες . . . ἐβαπτίσθημεν (*en heni pneumati hēmeis pantes . . . ebaptisthēmen* = We all were baptized in/by one Spirit). It is closest grammatically to Acts 1:5: ἐν πνεύματι βαπτισθήσεσθε ἁγίῳ (*en pneumati baptisthēsesthe hagiō* = You will be baptized in/by the Holy Spirit). In the Gospels, Jesus is the subject/agent of the verb βαπτίζω (baptize) in the narratives about John the Baptist, but in these two cases, the passive verb places the focus on the subject that receives the action (we/you), and neither specify Christ as the agent. In Acts 1:5, Jesus would be understood as an unspecified agent due to intertextuality with Luke 3:16 and 24:29, but contextually the Spirit is the specified agent when he comes upon them (Acts 1:8). Therefore, there could be two agents in the sense that Jesus sends (Luke 24:29), and the Spirit comes (Acts 1:8), so that the two are not mutually exclusive. However, ἐν is the most frequently used preposition in the New Testament and

with receiving the Spirit (1 Cor. 2:12; 2 Cor 11:4; Gal 3:2, 14; Rom 8:15) or simply having the Spirit (1 Cor 2:16; 7:40; Rom 8:15).[32] Luke also speaks of receiving the Spirit (Acts 2:38, 8:15, 19; 19:2), and uses the term interchangeably with the gift of the Holy Spirit (Acts 2:38; 10:45) and being baptized by the Holy Spirit (Acts 1:5, 2:38, 10:47; 11:16).[33] Paul explicitly associates receiving the Spirit with exercising faith, being washed, sanctified, and justified (1 Cor 6:11; Gal 3:1–5; Tit 3:5). Luke similarly associ-

---

has a broad range of meanings that include both agency and instrument (which are very close in the range of metaphorical senses for ἐν), but its basic meaning is "in" or "in the realm of" (Porter, *Idioms of the Greek New Testament*, 156–59). See Anthony Thistleton for the range of meanings that scholars, translators, and interpreters have assigned ἐν in this passage, and Fee for further discussion (Anthony C. Thistleton, *The First Epistle to the Corinthians*, 997; Fee, *God's Empowering Presence*, 178–82). If agency is expressed with ἐν and a passive verb, it is instrumental or impersonal agency, whereas the Spirit in 1 Cor 12 is portrayed as personal (Porter, *Idioms of the Greek New Testament*, 65). Therefore, Arrington's argument that ἐν refers to the agency of the Holy Spirit because of the previous use of ἐν πνεύματι in 1 Cor 12 requires a more a specific meaning of ἐν than the preposition, metaphor, syntax, or immediate context selects (Arrington, *Encountering the Holy Spirit*, 96–100). Regardless of how ἐν is understood, Arrington's attempt to distinguish being baptized by the Spirit in 1 Cor 12:13 from being baptized by the Spirit in the Gospels and Acts because of how he understands the force of ἐν and the Spirit's agency is unconvincing, particularly in the light of Acts 1:5. The immediate context of drinking the Spirit in v. 13b maintains the Gospels' parallels between the water of (John's) baptism and the Spirit (though Paul mixes the metaphor). David Garland insists that water baptism and Spirit baptism are not even mutually exclusive (Garland, *1 Corinthians*, 591). Furthermore, the intertextuality with the oral traditions in the early church anchor the phrase "baptized by the Holy Spirit" to all four Gospels and Acts where Jesus is the agent. As discussed above, Paul was a link in the transmission of the oral tradition in his churches, and furthermore, Luke was his close companion. In 1 Cor 12, it is more plausible that Jesus' agency was shared information between Paul, Luke, and the Corinthians, but not relevant to the point Paul was making about the Spirit's function in the body of Christ and Paul did not consider Jesus' role to be mutually exclusive of the Spirit's function. If this were yet another kind of baptism, Paul would have needed to signal the difference to avoid confusion in order to communicate adequately.

32. Paul also speaks of God supplying the Holy Spirit (Gal 3:5; Phil 1:19) or God placing the Holy Spirit in the believer (1 Thess 4:8; 2 Cor 1:22; 5:5; Rom 5:5; Eph 1:7; 2 Tim 1:7). See Fee, *God's Empowering Presence*, 830 and Witherington and Ice, *The Shadow of the Almighty*, 130.

33. Grammatically, there is no "*baptism* of the Holy Spirit" as such in the Greek; but rather the noun is the "*gift* of the Holy Spirit." From the believers' perspective, they receive the Holy Spirit. From the divine perspective, Jesus baptizes the believers with the Holy Spirit. French Arrington further expands the terminology connected with the baptism of the Spirit, equating "Spirit baptism" with the "promise of the Father," the "promise of the Spirit," the "Spirit's coming/falling upon," the "Spirit's being poured out by God," and being "filled with the Spirit" (Arrington, *Encountering the Holy Spirit*, 92–96).

ates the experience in his narrative with baptism, repentance, and faith (Acts 2:38; 19:2). All we have said about the Holy Spirit and the presence of God and service with spiritual gifts necessitates that the believer has received the Spirit (a.k.a. been baptized by the Holy Spirit). According to Paul, if anyone does not have the Spirit of Christ, he does not belong to Christ (Rom 8:9).

On the other hand, as in Acts 19:1–6, Paul could not imagine a believer who had been baptized in the name of Jesus claiming that he or she had never received the Holy Spirit or even heard that there was a Holy Spirit. I conclude from interpreting Luke and Paul together that believers not only should possess the Holy Spirit and all his fullness, but they should know they have been baptized by the Spirit and experience the manifestation of the Spirit from the beginning of their conversion. Often such is not the case today, and there is the rub.

When we speak of the Holy Spirit's role in conversion in a Pentecostal context, the classical doctrines of subsequence and consequence must be addressed. The doctrine of subsequence states that the gift of the Holy Spirit or the baptism of the Spirit is a separate experience subsequent to conversion. However, possession of the Holy Spirit must be part of the constellation of conversion, or a convert does not belong to Christ. I suggest that we are robbing both our converts and God when we invite people to come to Christ with anemic and insufficient gospel tools—people "receive Christ," but have no concept of his Lordship and do not even know that there is a Holy Spirit, let alone that they need to receive him. By our unbiblical praxis, we have created a Gordian knot and the puzzle becomes manifest in the doctrine of subsequence. I agree with Amos Yong, that the way forward is in invoking the Spirit in our baptismal practice, but we must also address our presentation of the gospel, which, according to the pattern of Acts, should include baptism and receiving the Holy Spirit in the invitation.[34]

Much of the Pentecostal discussion involves tongues as an essential boundary-crossing experience in the doctrine of subsequence.[35] However, according to Paul, not all believers in the body of Christ speak in tongues (1 Cor 12:30), though they are all baptized by the Holy Spirit (1 Cor 12:13). This contradicts the Classical Pentecostal doctrine of sub-

---

34. Yong, *The Spirit Poured Out on All Flesh*, 158–59.

35. Macchia, *Baptized in the Spirit*, 36. The evidence of tongues is basically competitive.

sequence, but supports the assertion that the gift of the Spirit is accompanied by an experiential manifestation. In addition, Paul specifies that tongues are a sign to unbelievers (1 Cor 14:22). While this verse has been subject to various interpretations, the global spread of Pentecostalism provides enlightenment. It indicates that there is a direct connection between revival and the manifestation of phenomena at conversion that validates the message.

Paul is characterized as a charismatic evangelist who leads the way in global evangelism in both Acts and his epistles. He is called and gifted by the Holy Spirit as an apostle, and preaches by the power of the Spirit with the signs and miracles that are part of the focus of Pentecostalism. Paul provides further insight into the conversion process that is reported through narrative in Acts, though he does not provide us with a systematic theology by any means. In both Acts and the epistles, receiving the Holy Spirit is an essential part of the constellation of conversion. Believers should know they have been baptized by the Spirit and experience the "manifestation of the Spirit" as well as the filling of the Holy Spirit.

Holistic Salvation, Sanctification, and Healing

A concern for holistic renewal or sanctification is central to Pentecostalism, and healing, that often extends to a theology of success and power, is a primary distinctive. Holistic sanctification includes spiritual, emotional, and physical sanctification or salvation. Similarly, for Paul, the Spirit is primarily at work in spiritual and emotional sanctification and healing. However, the role of the Spirit in the concern for physical care and healing is less transparent in Paul's epistles than it is in Luke–Acts. Furthermore, both Paul and Luke relate a theology of success and power that is counter-intuitive and a corrective to the contemporary church.

Paul sees continuity between the entry point of receiving the Spirit and Spirit renewal.[36] As he implies to the Galatians, after beginning with the Spirit, believers must complete the process with the Spirit (Gal 3:3). In fact, the Holy Spirit is the first-fruits of sanctification (1 Thess 2:13).[37]

---

36. Russell P. Spittler states that Pentecostals are more concerned with renewal than with creating a new *ordo salutis*, in contrast with the Classical Pentecostal doctrines of subsequence and consequence (Spittler, "Suggested Areas for Further Research," 39–57, esp. 43).

37. Steven Land says that the sanctification of the affections is really distinctive about

When Paul depicts life through the Sprit in Rom 8:1–17, he explains that the law of the Spirit sets the believer free at the salvation experience. This results in a profound complex of on-going benefits.[38] Believers receive life, peace, control, and leading by the Spirit, assurance that they are God's children, and intercession in prayer by the Spirit when they do not know how to pray.

The fruit of the Spirit, the filling of the Spirit, and the waging of spiritual warfare illustrate particularly the spiritual and emotional aspects of sanctification. The discussion of the fruit of the Spirit in Gal 5:22–23 shows that the Holy Spirit produces both experiences given by God (love, joy, and peace) and aspects of Christian character (kindness, goodness, faithfulness, gentleness, and self control). Ephesians 5:18 shows that as a result of the filling of the Holy Spirit, what starts with worship works out in a seamless way in transformed relationships effectively revolutionalizing and reversing the relationships of privilege between husband and wife, parents and children, and slaves and masters. The concepts of spiritual warfare can also belong here. Being "strong in his mighty power" alludes to the power of the Spirit. The only offensive weapon is the sword of the Spirit, which is the word of God, and all occasions are underpinned with praying in the Spirit (Eph 6:10–18). Spiritual weapons have the divine power of the Spirit to demolish strongholds of arguments and pretensions that are set up against the knowledge of God, because our weapons can take every thought captive (2 Cor 10:3–6).[39]

Paul demonstrates a pragmatic concern for physical needs, but the Spirit's role is only explicit in the sense that he interprets our prayers because we do not know how to pray as we should (Rom 8:27). The im-

---

Pentecostal theology (Land, *Pentecostal Spirituality*, 62–63).

38. Amos Yong further draws from Rom 8: "my main thesis is that Christian salvation includes both the transformation of human beings into the image of Jesus by the power of the Holy Spirit and the transformation of all creation into the new heaven and new earth by the triune God" (Yong, *The Spirit Poured Out on All Flesh*, 91). Preceding this statement, Yong outlines "Spirit soteriology" in Luke–Acts, claiming that "the transition from Luke to Acts is the transition from Spirit Christology to Spirit soteriology" (88). The gospel includes (1) the forgiveness of sins, (2) deliverance from the devil, (3) healing of the sick, (4) concern for the needs of the poor, the freeing of captives, and the liberation of the oppressed, and (5) an eschatological dimension that is both realized and future (89–90).

39. While I recognize that the Spirit is not explicitly mentioned in 2 Cor 10:3–6, the contrast of the weapons of the world with the weapons of divine power implies the Spirit's work.

portance of prayer and the Spirit's role in it is a consistent theme in Paul's letters. Paul prays continually for the churches, and encourages them to pray without ceasing (Rom 1:9–10; Eph 6:18; Col 1:3; 1 Thess 1:3; 2:13; 5:17; 2 Tim 1:3). He expresses confidence that God will meet the needs of those he loves according to his glorious riches in Christ Jesus (Phil 4:19; Rom 8:32). But primarily, Paul's concerns are that prayer be in accordance with God's will, that believers grow spiritually, and that the gospel advance (Rom 8:27; Eph 6:20; 2 Thess 3:1).[40] Within this framework, Paul can interpret life's worst-case scenarios as "working together for good" for believers (Rom 8:28–39), and as far as he is concerned, being beaten and confined to prison mean success if the gospel is preached as a result (Phil 1:12–18). However, he also prays for personal healing (2 Cor 12:7–10), identifies healing as a spiritual gift (1 Cor 12:28, 30), and takes collections for the poor in Jerusalem, urging generosity from the churches (1 Cor 16:1–4; 2 Cor 8–9). He urges people to work so that they will have something to share with those in need (Eph 4:28).

On the other hand, personal success or prosperity for Paul is characterized by paradox. Paul serves as a model for hard work (2 Thess 3:7–9; 2 Cor 11:8), and commonly refuses to be supported or helped by the people he is reaching. He embraces weaknesses, insult, hardships, persecutions, and difficulties—he claims that when he is weak he is strong and that he wants to share in Christ's sufferings (2 Cor 1:5; 12:10; Phil 3:10–11; Col 1:24). He voluntarily gives up rights and privileges in order to minister more effectively (1 Cor 9:19–23). He has learned to be content in every situation, whether well-fed or hungry, and whether living in plenty or in want (Phil 4:12–13). For Paul, personal success comes from following his call and gifting as an apostle and responding to God's guidance with radical obedience in his identification with Christ. Paul's interpretation of what it means to identify with Christ parallels Martin Mittelstadt's analysis of Luke–Acts, where the stories of Jesus and the apostles portray suffering and opposition as paradigmatic for the Christian community.[41]

One of the most magnificent statements concerning our sanctification and the Spirit's participation in it is how we are transformed into the Lord's likeness by reflecting God's glory that comes from the Spirit

---

40. This is consistent with Martin Mittelstadt's characterization of the Lukan view of the Spirit, where the role of the Spirit is primarily to inspire confession with uninhibited freedom (Mittelstadt, "Life in the Spirit and the Way of the Cross," 26–30, esp. 29).

41. Mittelstadt, *The Spirit and Suffering in Luke–Acts*.

(2 Cor 3:17–18). Paul teaches that the experiential transformation by the Spirit changes us into the image of Christ. Paul also models a Christ-like concern for others physically, spiritually, and emotionally. He models a Christ-like life, picking up his cross and following Jesus—and invites others to share in his journey and his suffering. What is true about suffering for Jesus and his followers in Luke–Acts is also true about suffering in the Pauline epistles.

The Holy Spirit and Eschatology

There is general agreement that Pentecostalism is characterized by an eschatological passion.[42] This eschatological passion appears to have a direct correlation with the Pentecostal focus on the experience of the Holy Spirit. According to Gordon Fee, the Pentecostal experience of the Holy Spirit is an eschatological reality because he belongs to the future.[43] This is consistent with both Paul's pneumatology and eschatology (2 Cor 1:22), though the content of his eschatology features the imminent return of Christ, the resurrection of the believer, the judgment of unbelievers, and the sanctifying effect of the eschatological hope.

Paul describes the Spirit as a down payment or first installment of our future reality in Christ at his second coming, and as a seal that marks believers as God's possession and places them under his protection (2 Cor 1:21–22; 5:5; Eph 1:13–14; 4:30). He also calls the Spirit the "firstfruits" of our adoption, which is the redemption of our bodies (Rom 8:23), and the Holy Spirit is linked with the language of "promise" (Gal 3:14; Eph 1:13–14). These metaphors correspond with Luke's connection of the coming of the Spirit with the eschatological fulfillment of the prophet Joel on the Day of Pentecost related by Luke (Acts 2:16–21; cf. Joel 2:28–32). The Spirit indicates that the Messiah's age has come and we are living in the end-time when God's promises are being fulfilled.

---

42. For Steven Land, the sanctification of the affections is part of an eschatological passion for the kingdom of God yet to come (Land, *Pentecostal Spirituality*, 62–63).

43. This expression is drawn from the argument of Gordon Fee, "The Issue of Separability and Subsequence," 105–19, esp. 111–16. Fee suggests on p. 113 that the fact that the Spirit belongs to the future is the key to everything in the New Testament, parallel to Jesus' announcement of the coming of the kingdom of God and the coming of the church age at Pentecost instead of the end. Macchia also states that the Spirit is an eschatological gift (Macchia, *Baptized in the Spirit*, 48).

One of the eschatological promises that most interests both Paul and Luke is the blessing for the Gentiles through Abraham (Gen 12:3). Paul links the inclusion of the Gentiles in the people of God with receiving the promise of the Spirit through faith (Gal 3:14).[44] Without a doubt, he has in mind the breaking down of the dividing wall between Jews and Gentiles and other boundaries between humans when he speaks of the unity created by the Spirit in which there is no longer Jew nor Gentile, male nor female, slave nor free (Eph 2:11–22; 4:3; 1 Cor 12:13; cf. Gal 3:28).[45] Luke demonstrates strikingly similar associations when he connects the baptism of the Holy Spirit and baptism into Christ with the account of the precedent-setting conversion of the Gentile Cornelius and his household (Acts 10:44–48). According to Luke, Peter repeated the account at the Jerusalem Council with focus on the significance of the gift of the Holy Spirit in the inclusion of the Gentiles in the people of God (Acts 15:6–9). Paul's mission to the Gentiles is the defining feature of his ministry. In crossing religious, social, and cultural boundaries to reach the Gentiles, Paul provides the best example in the New Testament of the contextualization of the gospel, both in Acts and in his epistles. It is probably no coincidence that the focus on the Spirit in the worldwide spread of Pentecostalism distinctively exhibits contextualization that makes the gospel relevant to social change and economic and political contexts. While contextualization is not normally considered to be eschatological, it must be seen as an expression of the fulfillment of the Abrahamic Covenant. The connections of this Pentecostal distinctive to Pauline practice are stronger than to any other model in the New Testament.

Therefore, Paul's association of the Spirit with the fulfillment of eschatological promise is consistent with a connection between the Pentecostal focus on the Spirit and Pentecostals' eschatological passion. Furthermore, the worldwide mission emphasis of Pentecostalism, which features contextualization, is an extension of Paul's mission to the Gentiles and the fulfillment of the Abrahamic Covenant, where the Spirit creates unity in the body of Christ among those who have been living in mutual

---

44. See Fee's discussion on the Spirit and the inclusion of the Gentiles in *God's Empowering Presence*, 811–12.

45. Though the Spirit is not explicitly mentioned in the well-known passage in Gal 3:28 ("neither male nor female"), the parallels with 1 Cor 12:13 are transparent, so that the contents can be conflated.

hostility, and reaches people groups who have been alienated from the people of God.

Conclusions and Concerns

Paul commanded the churches he planted to follow him as he followed Christ (1 Cor 11:1; 2 Thess 3:9). We too see him as a model. Obviously there should be some relationship between his actual life and behavior and our imitation of him. However, rationalistic interpretations and the systematizing of Paul's propositional statements in his epistles have had the effect of washing out the road between Paul's life and experience and our own. The imitation of Paul has been reduced to a set of theological dogmas and ethical character qualities. We need to rediscover Paul with different categories and embrace the patterns of his charismatic experience as well as his propositions. He validates and exemplifies many of the Pentecostal distinctives.

However, there are some concerns about the practice of prioritizing certain interpretations of Luke over Paul in order to maintain and justify historic Pentecostal doctrines. First, although Luke selected his material on the Holy Spirit for his narrative with a purpose, it does not follow that his purpose is to fully explain the theology of the Spirit. That is to say, he may well leave out aspects of his own theology that Paul in turn elucidates. It is not inconceivable that Luke and Paul would use similar terminology, since Luke was part of Paul's ministry team and half of Acts is devoted to Paul's story—in fact, one can make a case that Paul is the focus of Acts, and Luke highlights Paul's actions, stories, and speeches, whereas Luke is not an obvious participant in his own narrative and is not reporting his own experience. Do we interpret Luke's accounts of Paul's personal and pastoral experiences in contradiction to Paul's own understanding? Can we trust Paul to both interpret his own experiences and to provide correctives or adjustments to our own theological reflection? To do so would be more consistent with the Pentecostal commitment to personal experience.

I suggest that we can find numerous correlations between Paul, Luke–Acts, and the Pentecostal worldview. Though we interpret Luke and Paul as individual theologians in their own right, I suggest that we are not compelled by the Lukan text to interpret them in direct contradiction and conflict. Rather, they are complementary, and in regards to receiving the Spirit, one nuances the understanding of the other. Paul considers receiving the Spirit as essential in the constellation of initial conversion experiences, while Luke resists an *ordo salutis*—particularly one that subordinates the Spirit. Both writers support and expect an experiential manifestation when one receives the gift of the Spirit. When addressing healing and concern for the poor and oppressed, the marginalized and the disenfranchised, Luke's distinctive theology is complementary to Paul's, but contributes more to the heart and soul of a valid Pentecostal distinctive, and must be embraced. However, there also needs to be the initiation of a significant welcome and place for Paul in the Pentecostal discussion.

Bibliography

Anderson, Allan. *An Introduction to Pentecostalism*. New York: Cambridge University Press, 2004.

Arrington, French L. *Encountering the Holy Spirit: Paths of Christian Growth and Service*. Cleveland, TN: Pathway Press, 2003.

Dunn, James D. *The Theology of Paul the Apostle*. Grand Rapids: Eerdmans, 1998.

Fee, Gordon D. "Baptism in the Holy Spirit: The Issue of Separability and Subsequence." *Pneuma* 7 (1985) 87–99.

———. *God's Empowering Presence: The Holy Spirit in the Letters of Paul*. Peabody, MA: Hendrickson, 1994.

———. "The Issue of Separability and Subsequence." In *Gospel and Spirit: Issues in New Testament Hermeneutics*, 105–19. Peabody, MA: Hendrickson, 1991.

———. *Paul, the Spirit, and the People of God*. Peabody, MA: Hendrickson, 1996.

Garland, David E. *1 Corinthians*. BECNT. Grand Rapids: Baker, 2003.

Hollenweger, Walter J. "Priorities in Pentecostal Research: Historiography, Missiology, Hermeneutics, and Pneumatology." In *Experiences in the Spirit*, edited by J. A. B. Jongeneel, 9–10, Bern: Peter Lang, 1989.

Land, Steven J. *Pentecostal Spirituality: A Passion for the Kingdom*. Journal of Pentecostal Theology Supplement Series 1. Sheffield: Sheffield Academic Press, 1993.

Leckie-Tarry, Helen. *Language and Context: A Functional Theory of Register*. Edited by David Birch. London: Pinter, 1995.

Longenecker, Richard N., ed. *The Road from Damascus: The Impact of Paul's Conversion on his Life, Thought, and Ministry*. Grand Rapids: Eerdmans, 1997.

Macchia, Frank D. *Baptized in the Spirit: A Global Pentecostal Theology*. Grand Rapids: Zondervan, 2006.

Matera, Frank J. *New Testament Christology*. Louisville: Westminster John Knox Press, 1999.

Mittelstadt, Martin. "Life in the Spirit and the Way of the Cross: Following Jesus via Luke–Acts." *Enrich: A Journal for Pentecostal Ministry* 4:2 (2005) 26–30.

———. *The Spirit and Suffering in Luke-Acts: Implications for a Pentecostal Pneumatology*. Journal of Pentecostal Theology Supplement Series 26. London: T&T Clark International, 2004.

Porter, Stanley E. "Dialect and Register in the Greek of the New Testament Theory." In *Rethinking Context, Rereading Texts: Contributions from the Social Sciences to Biblical Interpretation*, edited by M. D. Carroll R., 190–208. JSOTSup 299. Sheffield: Sheffield Academic Press, 2000.

———. *Idioms of the Greek New Testament*. 2d ed. Biblical Languages: Greek 2. Sheffield: Sheffield Academic Press, 1994.

———. "Register in the Greek of the New Testament: Application with Reference to Mark's Gospel." In *Rethinking Context, Rereading Texts: Contributions from the Social Sciences to Biblical Interpretation*, edited by M. D. Carroll R., 209–29. JSOTSup 299. Sheffield: Sheffield Academic Press, 2000.

Porter, Stanley E., and Cynthia Long Westfall. "Mission in Acts: A Cord of Three Strands." In *Mission in the New Testament*, edited by Stanley E. Porter and Cynthia Long Westfall. Grand Rapids: Eerdmans, forthcoming.

Schreiner, Thomas R. *Paul, Apostle of God's Glory in Christ: A Pauline Theology*. Downers Grove, IL: InterVarsity, 2001.

Spittler, Russell P. "Suggested Areas for Further Research in Pentecostal Studies." *Pneuma* 5 (1983) 39–57.

Stronstad, Roger. *The Charismatic Theology of St. Luke*. Peabody, MA: Hendrickson, 1984.

Thistleton, Anthony C. *The First Epistle to the Corinthians: A Commentary on the Greek Text*. NIGTC. Grand Rapids: Eerdmans, 2000.

Witherington, Ben III. *The Christology of Jesus*. Minneapolis: Fortress Press, 1990.

———. *Paul's Narrative Thought World: The Tapestry of Tragedy and Triumph*. Louisville: Westminster John Knox Press, 1994.

Witherington, Ben III and Laura M. Ice. *The Shadow of the Almighty: Father, Son, and Spirit in Biblical Perspective*. Grand Rapids: Eerdmans, 2002.

Yong, Amos. *The Spirit Poured Out on All Flesh: Pentecostalism and the Possibility of Global Theology*. Grand Rapids: Baker, 2005.

7

Spirit and Suffering in Contemporary Pentecostalism: The Lukan Epic Continues[1]

Martin William Mittelstadt

Introduction: A Twentieth-century Epic of Lukan Proportions

On the morning of Saturday, November 26, of this past year, I opened my local newspaper to read of a story of epic proportions. The front-page headline of the *Springfield News-Leader* read: "Family Honors Missionary's Memory."[2] To my delight, I began a journey into the riveting story of Assemblies of God missionary to the Congo, Jay Tucker. After reading the newspaper reports, I felt compelled to purchase the biography by his wife, Angelina, which I promptly devoured.[3] Jay and Angelina served together in the Congo from 1939 to 1964 and experienced Acts-like ministry. Angelina chronicles numerous accounts of incredible conversions coupled with miraculous signs and wonders akin to the experiences of the early community in Acts. Today, the church in Paulis planted by the Tuckers is a thriving indigenous congregation numbering around 2,500 congregants.

---

1. This paper is both a synopsis and survey of recent developments relating to my earlier work, Mittelstadt, *Spirit and Suffering*.

2. Wes Johnson, "42 Years of Grief," *Springfield News-Leader*, November 26, 2006, sec. 1A, 4A. The next day reflections on the memorial service are offered by Ryan Slight, "Family Celebrates Missionary's Legacy," *Springfield News-Leader*, November 27, 2006, sec. 1B.

3. Tucker, *"He is in Heaven."*

Spirit and Suffering in Contemporary Pentecostalism 145

The riveting part of the story, however, is its apparent dark or tragic side. The newspaper headline also read:

> 42 years of grief: Family members hope to come to terms with the brutal 1964 killing of an Assemblies of God missionary at the hands of Congolese rebels. Today at a Springfield cemetery, survivors will dedicate a memorial to JW "Jay" Tucker.

As I read this story I felt like I was reading a Pentecostal version of the Jim Elliot story. To my disappointment, as a biblical scholar all too familiar academically with a theology of suffering, I never knew that we Pentecostals possessed our own comparable missionary epic.[4] This is the story. Tucker was held in custody by Simba rebels for several weeks until on November 4, 1964, he was beaten with clubs, bottles, and sticks, and eventually tossed into the crocodile-infested Bomokande River. His body was never found. In the days that followed, this story traveled downstream to the land of the Mangbetu tribe, who had a strange custom. The Mangbetu believed that if the blood of any man flowed in their river, they had to listen to his message. Until this time, the gospel message had struggled to connect with them, but in an ironic turn of events, the horrific death of Jay Tucker opened doors for the gospel in a way not all that different from what happened when followers of Jesus were scattered by persecution and martyrdom in Acts. A great revival broke out among the Mangbetu with reports of conversions, healings, miracles, and a host of church plants.

Why is the Tucker story rarely heard in Pentecostal contexts? It seems that Pentecostals love to pontificate on the will of God and his

---

4. Jim Elliot and four other missionaries, Ed McCully, Roger Youderian, Peter Fleming, and their pilot Nate Saint, tried to reach the Auca (Huaorani) Indians of Ecuador, who had never been contacted by missionaries. On their first visit to the Huaorani in 1956, they were all murdered. Almost immediately, Elliot and his friends became known worldwide as martyrs. Their deaths are credited with sparking an interest in Christian missions among the youth of their time, and their dedication is still considered an encouragement to Christian missionaries working throughout the world. After her husband's death, Elisabeth Elliot and other missionaries began working among the Huaorani, where they had a profound impact and won many converts. She later published two books *Shadow of the Almighty* and *Gates of Splendor*, which describe the life and death of her husband. Jim Elliot's journal entry for October 28, 1949, contains his now famous quotation, expressing his passion for missions: "He is no fool who gives what he cannot keep to gain that which he cannot lose."

leading, but primarily when life and ministry are going well.[5] We often convey a dominant pragmatism that suggests any idea or act that produces good results is obviously approved by God. Conversely, when we struggle, there is often at least a hint of suspicion that we are off the correct path, or our methods are flawed, or God is not pleased with our activity. But do these notions resonate with the Scriptures? Do they resonate with global Christianity, especially beyond the comforts of North America? The growth of the movement is bringing contemporary Pentecostals to a crossroads. On the one hand, there is evident maturation in our development of Pentecostal theology and praxis, particularly as we gain prominence in an ecumenical world. On the other hand, this maturity brings with it a subtle comfort, a relaxed status, whereby the mission and passion of our forefathers may be threatened. As I appraise the current status of North American Pentecostalism, I am compelled to consider the convergence of the Spirit and suffering in the Scriptures, specifically Luke–Acts, a favorite corpus for Pentecostals. It is my purpose to examine Luke's ability to sustain elements of triumph and tragedy, acceptance and rejection of the gospel message through Spirit-led witness in order to stimulate discussion toward a more comprehensive Pentecostal pneumatology.

Getting Started: Methodological Considerations

Reading Luke–Acts

The feasibility of this thesis rests on a number of preliminary considerations. First, the term "Luke–Acts" is fundamental to this essay. While it is possible to read Luke and Acts apart from each other, an approach encouraged by their division in the canon, I examine the third Gospel and

---

5. I use the term "Pentecostal" to refer to those who share in the experience of Spirit-Baptism in the classical sense. Representative North American Pentecostal denominations include the Assemblies of God, Pentecostal Assemblies of Canada, International Pentecostal Holiness Church, Church of God in Christ, Church of God (Cleveland, Tennessee), and the International Church of the Foursquare Gospel. I distinguish Pentecostals from Charismatics, namely, those of the renewal movement in the late 50s and early 60s in the mainline denominations. Charismatics usually did not form new denominations but remained within their established Protestant, Catholic, and Orthodox traditions. For excellent summaries of the Pentecostal and Charismatic traditions, see Lederle, *Treasures Old and New*; Anderson, *Introduction to Pentecostalism*; and various articles in Burgess and Van Der Maas, *Pentecostal and Charismatic Movements*.

Acts as a two-volume work.⁶ When viewed together, Luke and Acts form a comprehensive and coherent narrative, so that themes that begin in the Gospel often find their fulfillment in Acts.⁷ This is not surprising, given Luke's own connection between the two volumes: the acts of the early church serve as a continuation of all that Jesus did and taught (Acts 1:1). Luke's innovation is to show that the gospel story is incomplete without the story of the emerging disciples and the formation of the new community.⁸ Luke Timothy Johnson suggests that Luke's presentation of the meaning of Jesus and the early Church for the world is found in a single vision, so that what happens in Jesus foreshadows the church's experience and what happens in the church finds meaning in the continuation of Jesus' story.⁹

Literary Criticism

Second, in light of the connection between the two volumes, I also adopt a narrative/literary approach. Such an approach recognizes Luke not only as a writer of short vignettes, but a gifted storyteller with his most impressive accomplishment possibly the forging of these short stories into

---

6. The contemporary term "Luke–Acts," was coined by Cadbury, *Making of Luke-Acts*, and refers to the literary connection between the Third Gospel and Acts. Following in this scholarly tradition, I assume that Luke–Acts is the product of a single author resulting in a two-volume work with a definite narrative unity and inner integrity, characterized by overarching themes and repeated patterns. I also use the name "Luke," to refer either to the Gospel of Luke or to the author of the Third Gospel and the Acts of the Apostles. I should point out that a high regard for the historical reliability of the biblical text leads most Pentecostal scholars to affirm the traditional identification of Luke as a physician and a co-worker of Paul. While there is a near consensus on the unity of Luke–Acts, an important challenge to this position comes from Parsons and Pervo, *Luke and Acts*. Pentecostals should also consider the canonical approach in Wall, "Purity and Power." Wall calls for a separate reading of Luke and Acts more in continuity with their canonical alignment. Finally, see my trajectory of Luke–Acts research in the Pentecostal tradition in Mittelstadt, "Reading Luke–Acts."

7 Johnson says it well: "The decision to read these separate texts together as a single literary work represents the triumph (or giving up) of the literary-critical approach to the NT writings, concerned less for the historical data contained in a writing, or the prehistory of its discrete parts, than with its distinctive voice.... To adopt the category 'Luke–Acts' therefore, means to accept a contemporary literary designation in preference to the traditional perception of the texts or even their canonical placement" ("Luke–Acts," 404).

8. Barrett, *Acts of the Apostles*, 54.

9. Johnson, *Writings of the New Testament*, 199.

one long coherent narrative. Luke–Acts stands as a single story, and, by implication, Luke's purposes and/or understanding of any specific motif must take the whole story into account, precisely in its literary development. This approach, while broadly termed "literary criticism," offers widely divergent connotations for various scholars.[10] My approach shares methodological perspectives of literary/narrative criticism as employed by scholars who discern Luke's theological purposes by tracing narrative developments, plot lines, character roles, and the use of irony, repetition, anticipation, and other literary features commonly associated with modern novels, short stories, and films.[11] Literary critics affirm that Luke is an author of considerable literary skill and rich imagination, who conveys a vision of the significance of Jesus Christ and of the mission that follows his ascension.[12] Luke does not provide a theological thesis wrapped in a narrative from which it can be separated; on the contrary, Lukan theology is inextricably bound up with the narrative. Using these literary devices, I seek to discover Luke's literary connections and patterns, and to trace internal developments within the narrative as they relate to the primary theme under observation.[13]

---

10. In secular literary studies this method is called "narratology," but biblical scholars use the term "literary/narrative criticism," probably as a counterpoint to and improvement upon source, form, and redaction criticism. See A. B. Spencer, who lists some 15 contrasting definitions of literary criticism ("Literary Criticism," 225–36), and F. S. Spencer, who offers an excellent summary of various literary approaches applied to Luke–Acts ("Modern Literary Approaches"). In light of the proposed literary analysis, this study will not comment on questions of historicity. This does not imply hostility to such analysis but rather brackets historical questions in order to pursue literary components. The focus is not on whether Luke writes an accurate account of historical events, but rather his theological emphases as discerned through the narrative. On the relationship between historical-critical and literary approaches, see Sternberg, *Biblical Narrative*, 6–23 and Powell, *Narrative Criticism*, 96–98.

11. Gaventa, "Theology of Acts;" Johnson, "Luke–Acts," *Writings of the New Testament*, and *Possessions in Luke–Acts*; Kurz, "Narrative Approaches," "Narrative Models," and *Reading Luke–Acts*; and Tannehill, *Narrative Unity*.

12. Pentecostals interested in the application of a narrative-critical methodology in Luke–Acts should consult the valuable work of Kurz, *Reading Luke–Acts*. Kurz, a charismatic Catholic, was my dissertation mentor at Marquette University and is an occasional visitor of the Society for Pentecostal Studies.

13. I am aware of the potential concerns surrounding "parallelomania" and cross-referencing. For example, see Praeder, "Parallelisms in Luke–Acts," 35. She cautions: "Parallel reading requires close reading of the passages, sensitivity to similarities in language and sequence, and knowledge of the literary and theological character of Luke–Acts."

Contemporary Implications

Third, since the goal of this project is to offer implications for a contemporary Pentecostal pneumatology, a literary analysis, which focuses on specific passages and remains grounded in the Lukan text, is well suited to this task. Exegesis within a literary framework places Luke in a position to speak to readers of any generation. Modern readers are encouraged to consider not only how original readers are affected by their understanding of the text but also how the text should affect contemporary readers.

Pentecostals have engaged in such reading of the Scripture throughout their short history. In other words, Pentecostals see their own experience as a re-enactment or continuation of the biblical story. For example, in a popular homiletical exhortation in the official organ of the Pentecostal Assemblies of Canada, *The Pentecostal Testimony*, the late Canadian educator Karel Marek titles his comments, "Acts Chapter 29," with a subtitle stating: "In case you hadn't noticed recently there are only 28 chapters recorded in the Book of Acts in your Bible."[14] In his opening paragraph, writing a vintage Pentecostal refrain, he declares, "I've frequently heard of churches with a desire to 'write' Acts chapter 29. Is it not the dream of every preacher? Is this not what the world needs to see?"[15] As "living texts," Marek calls Pentecostals to a renewed posture for reception of a contemporary Pentecost and the ensuing empowerment in order to continue the Lukan narrative into the present day.[16]

Any larger survey of the history of Christian doctrine regularly points to the importance of creeds and propositional statements as the basis for theological belief and praxis. However, as John Goldingay notes:

> Narrative, story, dominates Scripture. . . . At one level, Christian tradition has indeed always recognized the importance of story, but you would not guess this from the nature of Christian theol-

---

14. Marek, "Acts 29," 24.

15. Marek, "Acts 29," 24.

16. According to Land, *Pentecostal Spirituality*, the Pentecostal story also may be framed by the ongoing metaphor of journey as a powerful language of transcendence, crossing over and moving beyond. While there is a constant recognition that we are not yet what we ought to be, this metaphor of journey evokes adventure, courage, and daring. For Pentecostals, the life we are called to live is one where we seek to walk in continuity with first-century Christian communities, hoping to transform and embrace the neighborhood, the society, and the world. Concerning this motif in Luke–Acts, see also the early but still valuable contribution by Filson, "Journey Motif."

ogy, or from the nature of most writing on spirituality . . . It is a natural and biblical way to do theology . . . narrative is Scripture's more dominant way of doing theology.[17]

In reflecting upon the last century, I think it is possible that Pentecostals are now receiving their most positive turning point for sustainable scholarship due to the recent migration of the literary/narrative critical methodologies from the humanities into biblical studies. In fact, possibly more than any other contemporary tradition, Pentecostals are finally able to utilize technical language for the kind of exegesis they have been using since the beginning of the twentieth century. Pentecostal scholars are beginning to engage in methodological discourse, to argue that Pentecostals have long been aware that the power of the Holy Spirit is unleashed through orality (in witnessing, telling, and hearing the stories of God's mighty love and actions), in ways otherwise not possible through mere theological argument.[18] Consider the following correspondence from Assemblies of God scholar Jerry Camery-Hoggatt:

> Pentecostals have been doing narrative theology for years although without the added dimension of critical self-reflection. Hence there is a critical need for hermeneutical theorizing along these lines. And narrative theology as it is developing outside of Pentecostalism may often provide helpful vocabulary and criteria of evaluation as we become self-conscious about what we have for so long done naturally. . . . With the discovery of narrative theology we are suddenly on the cutting edge of the contemporary theological scene."[19]

Accordingly, narrative theology aids Pentecostals in counterbalancing a propositional theology and hermeneutic with one that is more experiential, imaginative, story-based, and Spirit-led. While Pentecostals continue to appeal to critical insights from source criticism, form criticism, redaction criticism, and other "historical-critical" approaches, these tools offer only pre-interpretive work. The power of the Christian story and of individual biblical stories is found not only in their dissection, but also in their ability to grab attention, capture the imagination, and so draw in

---

17. Goldingay, "Biblical Story," 5–6.
18. Dowd, "Contours," 16.
19. Correspondence between Michael Dowd and Jerry Camery-Hoggatt from a personal letter written July 23, 1985, cited in Dowd, "Contours," 18.

and change the reader. Pentecostals begin to reap great dividends with the emergence of a narrative theology by being able to proclaim that propositional truth cannot report the whole truth. Narrative approaches to Scripture create expectations for future encounters with God helping the believing community transform "the story" into "our story."[20]

The near-triumph of literary analysis does not leave Pentecostals without confrontation from academic or ecclesial communities. In still another hermeneutical essay, Paul Elbert finds it necessary to remind members of the Evangelical Theological Society:

> Historicity, not narrative theology and pneumatology, has dominated Evangelical scholarship in Acts. And this is, of course a proper and important enterprise. But if it becomes an exclusive vision, the interpretation of Paul (dispensational and otherwise) can unduly overshadow the Christian tradition, description, and practice as portrayed by Luke.[21]

In a footnote to this quotation Elbert makes a bold observation concerning the potential practical implications for such Evangelical conclusions: "We believe that the events of Acts happened, we just don't want them to happen to us." Ironically, conservative Evangelicals will fight alongside Pentecostals in defending the historical reliability of the Lukan narratives, but Pentecostals, utilizing a literary methodology, expect these same events to occur as part of contemporary experience.

Pentecostal Challenge and Neglect

While I agree wholeheartedly with Elbert's accusations against Evangelicals, I believe Pentecostals may also be guilty of the same criticism we apportion against others. Pentecostals want to recapture the life of the early church, but do we really know of what we speak? We are champions

---

20. Goldingay, "Biblical Story," 6. Similarly, Wright argues for the contemporary application of biblical narrative by using the analogy of a Shakespearean play that is missing the final act. He suggests that "highly trained," sensitive, and experienced actors, who would immerse themselves in the previous acts, could write a final act. The book of Acts also seems to end in an abrupt, unfinished way. Wright proposes that Luke challenges his readers to "adopt the model" and write the last act by pressing ahead with the unfinished task of spreading the gospel (*New Testament*, 139–43). I am indebted to Brian Rosner for this reference. Concerning the ending of Acts, see Rosner, "Progress of the Word," 229–33.

21. Elbert, "Pentecostal/Charismatic Themes," 207.

of the language of Spirit-empowerment and the triumph of the gospel, but should not the entire Lukan story continue to speak to contemporary readers, even when it includes the fact that believers are rejected and persecuted? Luke challenges the notion of an idealized and romanticized gospel by offering a narrative filled with consistent rejection and opposition. He describes how witnesses beleaguered by opposition and persecution are prepared, assisted, and encouraged to fulfill the plan of God. Through utilization of a literary analysis, contemporary Pentecostals ought to be encouraged to continue pursuit of the Spirit and engage the world envisioned by Luke, even though it is a hostile world.

Any brief review of Lukan scholarship reveals a commensurate Lukan interest in the theme of opposition, which leads to rejection, suffering, and persecution. Luke navigates his story of Jesus and emerging witnesses, a story of epic proportions, from humble origins in Palestine to expansion and success in the Mediterranean world. Scholars are quick to note the artistry of Luke demonstrated through his narration of the fate of Jesus, his witnesses, and the gospel message, through a series of reversals and irony. His story is not merely a narration of persistent triumph, but one of consistent conflict, opposition, and persecution of God's agents.

But what might be the reason for Pentecostal neglect of this motif? Before examining specific texts, I suggest that the initial academic era of Pentecostal scholarship in Lukan studies was not immediately prepared for exploration of such specific motifs. Out of necessity, Pentecostal scholars entered the academic marketplace in response to outside challenges concerning pneumatology. The first wave of Pentecostal scholarship on Luke–Acts was prompted by the watershed work of James D. G. Dunn, *Baptism in the Holy Spirit* in 1970. While sympathetic to Pentecostal experience, Dunn set out to prove that a Pentecostal interpretation of the Spirit is irreconcilable with Scripture. He states: "I hope to show that for the writers of the NT the baptism in or gift of the Spirit was part of the event (or process) of becoming a Christian . . . that it was the chief element in conversion-initiation so that only those who had thus received the Spirit could be called Christians."[22] For Dunn, reception of the Spirit is soteriological, thus initiatory in character and something that brings the recipient into the salvation experience. He goes on to say: "These two

---

22. Dunn, *Holy Spirit*, 4.

are one—two ways of describing the same thing ... baptism in the Spirit is God's act of acceptance, of forgiveness, cleansing, and salvation."[23] For nearly an entire generation, Pentecostal scholarship concerning Luke–Acts remained focused on defense against Dunn and Dunn-like positions. Pentecostals, concerned with the development and defense of their Pentecostal distinctives and experience, offered numerous substantial responses to Dunn's thesis. The monumental efforts of four Pentecostal scholars are well known for their contributions to a Pentecostal pneumatology; namely, Roger Stronstad, James Shelton, Robert Menzies, and Howard Ervin.[24] While Dunn's work led to an initial scholarly awakening and continues to stimulate ongoing discussion for Pentecostal scholars, Pentecostals have appeared so focused on defense of post-conver-

23. Dunn, *Holy Spirit*, 82. While Dunn's work evokes the greatest response from Pentecostals, the newest dialogue partner to reject the classic two-stage view of Spirit baptism is Turner, *Power from on High*. Other previous challenges include Bruner, *Holy Spirit* and Stott, *Baptism and Fullness*. One further challenge to the classic Pentecostal experience of Spirit-baptism is offered by a self-professing Pentecostal, Gordon Fee. See Fee, "Hermeneutics," 122, where he states: "In a sense, the Pentecostal tends to exegete his experience. For example, the doctrine of Spirit-baptism as distinct from and subsequent to conversion did not flow naturally out of his reading of Scripture." Other contributions include Fee, "Baptism" and *Gospel and Spirit*. A review by Menzies concludes: "I do not question Gordon Fee's personal Pentecostal experience. I am not clear, however, about how he expresses Pentecostal theology" (Review of *Gospel and Spirit*, 32).

24. While other Pentecostals have contributed to a Pentecostal pneumatology, the works of these four scholars are most enduring in terms of ongoing publication, scholarship, and citation within and outside of the Pentecostal tradition.
   1. Roger Stronstad: His most important work to date is *Charismatic Theology*, which was originally submitted as a master's thesis at Regent College under Ward Gasque. A more recent work is *Prophethood*. Other related works include "Lucan Historiography," "Trends," "Pentecostal Experience," and "Pentecostal Hermeneutics."
   2. James Shelton: See *Word and Deed*, "'Filled with the Holy Spirit'," and "Reply to James D. G. Dunn."
   3. Robert Menzies: His most important work is his dissertation, *Early Christian Pneumatology*, now revised and updated as *Empowered for Witness*. His most recent project, *Spirit and Power*, is co-authored with his father, William Menzies. Chapter titles include, "The Issue of Subsequence," "Evidential Tongues," and "Tongues: Available to All." Other related works include: "Luke's Pneumatology," "James Shelton," and "Luke and the Spirit."
   4. Howard Ervin is an American Baptist charismatic who is sympathetic to the classical Pentecostal doctrine. Of the works of those scholars under review, his *Conversion-Initiation* is the most direct reply to Dunn. An earlier work is *These Are Not Drunken*.

For further discussion concerning these works see my monograph, *Spirit and Suffering*, 20–28 and Atkinson, "Pentecostal Responses."

sion Spirit-baptism that they have often ignored other motifs.[25] Today, Pentecostal scholars are not only positing impressive contributions on Lukan pneumatology, but are also beginning to engage with and enlarge the scholarly discussion concerning other Lukan contributions to the people of God.[26]

I focus on one particular lacuna in our understanding of and presentation of Luke's pneumatology. It is my contention that the Pentecostal tradition, at the scholarly and ecclesial levels, has generally neglected to address and to apply the role of the Holy Spirit in contexts of suffering and persecution.[27] I should add that I am not the first to notice this gap.

As early as 1982, Russell Spittler, in his plenary address to the Society for Pentecostal Studies, suggested that a study be done on the relationship between charismatic phenomena and martyrdom in the early church. He states, "When life was threatened—surely that counts for psychological stress on anyone's measure—did use of spiritual phenomena increase among early Christians? Such an inquiry might present an opportunity for a psycho-historical investigation."[28] In 1991, James Bradley of Fuller Theological Seminary wrote of the paradox of miracle and martyrdom in the early church:

> The same God who healed early Christians often led them to sudden, violent death, even in the flower of youth. The ever-present reality of confessing Christ at the risk of one's life (confessorship) and martyrdom itself in relation to supernatural healing is a vital but almost wholly neglected aspect of the early church's life. . . . The early church's concern [was] to remind believers that any temporary relief from suffering found in healing in no wise exempted them from the setbacks, limitations, suffering and possibly even death that were necessarily involved in following Christ.[29]

---

25. For example, thirty years after Dunn's initial project on Spirit-baptism, the most recent work of Robert and William Menzies (*Spirit and Power*) still includes a chapter entitled "Exegesis: A Reply to James Dunn."

26. Mittelstadt, "Reading Luke–Acts."

27. Cunningham defines persecution as rejection of or unbelief in a particular teaching, which progresses to rejection of the messenger, ever escalating in intensity to the point of violent response (*Through Many Tribulations*, 301). I will follow this definition, thereby limiting my focus to suffering in the context of witness.

28. Spittler, "Suggested Areas," 54.

29. Bradley, "Miracles and Martyrdom," 70–71.

Although Spittler and Bradley provided the call for such a Pentecostal project, there had been no comprehensive Pentecostal effort on the convergence of the Holy Spirit and suffering in Luke–Acts prior to my monograph. In light of this oversight, I examine Luke's ability to sustain both elements of triumph and tragedy, acceptance and rejection of the gospel message, through Spirit-led witness, in order to stimulate discussion toward a more comprehensive Pentecostal pneumatology. The following exegesis is an examination of six passages in the original Lukan epic that encourage not only original readers but also contemporary Pentecostals to adopt a rigorous pneumatic discipleship that perseveres in the midst of suffering and persecution.

The Original Epic: Exegesis[30]

Simeon's Preview of the Gospel Message (Luke 2:25–35)

After the impact of the infant Jesus is experienced by a host of Spirit-inspired individuals, who announce joyous words of anticipation and praise, the somber words of Simeon near the climax of the Lukan birth narrative launch the first intersection of the Spirit and suffering. In Luke 2:25–35, Simeon arrives on the scene and forecasts division. Through a triple reference to the presence of the Holy Spirit as inspiration for Simeon, Luke establishes Simeon as a reliable witness concerning the infant Jesus (2:25, 26, 27). The Lukan Jesus, who brings salvation and is received by many, will also be rejected, which will lead to opposition and, in turn, suffering and persecution. Consequently, Simeon's words serve as a Lukan literary prophecy: God's work in Jesus brings all people to a point of decision, namely one of acceptance or rejection.[31] For Luke,

---

30. Once again, for comprehensive analysis of these passages I strongly recommend a look at chap. 2 and 3 of Mittelstadt, *Spirit and Suffering*.

31. Luke uses several elements to disclose his theological purposes:
   1. Literary prophecy is a Lukan device where utterances by characters are explicitly fulfilled in the subsequent narrative. Other examples include Jesus' words to his disciples in Luke 12:1–12 fulfilled in Acts 3–5 and 7; the passion predictions of Jesus (Luke 9:22, 44; 18:32–33; fulfilled in Luke 24:6–8, 44); Jesus' predictions concerning the tribulations of the disciples (Luke 21:12–15; fulfilled in Acts 4:3–5, 14; 5:17–42); Jesus' instruction concerning the proper response to unbelieving cities (Luke 9:5; 10:11; fulfilled in Acts 13:51); and Agabus's prediction of sufferings for Paul (Acts 21:10–14; fulfilled in Acts 21:30–35).
   2. Programmatic prophecy is a form of literary prophecy where Luke directs the

Simeon's inspired words place rejection and opposition to Jesus in the plan of God.

Jesus in Nazareth: A Preview of Jesus' Ministry (Luke 4:16–30)

As Luke embarks upon narration of Jesus' ministry tour, it is in dramatic fashion that the Spirit-led Jesus is met with rejection and persecution in his inaugural mission. While worshiping in the synagogue at his home town of Nazareth, Jesus reads from Isa 61 and, according to his fellow worshipers, presumptuously interprets the prophecy as fulfilled in him. In ironic fashion, the Lukan Jesus, also under the direction of the Holy Spirit (Luke 3:15–16, 22; 4:1, 14), is rejected, thereby serving as Luke's first explicit example of Simeon's forecasting of acceptance and rejection. These accounts not only offer the first fulfillment of Simeon's words, but also serve a paradigmatic purpose for Luke's readers: future witnesses of Jesus will not only proclaim the message of Jesus, but may also experience a similar fate, namely, acceptance and rejection.

Jesus Prepares his Disciples (Luke 12:1–12)

As the Lukan narrative unfolds, Jesus ventures into a powerful mission expressed through miraculous deeds and potent teaching. As Jesus travels to Jerusalem for his impending death (beginning with Luke 9:51), several teaching discourses serve a preparatory purpose for Jesus' disciples. Luke's travel narrative not only prepares his readers for the death of Jesus, it also prepares readers for the anticipated ministry of the disciples. By way of another literary prophecy, the Lukan Jesus assures his disciples that the same Spirit who functions as the source of power for Jesus' mis-

---

development of the plot as a fulfillment of the prophecy. For example, the inauguration of Jesus' ministry in Nazareth in Luke 4 is a preview of Jesus' ministry in fulfillment of Isa 61; or note the critical position of Acts 1:8 as programmatic for the geographical and ethnic expansion of the gospel from Jerusalem, to Judea, Samaria, and beyond.

3. Speech-narrative prophecy is the Lukan arrangement of speeches within the narrative to form a "prophecy-fulfillment" pattern. Luke places speeches so that the narrative following them fulfills their point, often ironically (for example, in Luke 4:14–30, Jesus declares a prophet is not accepted in his home town and he is rejected; and in Acts 7, Stephen accuses his listeners of rejecting the prophets and of resisting the Holy Spirit, then they respond by killing him). These literary elements are detailed further in the respective exegetical units of chap. 3 and 4 of Mittelstadt, *Spirit and Suffering*. See also Peterson, "Motif of Fulfillment" and Frein, "Narrative Predictions."

sion will be available and a guarantee for the disciples in the midst of opposition that amounts to blasphemy against the Holy Spirit (12:10–12). As the disciples are commissioned to carry forth the message of Jesus, they are also assured of the anointing of the Spirit in what will be a hostile world. For Luke's readers, this pericope (among others) serves to place the disciples in continuity with their master. Pneumatic discipleship will receive a divided response!

The Apostles Meet Resistance (Acts 3–5)

Luke's contribution to the story of Jesus does not end with the death and resurrection of Jesus as in the other Gospels. His second volume continues the impact of Jesus through the lives of the disciples and other witnesses to the gospel (Acts 1:1). The experiences of the disciples continuously afford explicit fulfillment of Jesus' words in Luke 12:1–12 that his followers would be persecuted by opponents but honored by God. Through the lives of Peter, John, and the other apostles, Luke communicates the great strength of the emerging Jesus movement. In Acts 3–5, as Jesus' followers share their new understanding of Jesus as Savior and Lord, they are met not only with acceptance but also with rejection. This rejection comes in the form of hatred and persecution, similar to the lot of Jesus himself. When they are maligned, arrested, and flogged, when they are forced to choose between denial and safety or confession and pain, it is the Holy Spirit who inspires their actions and words, as Jesus promised in Luke 12:12 (see Acts 4:8, 31).[32]

---

32. I know of only one essay by a Pentecostal scholar on the nature of suffering in Acts 3–5, and another related paper on suffering in Acts 12. Gallagher offers a moving pastoral autobiography by comparing his own sense of calling and then wrestling with implications of healing, to those of the emerging community in Acts ("From Doing to Being"). First, in his analysis of the "little Pentecost" (Acts 4:23–31), he charts how his own ideas of ministry success often parallel contemporary values of Western society without critical evaluation. By way of a fresh reading of Acts 4, Gallagher recognizes the early church pattern of prayer, Spirit, and mission, which ought to call for contemporary readers to see mission as flowing out of "beingness" rather than "doingness." In Gallagher's second paper, "Hope in the Midst of Trial," he paradigmatically parallels the journey of his wife Dolores, as she struggles against and eventually dies of colon cancer, to the respective tragedies and triumphs of James and Peter as recorded in Acts 12. Gallagher then places his own family story in light of the persecution of the church in Jerusalem (Acts 12:1–5) versus Peter's miraculous escape from prison (Acts 12:6–11).

Stephen: The First Christian Martyr (Acts 6–7)

As the emerging community expands, the opposition experienced by Jesus and the apostles also extends to other witnesses. Stephen advances the convergence of the Spirit and suffering in three ways. First, Stephen faces opposition similar to that faced by the Twelve, but opposition to him is even more intense. Peter and John are threatened and released, and the Twelve are maligned and flogged, but Stephen is stoned to death. Second, readers should immediately recognize that the death of Stephen mirrors the death of Jesus (Acts 7:54–60). The parallel is striking: followers of Jesus are not only continuing Jesus' ministry (as suggested by Acts 1:1) but also experiencing continuity with the rejection of Jesus. Third, Stephen's speech roots rejection in salvation history. Luke uses Stephen's speech to demonstrate that the rejection of Jesus, the apostles, and Stephen himself, finds its origin in the history of the people of God. Chosen salvific agents such as Joseph, Moses, and the prophets advance Luke's pattern of acceptance and rejection by demonstrating its continuity with God's activity in history (Acts 7:2–53). It seems reasonable to conclude that Luke's ominous history of salvation is intended to place rejected followers in "good company." Finally, it is not without significance that Stephen is a man "full of the Holy Spirit" (Acts 6:3, 5, 10; 7:51). For Luke's readers, Stephen's story cultivates bold commitment in the face of opposition by suggesting that witness for Jesus may summon a fate similar to that of previous Spirit-led witnesses.[33]

Paul: Spirit-led Witness Par Excellence (Acts 20)

The apostle Paul affords Luke a final opportunity to further his explicit emphasis on the Spirit in contexts of suffering. Paul's story is not only one

---

33. Pentecostal scholar Holm offers the only focused essay specifically on the Stephen narrative. Holm examines the Stephen narrative (Acts 7) in an attempt to import the significance of Stephen's polemical words into the contemporary church. In the hands of Luke, Stephen's martyrdom functions as an ironic geographic segue to church expansion beyond Jerusalem and into the Gentile community. Further, at the level of the story, witnesses are forced either to resist the Holy Spirit and be complicit in Stephen's death or cast their own lot with the "Son of Man standing at the right hand of God" (Acts 7:56). Holm raises important issues concerning Pentecostal reflection upon history, specifically a call to move beyond nostalgic desire for the "old and venerable" to a rigorous spiritual formation and discipline aligned with God's purposes/destiny that may include opposition ("Acts 7," 15).

of remarkable missionary success, but also one of immense difficulty, as he is consistently rejected, abused, and beaten, and often has to flee for his life. Through irony, Luke roots this persecution in divine providence. Paul's successful journey to Rome as a persecuted witness is not accidental or simply an obstacle to be overcome, but places him in continuity with Jesus. As the journey of Jesus in the Third Gospel is a journey for his ordained suffering, so also, in a twist of fate, the Lukan Paul goes to Rome, not as a free man but as a prisoner in chains and ultimately "bound by the Spirit" (Acts 20:22).

While Luke's entire presentation of Paul is one of proclamation in the midst of opposition (see Acts 9:15–16), the Lukan Paul also offers a fitting "farewell discourse" to the Ephesian elders, and, by inference, to all future witnesses of Jesus (Acts 20:18–35). By implication, Paul's life, directed by the Spirit, serves as an example to the Ephesian community. When under duress, they (and Luke's readers) need not lose heart, for their own present and/or potential future persecution places them in continuity not only with the prophets, Jesus, the Apostles, and Stephen, but also with their own pastor, Paul (see Table 1, p. 168: Summary).

The Epic Continues:
Spirit and Suffering in Contemporary Pentecostalism

Observations

At a fundamental level, this investigation ventures into an area not previously given its due in Classical Pentecostal projects. While this is partially due to the previous generation's need to defend its distinctive doctrines, as a new generation of Pentecostal scholars move beyond a limiting defense, new areas of research are already proving fruitful. With the emergence of literary criticism, students of Luke–Acts are less likely to settle for mere defense of a traditional doctrine of the Holy Spirit but rather call attention to more holistic possibilities and responsibilities of the Spirit-filled life. My observation of apostolic witness points to disciples with a new-found certainty that Jesus has risen from the dead and a conviction that they have received the Holy Spirit, which, in turn, sets them upon a path characterized by suffering and death. When empowered by the Spirit, the life of a witness becomes continuous with the life and suffering of Jesus (Acts 14:22). A primary Lukan purpose is undoubtedly to introduce his readers to a responsible Christian life of perseverance in the course of ongoing missionary work.[34] While numerous extended Lukan scenes close by testifying to the triumph of the church over its adversaries (Acts 4:32–37; 9:31; 12:25; 16:5), the episodes that follow demonstrate that neither the Word of God nor its adversaries will be stopped. Luke's theology is intricately and irreversibly bound up with the story he tells and cannot be separated from it. This pattern does not disappear; it is one of positive response and rejection. Both of these threads, the triumph of the God who will not allow the gospel to be overcome as well as the rejection of the gospel and the persecution of its apostles, belong to the narrative Luke develops. To eliminate either of them is to miss something essential to the Lukan story.

A second observation is a call for Pentecostals to see that suffering due to opposition to the gospel is a constant in Lukan theology. While an important Lukan interest is to celebrate the triumph of Christianity in a narrative that begins in Jerusalem and ends on the world stage of Rome, it is not one of uninterrupted triumph from glory to glory. Similarly, any review of the emergence of the Pentecostal tradition will celebrate its strong missionary successes but also note its sufferings.

The consistent call of Pentecostal leadership is to continue writing the book of Acts. This can only be fulfilled through the same empowering of the Holy Spirit and his commissioning to a mission of gospel proclamation. Often lacking, however, is Luke's emphasis on the importance of the Spirit's work in contexts of persecution and martyrdom. It is not accidental that the entire cast of key characters in Luke–Acts suffers "for the name," on account of their proclamation concerning Jesus. The lives of Jesus, Peter and John, the Twelve, Stephen (and his inclusion of the prophets of old), and Paul testify that though God will not allow the gospel to be overcome, its rejection and the persecution of its apostles is as inevitable as the moments of triumph. The oft-cited Pentecostal "triumphalism" is only half of Luke's narrative complexity; he sustains both elements of triumph and tragedy. Luke calls for recognition of the persistent connection between persecution, Christian suffering, and

---

34. Karris describes Luke as a pastoral theologian: "Luke uses the sources of Christian tradition available to him to answer the faith questions of his communities. In consoling, guiding, and challenging these communities, he is like a good pastor who creatively adapts traditions to speak to both the felt and real needs of the people" ("Missionary Communities," 83).

Spirit-inspired mission: witnesses are persecuted because they are sent. Furthermore, persecution and suffering ironically extend the mission (e.g., Acts 8:1–4).

A third observation flows naturally out of Luke's ability to sustain a narrative filled with intense conflict. Since one of the methodological implications of a literary analysis is a commitment to discern Luke's objectives for his readers, various ethical, homiletical, and other applications of the Lukan narrative are bound to emerge. Although one can assume that Luke's message was needed in the early church, the more difficult question rests in finding sensitive contemporary answers, which are not always easily discerned in biblical narrative. With this in mind, I proceed with caution.

It seems reasonable to conclude that readers to whom Luke originally writes are under pressure due to opposition and persecution, and need to know that endurance is possible. Such a background calls for theological and practical consideration of how to deal with this reality. Luke answers by narrating the struggles and survival of the emerging church, for readers familiar with its origin will have confidence in its present and future survival. Luke describes how the Holy Spirit works irresistibly to spread the gospel, giving readers courage and confidence to take their own share in the witness to Christ, to which the whole church is called.

Luke also teaches that suffering accompanies serious ministry and the expansion of Christianity. While those who kill Christ and the martyrs will always exist, it is through personal witness and sacrifice that Christianity advances. For Luke, the greatest defense of the gospel and its representatives is that it is worth dying for. These trials are not "mere annoyances" or slight setbacks, for they cost the church its best people. A Lukan view of the Spirit offers ironic reassurance to readers. Through the witness of rigorous pneumatic disciples, the church not only survives but also advances. While witness may lead to ostracism, imprisonment, or death, the role of the Spirit is not primarily to bring consolation and strength in physical suffering, but to inspire confession with uninhibited freedom.[35] This call to sacrifice life and comfort is at the heart of Luke's message to second-generation Christians.[36]

Recent Scholarly Developments

In the years since the release of my monograph *Spirit and Suffering in Luke–Acts*, I continue to observe and track the theological attention given by Pentecostals to the motif of suffering in general and in Luke–Acts specifically.[37] The advance of global Pentecostalism outside of the global north makes this topic all the more important.[38] Consider China. Pentecostal scholar and missionary Luke Wesley may in fact supply some of the best contemporary parallels to the Third Gospel and Acts. Wesley provides an insider portrait of "The Church in China" as consisting of the paradoxical combination of Pentecostal, powerful, and persecuted. His work substantiates firsthand the convergence of the Spirit and suffering. Wesley considers first the lives of Chinese Christians connected with the state church, and concludes that their minimal liability to persecution makes texts which promise power for bold witness in the face of opposition (e.g., Luke 12:11–12; Acts 1:8; 7:55) of minimal importance. On the other hand, house church believers, a majority of whom he argues are Pentecostal, must make a different choice. Again, their context shapes how they read and appropriate Scripture. These believers, who face persecution or its ever-present threat, view texts that promise God's power

---

35. Concerning the survival of the Christian mission, Lampe points to the almost three centuries of intermittent persecution during the critical period of its formation and growth demonstrated by a clear and uncompromising idea of martyrdom and endurance as the pivotal reason for its success ("Martyrdom and Inspiration," 118).

36. The accusation against Luke that he merely expresses a *theologia gloriae* (theology of glory) at the expense of a *theologia crucis* (theology of the cross) is not warranted. Though Luke might not use cross language, it nevertheless appears in the way in which he tells his story. See Barrett, "*Theologia Crucis*," and Gaventa, "To Speak Thy Word."

37. Pentecostal readers interested in further data concerning persecution should consult Newberg, "Persecution and Martyrdom;" Cunningham, "Contemporary Martyrs;" and McGee, "Historical Perspectives," which focuses on persecution and martyrdom from an Assemblies of God perspective.

38. The global North is generally synonymous with Western Europe and North America. These categories are highlighted in the invaluable work of Jenkins, *Next Christendom* and *New Faces of Christianity*.

Spirit and Suffering in Contemporary Pentecostalism

for bold witness in the face of opposition as tremendously significant.[39] When speaking of these Chinese Christians, Wesley states:

> The stories in the book of Acts take on new meaning. The experiences of Peter, Stephen, and Paul often parallel their own. House church believers identify with their vulnerability, their weaknesses and their need for divine strength. Stories of bold, Spirit-inspired witness in the face of opposition offer much-needed encouragement. Indeed, the Pentecostal reading of the text and the experience of which it speaks are often exactly what is needed to face the opposition and persecution that lie ahead.[40]

Wesley's analysis of believers in a hostile environment supplies a very different reading of Luke–Acts than readings by Classical Pentecostal (and Christian) Euro-American readers. The experiences and perspectives of persecuted Christians in China (and elsewhere) call for a recognition that persecution and Pentecostal power go hand in hand.[41]

If Wesley sheds light on a specific part of the world, a recent and complementary text with a more global outlook is also worth examination. Cecil Robeck and Harold Hunter combine to edit a new volume on the plight of suffering Christians around the world. In the introduction, the editors echo the conclusion above:

> In North America, at least, where both of us make our homes, Classical Pentecostalism as well as much of the later charismatic renewal has struggled with the place of suffering in the church. The minority voices that have pondered the divine mysteries have frequently been drowned out by those who have thundered from their pulpits that miracles remove the sting of pain.[42]

Robeck and Hunter have solicited essays from a wide range of traditions but with a special focus on Pentecostal/Charismatic Christianity in order to provide up-to-date theological and practical global reflections on Christian persecution, from class and racial discrimination to governmental restrictions, from inter-religious conflict to tensions arising from those outside of the Christian faith. In the chapter entitled: "A

---

39. Wesley, *Church in China*, 100–101.
40. Wesley, *Church in China*, 96.
41. Wesley, *Church in China*, 103.
42. Robeck and Hunter, *Suffering Body*, xv.

Spirit Theology of Suffering," Keith Warrington takes readers on a quick journey of suffering in the Scriptures by way of Judaism, the Synoptic Gospels, Luke–Acts, and Paul. Warrington notes:

> For Western Christianity, the experience of suffering is an infrequent one and that may have influenced our limited observation of suffering in relation to the Spirit-led lifestyle of the believer. If it does not happen to us, then it may not be a central characteristic of the work of the Spirit. However, the New Testament paints a different picture.[43]

Direction for Today

The final turn of this project is to transform exegesis into application, specifically, to posit implications for Luke's revelation to contemporary Pentecostal contexts. Since a benchmark of Pentecostal experience is pursuit of the Spirit-filled life as portrayed in the narratives of Luke–Acts, contemporary application is not a new concept. Pentecostals are comfortable using Luke–Acts as a story from which to learn, for a message needed in the early church is also relevant today. This is also consistent with a literary analysis, for paradigmatic uses of Luke–Acts today are in continuity with the paradigmatic uses originally envisaged for such texts.[44] Although careful application is evidently required when spanning centuries and cultures, Luke does provide models for imitation, not only for first century readers, but for Christians today. While Pentecostals continue to encourage witness in the power of the Spirit, there is a noticeable lack in their thinking concerning implications of the Spirit-filled life when juxtaposed with suffering.

One of the conclusions already reached is that Luke narrates why the early mission is not as successful as the early Christians had hoped. Major factors in the unfolding story include the harsh realities of resistance as faced by the emerging community. This strong experience of resistance and rejection in Acts results in a necessary tempering of the mission. Contemporary Pentecostals should learn from these struggles:

---

43. Warrington, "Spirit Theology," 24. I must admit my disappointment concerning the minimal analysis afforded not only to Luke–Acts but also Judaism and the Synoptics. Warrington spends more than two-thirds of the chapter on exegesis of Romans 8.

44. Kurz, "Narrative Models," 188–89.

patience and faithfulness while maintaining trust in God's power and purpose are necessary in a world we do not control. This trust ought to allow similar openness to the Spirit of God, who may even work by irony, that is, by using opponents of the mission to move the divine purpose forward.[45] Regrettably, this lesson has been a difficult one for Pentecostals to discern.

At the risk of oversimplifying Pentecostal demographics, I would propose two strains of Pentecostal Christians to which this study might find suitable application. The first grouping consists of Pentecostals in the global North. The difficulty in applying these findings to northern Pentecostals is mainly one of awareness and/or indifference. A significant trend in our ever-developing northern worldview is one that replaces objectivity with subjectivity, reason with feeling, and conviction with opinion, and that culminates with belief in an inherent right to happiness.[46] Since Pentecostal Christians expect "the blessing of God," suffering seems to infringe on this right to happiness, causing an increasing gap between expectations and any potential suffering connected with God and/or godliness. In a poignant analysis of contemporary Pentecostalism, Thomas Smail argues that far from being immune to this trend to view happiness as a right, Pentecostals are exhibiting growing similarities to the secular mindset of the general populace. His poignant criticism of the Pentecostal/Charismatic movement is that it "springs from a *theologia gloriae* that does not wrestle with a *theologia crucis* and so concentrates too one-sidedly on the triumphs of Easter and Pentecost and does not sufficiently take into account that they can only be reached by way of the cross."[47] It seems that a current paradigm for the Pentecostal tradition is one that does not generally relate well to the expectation of conflict, resistance, and opposition that was so much a part of its formative years. Instead, this expectation is being replaced with a tradition that fits comfortably into the status quo; it is no longer a mission-driven movement that sees itself with a message at odds with its culture. Given this mindset, contemporary pursuit of the Spirit is often relegated to a personal, self-

45. Tannehill, *Narrative Unity*, 2:2 and Moessner, "The Christ Must Suffer." Moltmann concurs: "Participation in the apostolic mission of Christ therefore leads inescapably into tribulation, contradiction and suffering" (*Church*, 361).

46. It may be added that this same manner of thinking also penetrates the belief and praxis of the broader North American Christian community.

47. Smail, "Cross and the Spirit," 15.

empowering experience, which gives further impetus to "the blessing of God," measured in terms of secular power and success. This form of pneumatic pursuit is far removed from the pages of Luke–Acts where Pentecostals originally found their reason for existence.[48]

The other strain consists of contemporary Pentecostals experiencing exponential growth in the global South. According to David Barrett, the explosion of worldwide Pentecostal growth, now at more than 500 million, has a new face, including more urban than rural people (active in 80% of the world's 3,300 largest cities); more Second and Third world (70%) than First World people (30%); and more impoverished (87%) than affluent people (13%).[49] Furthermore, a growing number of these Pentecostals experience various forms of persecution on account of their Christian beliefs, which leads to a very different response to a close reading of Luke–Acts than that of their First World counterparts.[50] As Pentecostals from the global South continue in their pursuit of the Spirit, emphasis should and will continue to be on an enduement of power. However, when people receive the Spirit, they are not all-powerful. On the contrary, a close reading of Luke–Acts is a vivid reminder of the limitations which follow Spirit-enablement. Global South Pentecostals are forced to learn the limits of witness. They must do so while maintaining trust in God's power to reach the ultimate goal. Such trust is supported by a perception of God as a God of surprises or reversals, indeed, a God who works by irony, who can use even opponents of the mission to move the divine purpose forward. While serving faithfully in mission, followers engage and affirm their God, whose exact moves cannot be anticipated as part of the ongoing struggle of faith.

---

48. Tannehill, *Narrative Unity*, 2:1.

49. Barrett, "Pentecostal/Charismatic Renewal." See also various categorical articles on the shifting demographics in contemporary Pentecostalism in Dempster, Klaus, and Petersen, *Globalization of Pentecostalism*, particularly Section III, entitled "Issues Facing Pentecostals in a Postmodern World" (pp. 261–396). While I am also aware that these statistics include all forms of Pentecostals from a host of mainline to independent traditions, Classical Pentecostals continue to invest in missionary endeavors, which reach many of these regions.

50. Moltmann states: "The number of martyrs in the 'young' missionary churches meanwhile exceeds the number of martyrs in the early church. There are many countries in which the apostolic witness is predominantly heard in prison, and nowhere so distinctly as there" (*Church*, 361).

Pentecostals in the global South not only remain confident in the validity and importance of the mission and continue in Spirit-empowered witness, but they are also continuing Luke's story of acceptance and rejection, triumph and tragedy, beyond the end of Acts.[51] As this study demonstrates, these Christians may, in fact, be more like the readers Luke had in mind when he wrote in the first century. One can only hope and pray that God will give them courage as well as arouse a seemingly indifferent and secularized global North to respond to their increasing need for encouragement and support.

May the holistic Lukan story continue to speak to all contemporary Pentecostals by providing a model for Christians, who are called to continue the task of proclamation! As Luke demonstrates how the pneumatic community overcomes difficult circumstances in the midst of persistent opposition, so also may contemporary Pentecostals adopt a rigorous pneumatic discipleship that perseveres in the midst of suffering and persecution.

---

51. Several excellent surveys of modern persecution of Christians include: Davis, "Religious Persecution;" Hefley and Hefley, *By Their Blood*; and Marshall, *Their Blood Cries Out*. While the Western world is generally untouched by persecution, a growing number of Christians around the world live with the ever-increasing realities of suffering for their faith. An increasingly secularized West and its leadership elites tend to be indifferent to and often uncomprehending of a spiritual worldview that endures persecution and death for the sake of belief. Paul Marshall cites two reasons for this indifference: (1) for the most part, North American Christians are not interested in anything that happens outside their own boundaries, and in many cases outside the boundaries of their own little community; (2) North American Christians have no experience of persecution or suffering for the faith which remotely resembles the experiences of believers in the Second or Third World. It is difficult for them to empathize with what is reported so far outside their experience. Marshall goes on to offer cultural and theological factors that he believes render contemporary responses to persecution negligible. These are:

1. A popular form of success theology which stresses prosperity and inner peace as results of spiritual value.
2. Nationalistic Christianity which confuses God and America.
3. An obsession with end-times prophecy which produces favoritism and fatalism.
4. Fierce competition for fund raising dollars by emphasizing an organization's own efforts.
5. A lack of information: because of an indifferent secular media, news of Christian persecution rarely reaches the West (*Their Blood Cries Out*, 5, 7, 152).

Finally, the most recent and comprehensive analysis of martyrdom is found in Barrett and Johnson, *World Christian Trends*. See particularly the chapter entitled: "Martyrology: The Demographics of Christian Martyrdom, AD 33–AD 2001," 225–64.

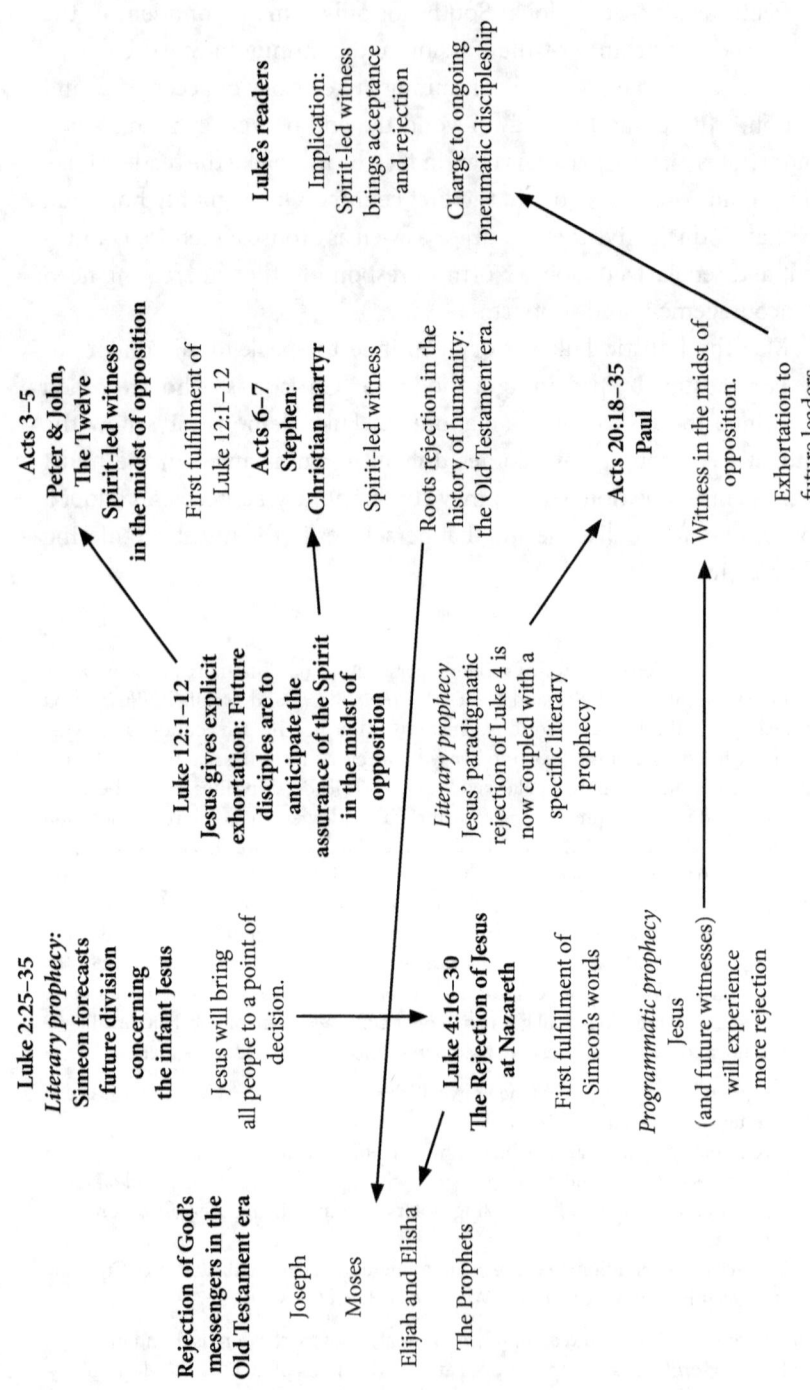

TABLE 1: Summary of Findings: Literary Connections on the Convergence of Spirit and Suffering

Bibliography

Anderson, Allan. *An Introduction to Pentecostalism: Global Charismatic Christianity*. Cambridge: Cambridge University Press, 2004.

Atkinson, William. "Pentecostal Responses to Dunn's Baptism in the Holy Spirit: Luke-Acts." *Journal of Pentecostal Theology* 3 (1995) 87-131.

Barrett, C. K. *A Critical and Exegetical Commentary on the Acts of the Apostles I: Preliminary Introduction and Commentary on Acts I–XIV*. Edinburgh: T&T Clark, 1994.

Barrett, David. "The Twentieth-Century Pentecostal/Charismatic Renewal in the Holy Spirit with its Goal of World Evangelization." *International Bulletin of Missionary Research* 12 (1988) 119-29.

Barrett, David, and Todd M. Johnson, ed. *World Christian Trends AD 30–AD 2200: Interpreting the Annual Christian Megacensus*. Pasadena, CA: William Carey Library, 2001.

———. "*Theologia Crucis*—in Acts?" In *Theologia Crucis-Signum Crucis: Festschrift für Erich Dinkler zum 70 Geburtstag*, edited by Carl Andresen and G. Klein, 73-84. Tübingen: J.C.B. Mohr, 1979.

Bradley, James E. "Miracles and Martyrdom in the Early Church: Some Theological and Ethical Implications." *Pneuma* 13 (1991) 65-81.

Bruner, F. D. *A Theology of the Holy Spirit: The Pentecostal Experience and the New Testament Witness*. Grand Rapids: Eerdmans, 1970.

Burgess, Stanley, and Eduard Van Der Maas, ed. *New International Dictionary of Pentecostal and Charismatic Movements*. Grand Rapids: Zondervan, 2002.

Cadbury, Henry. *The Making of Luke-Acts*. New York: Macmillan, 1927.

Cunningham, Lawrence. "On Contemporary Martyrs: Some Recent Literature." *Theological Studies* 63 (2002) 374-81.

Cunningham, Scott. *Through Many Tribulations: The Theology of Persecution in Luke-Acts*. JSNTSup 142. Sheffield: Sheffield Academic Press, 1997.

Davis, Derek. "Thoughts on Religious Persecution around the Globe: Problems and Solutions." *Journal of Church and State* 40 (1998) 279-87.

Dempster, Murray, et al., ed. *The Globalization of Pentecostalism: A Religion Made to Travel*. Irvine, CA: Regnum International, 1999.

Dowd, Michael B. "Contours of a Narrative Pentecostal Theology and Practice." Paper presented at the annual conference of the Society for Pentecostal Studies, Gaithersburg, MD, November 1985.

Dunn, James D. G. *Baptism in the Holy Spirit: A Re-examination of the New Testament Teaching on the Gift of the Spirit in Relation to Pentecostalism Today*. Philadelphia: Fortress, 1970.

Elbert, Paul. "Pentecostal/Charismatic Themes in Luke-Acts at the Evangelical Theological Society: The Battle of Interpretive Method." *Journal of Pentecostal Theology* 12 (2004) 181-215.

Elliot, Elisabeth. *Shadow of the Almighty: The Life and Testament of Jim Elliot*. San Francisco: Harper & Row, 1958.

———. *Through Gates of Splendor*. London: Hodder and Stoughton, 1962.

Ervin, Howard. *Conversion-Initiation and the Baptism in the Holy Spirit: An Engaging Critique of James D. G. Dunn's Baptism in the Holy Spirit*. Peabody, MA: Hendrickson, 1984.

———. *These Are Not Drunken as Ye Suppose*. Plainsfield, NJ: Logos, 1968.

Fee, Gordon. "Baptism in the Holy Spirit: The Issue of Separability and Subsequence." *Pneuma* 7 (1985) 87–99.

———. *Gospel and Spirit: Issues in New Testament Hermeneutics*. Peabody, MA: Hendrickson, 1991.

———. "Hermeneutics and Historical Precedent: A Major Problem in Pentecostal Hermeneutics." In *Perspectives on the New Pentecostalism*, edited by R. Spittler, 118–32. Grand Rapids: Baker, 1976.

Filson, Floyd V. "The Journey Motif in Luke–Acts." In *Apostolic History and the Gospel*, edited by W. Ward Gasque and Ralph P. Martin, 68–77. Exeter, UK: Paternoster, 1970.

Frein, Brigid Curtin. "Narrative Predictions, Old Testament Prophecies and Luke's Sense of Fulfillment." *New Testament Studies* 40 (1994) 22–37.

Gallagher, Robert. "From Doing to Being: A Missiological Interpretation of Acts 4:23–31." *Journal of Asian Mission* 5 (2003) 153–74.

———. "Hope in the Midst of Trial: A Missiological Interpretation of Acts 12:1–11." Paper presented at the annual conference of the Society for Pentecostal Studies, Milwaukee, WI, March 2004.

Gaventa, Beverly Roberts. "To Speak Thy Word with All Boldness: Acts 4:23–31." *Faith and Mission* 3 (1986) 76–82.

———. "Toward a Theology of Acts: Reading and Rereading." *Interpretation* 42 (1988) 146–57.

Goldingay, John. "Biblical Story and the Way It Shapes Our Story." *Journal of the European Pentecostal Theological Association* 17 (1997) 5–15.

Hefley, James and Marti Hefley. *By Their Blood: Christian Martyrs in the Twentieth Century*. 2d ed. Grand Rapids: Baker, 1996.

Holm, Randall. "Acts 7 and the Destiny of the Holy Spirit." Paper presented at the annual conference of the Society for Pentecostal Studies, Wilmore, KY, March 2003.

Jenkins, Philip. *The New Faces of Christianity: Believing the Bible in the Global South*. New York: Oxford University Press, 2006.

———. *The Next Christendom: The Coming of Global Christianity*. New York: Oxford University Press, 2002.

Johnson, Luke Timothy. *The Literary Function of Possessions in Luke–Acts*. Missoula, MT: Scholars Press, 1977.

———. "Luke–Acts, Book of." In *The Anchor Bible Dictionary*, edited by David Noel Freedman, 4:403–20. New York: Doubleday, 1992.

———. *The Writings of the New Testament: An Interpretation*. Philadelphia: Fortress, 1986.

Karris, Robert. "Missionary Communities: A New Paradigm for the Study of Luke–Acts." *Catholic Biblical Quarterly* 41 (1979) 80–97.

Kurz, William. "Narrative Approaches to Luke–Acts." *Biblica* 68 (1987) 195–222.

———. "Narrative Models for Imitation in Luke–Acts." In *Greeks, Romans and Christians: Essays in Honor of Abraham J. Malherbe*, edited by Wayne Meeks, et al., 171–89. Minneapolis: Fortress, 1990.

———. *Reading Luke–Acts: Dynamics of Biblical Narrative*. Louisville, KY: Westminster, 1993.

Lampe, Geoffrey W. H. "Martyrdom and Inspiration." In *Suffering and Martyrdom in the New Testament*, edited by William Horbury and Brian McNeil, 118–35. Cambridge: Cambridge University Press, 1980.

Land, Steven J. *Pentecostal Spirituality: A Passion for the Kingdom*. Journal of Pentecostal Theology Supplement Series 1. Sheffield: Sheffield Academic Press, 1997.

Lederle, Henry. *Treasures Old and New: Interpretations of "Spirit-Baptism" in the Charismatic Renewal Movement*. Peabody, MA: Hendrickson, 1988.

Marek, Karel. "Acts 29." *The Pentecostal Testimony* 70 (1989) 24–25.

Marshall, Paul. *Their Blood Cries Out: The Worldwide Tragedy of Modern Christians Who Are Dying for Their Faith*. Dallas: Word, 1997.

McGee, Gary. "Historical Perspectives on Pentecostal Missionaries in Situations of Conflict and Violence." *Missiology* 20 (1992) 33–43.

Menzies, Robert P. *The Development of Early Christian Pneumatology with Special Reference to Luke–Acts*. JSNTSup 54. Sheffield: Sheffield Academic Press, 1991.

———. "The Distinctive Character of Luke's Pneumatology." *Paraclete* 25 (1991) 17–30.

———. *Empowered for Witness: The Spirit in Luke–Acts*. Journal of Pentecostal Theology Supplement Series 6. Sheffield: Sheffield Academic Press, 1994.

———. "James Shelton's *Mighty in Word and Deed*: A Review Article." *Journal of Pentecostal Theology* 1 (1993) 105–15.

———. "Luke and the Spirit: A Reply to James Dunn." *Journal of Pentecostal Theology* 2 (1994) 115–38.

Menzies, William W. Review of *Gospel and Spirit: Issues in New Testament Hermeneutics*, by Gordon Fee. *Paraclete* 27 (1993) 29–32.

Menzies, William W. and Robert P. Menzies. *Spirit and Power: Foundation of Pentecostal Experience*. Grand Rapids: Zondervan, 2000.

Mittelstadt, Martin William. "Reading Luke–Acts in the Pentecostal Tradition: The History and Status of Luke–Acts Research." Paper presented at the annual conference of the Society for Pentecostal Studies, Cleveland, TN, March 2007.

———. *The Spirit and Suffering in Luke–Acts: Implications for a Pentecostal Pneumatology*. Journal of Pentecostal Supplement Series 26. London: T&T Clark, 2004.

Moessner, David. "'The Christ Must Suffer': Rethinking the Theology of the Cross in Luke–Acts." In *Society of Biblical Literature 1990 Seminar Papers*, edited by David J. Lull, 165–95. Atlanta: Scholars, 1990.

Moltmann, Jürgen. *The Church in the Power of the Spirit: A Contribution of Messianic Ecclesiology*. Translated by Margaret Kohl. San Francisco: Harper & Row, 1977.

Newberg, Eric. "Persecution and Martyrdom." In *Encyclopedia of Pentecostal and Charismatic Christianity*, edited by Stanley Burgess, 366–70. New York: Routledge, 2006.

Parsons, Mikeal, and Richard I. Pervo. *Rethinking the Unity of Luke and Acts*. Minneapolis: Fortress, 1993.

Peterson, David. "The Motif of Fulfillment and the Purpose of Luke–Acts." In *The Book of Acts in Its Ancient Literary Setting*, edited by Bruce Winter and Andrew Clarke, 83–103. Book of Acts in Its First Century Setting 1. Grand Rapids: Eerdmans, 1993.

Powell, Mark Allan. *What is Narrative Criticism?* Minneapolis: Fortress, 1990.

Praeder, Susan Marie. "Jesus-Paul, Peter-Paul, and Jesus-Peter Parallelisms in Luke–Acts: A History of Reader-Response." *SBL Seminar Papers* 23 (1984) 23–39.

Robeck, Cecil, and Harold Hunter, ed. *The Suffering Body: Responding to the Persecution of Christians*. Peabody, MA: Paternoster Press, 2006.

Rosner, Brian S. "The Progress of the Word." In *Witness to the Gospel: The Theology of Acts*, edited by I. Howard Marshall and David Peterson, 215–33. Grand Rapids: Eerdmans, 1998.

Shelton, James. "'Filled with the Holy Spirit' and 'Full of the Holy Spirit': Lucan Redactional Phrases." In *Faces of Renewal: Studies in Honor of Stanley M. Horton*, edited by Paul Elbert, 82–107. Peabody, MA: Hendrickson, 1988.

———. *Mighty in Word and Deed: The Role of the Holy Spirit in Luke–Acts*. Peabody, MA: Hendrickson, 1991.

———. "A Reply to James D. G. Dunn's *Baptism in the Spirit*: A Response to Pentecostal Scholarship on Luke–Acts." *Journal of Pentecostal Theology* 2 (1994) 139–43.

Smail, Thomas. "The Cross and the Spirit: Toward a Theology of Renewal." In *The Love of Power and the Power of Love*, edited by Thomas Smail, et al., 15–36. London: SPCK, 1993.

Spencer, A. B. "Literary Criticism." In *New Testament Criticism and Interpretation*, edited by D. A. Black and D. S. Dockery, 225–51. Grand Rapids: Zondervan, 1991.

Spencer, F. Scott. "Acts and Modern Literary Approaches." In *The Book of Acts in Its Ancient Literary Setting*, edited by Bruce Winter and Andrew Clarke, 381–415. Book of Acts in Its First Century Setting 1. Grand Rapids: Eerdmans, 1993.

Spittler, Russell P. "Suggested Areas for Further Research in Pentecostal Studies." *Pneuma* 5 (1983) 39–56.

Sternberg, Meir. *The Poetics of Biblical Narrative: Ideological Literature and the Drama of Reading*. Bloomington: Indiana University Press, 1985.

Stott, John. *The Baptism and Fullness of the Holy Spirit*. Downers Grove, IL: InterVarsity Press, 1964.

Stronstad, Roger. *The Charismatic Theology of St. Luke*. Peabody, MA: Hendrickson, 1984.

———. "The Hermeneutics of Lucan Historiography." *Paraclete* 22 (Fall 1988) 5–17.

———. "Pentecostal Experience and Hermeneutics." *Paraclete* 26 (Winter 1992) 14–30.

———. "Pentecostal Hermeneutics." *Pneuma* 15 (1993) 215–22.

———. *The Prophethood of All Believers: A Study in Luke's Charismatic Theology*. Journal of Pentecostal Theology Supplement Series 16. Sheffield: Sheffield Academic Press, 1999.

———. "Trends in Pentecostal Hermeneutics." *Paraclete* 22 (Summer 1988) 1–12.

Tannehill, Robert C. *The Narrative Unity of Luke-Acts: A Literary Interpretation*. 2 vols. Philadelphia: Fortress, 1986–1990.

Tucker, Angelina. *He is in Heaven: The Story of J. W. Tucker, Martyred Missionary to the Congo, Told by His Widow*. New York: McGraw Hill, 1965.

Turner, Max. *Power from on High: The Spirit in Israel's Restoration and Witness in Luke-Acts*. Journal of Pentecostal Theology Supplement Series 9. Sheffield: Sheffield Academic Press, 1996.

Wall, Robert W. "'Purity and Power' according to Acts of the Apostles." *Pneuma* 21 (1999) 215–31.

Warrington, Keith. "A Spirit Theology of Suffering." In *The Suffering Body: Responding to the Persecution of Christians*, edited by Cecil Robeck and Harold Hunter, 37–61. Peabody, MA: Paternoster Press, 2006.

Wesley, Luke. *The Church in China: Persecuted, Pentecostal and Powerful*. Asian Journal of Pentecostal Studies Series 2. Baguio, Philippines: AJPS Books, 2004.

Wright, N. T. *The New Testament and the People of God*. London: SPCK, 1992.

Epilogue

Clark H. Pinnock

More than a decade ago, I wrote the foreword to Roger Stronstad's important monograph entitled *The Charismatic Theology of St. Luke*. It had been written in 1975 as a Master's thesis in New Testament studies at the "other Regent," Regent College, Vancouver, British Columbia. At that time, most evangelicals were prepared to acknowledge Pentecostalism as a source for renewal in mission and church growth, but were not yet ready to honor it as a source of intellectual and theological substance. Well that was then, and this is now. Pentecostal scholarship nowadays is second to none in quality and seriousness. This book is testimony to that fact.

In closing, I see no point in repeating what our cohort of good scholars, some younger, some older, have put on the table for our enrichment. What I can do, and what I should do, is to draw a few threads together by way of an afterword. It was only right for Frank Macchia to lead off the discussion since he is the senior Pentecostal systematic theologian in the English-speaking world. Just for him to be here at McMaster Divinity College made this an important consultation. Frank is the man who can define the issues, expand boundaries, and open up new possibilities for our thinking. Frank is in his prime theologically and is even now polishing the crown jewel of Pentecostalism, Spirit Baptism, within the hearing of multitudes both inside and outside the movement. For what it is worth, I would say that his book *Spirit Baptism* is history in the making. He is offering the churches, Pentecostal and non-Pentecostal, a broad interpretation of Spirit Baptism that keeps the flame of the renewal burning while remaining open to the treasures of other ecclesial communities. We have needed this for a long time.

Already dazzled by Frank's contribution and quite breathless, we then found ourselves in the presence of a brilliant "young" (no pun intended) Asian Pentecostal philosopher from the Assemblies of God who intends to revolutionize our understanding about the Spirit's working among the religions of humanity. He boldly places before us the possibility of a pneumatological theology of religions. As an older chap who has advanced similar ideas about the generosity of God, I have experienced some hostility and opposition, especially from fundamentalists who are fearful about opening doors too widely. However, I think that Pentecostals are less likely to be governed by their fears and may be able to hear Amos in a more positive manner, as we did at the conference. Listen to Amos as he tracks the welcoming Spirit of our bountiful God without in any way compromising our trust in the uniqueness of Jesus Christ.

Frank and Amos were a hard act to follow! Happily though, the subsequent essays kept to the high standard that the first speakers set. Steve Studebaker, theology professor at McMaster Divinity College, offered an improved Pentecostal theology of grace. He thinks that too much time and effort have been given to the experiences of grace subsequent to salvation and too little to the centrality of the Spirit in the entire Christian experience. Following Steve, who is his dissertation advisor, was Andrew Gabriel, with a study on pneumatology and the doctrine of God. Andrew defends speaking of God in clearly trinitarian terms and aims to bring out the ways in which the Spirit presents us with the God whose face is turned toward us. In these two papers, we are hearing a new generation of Pentecostal theologians speaking out, and with no lack of professional competence.

Of course, we were all greatly disappointed when it turned out that Roger Stronstad was unable to attend the conference. Roger is also a senior Pentecostal and one who marches to his own drummer. Fortunately, we have his paper at hand in which he re-visits an original theme in his book *The Charismatic Theology of St Luke*. Roger has been resolute in defending Luke's charismatic (not soteriological) theology. He wants Pentecostals to stay faithful to Spirit Baptism as an empowering and charismatic "second blessing." Others see value in blending the different streams and not drawing lines of difference too sharply. It would have been good to have had Roger present so that we could have tended to what Frank calls "unfinished business."

The two final papers kept to the high standards set by the earlier ones. How apt I thought it was of Martin Mittelstadt to raise the issue of the Spirit and suffering in Luke–Acts, when you consider how many millions of our fellow Pentecostals live in poverty as we speak. What a great hermeneutical trumpet to blow at the end of this conference! Just imagine—what if the revolution that Luke–Acts stimulated in the past century in relation to world evangelism were to explode again and impact the world in the direction of the transformation of societies? And how fitting also was what Cynthia Westfall had to say about the lines of continuity, and not just the differences, between Paul's and Luke's pneumatology! She points us in the direction of a global theology of the Holy Spirit.

Pentecostal Studies Resource Guide

Martin William Mittelstadt

The following guide is not exhaustive but rather intended to introduce scholars and students to influential resources on the Pentecostal/Charismatic movement.* While the annotated bibliography is limited to books and monographs, outstanding journal articles and essays can be found not only via the journal sites but also in the bibliographies of many works cited below. The references are arranged under the following categories: (1) Print media, organized under bibliographical sources, general/edited works, history, theology, spirituality, and biblical studies, and (2) Internet sites for accessing organizations, research sites and archives, and journals and papers.

Annotated Bibliography

Bibliographical Sources

Burgess, Stanley M., and Eduard M. Van der Maas, ed. *The New International Dictionary of Pentecostal and Charismatic Movements*. Revised and expanded edition. Grand Rapids: Zondervan, 2002.

> ◆ The best topical, biographical, and global encyclopedia available to introduce and resource the Pentecostal and Charismatic movements. Concerning sources on Pentecostalism see the extensive article by A. Cerillo and G. Wacker: "Bibliography and Historiography" (382–405).

Jones, Charles Edwin. *A Guide to the Study of the Pentecostal Movement*. 2 vols. Metuchen: Scarecrow, 1983.

* Thank you to Jessica Johnson, my student worker, and Murl Winters, the Evangel University research librarian, for their invaluable assistance.

↬ An early comprehensive guide to primary and secondary materials in English. Entries include primary texts both doctrinal and devotional in nature.

———. *Black Holiness: A Guide to the Study of Black Participants in Wesleyan Perfectionist and Glossolalic Pentecostal Movements*. Metuchen: Scarecrow, 1987.

↬ An important bibliography highlighting the various groups to emerge from the Wesleyan and Pentecostal movements.

Mills, Watson E. *Charismatic Religion in Modern Research: A Bibliography*. Macon: Mercer University Press, 1985.

↬ A bibliography containing more than 2,100 scholarly entries on the emergence of the Charismatic renewal.

———. *Glossolalia: A Bibliography*. PLACE: Edwin Mellen Press, 1985.

↬ A supplement to *Speaking in Tongues* (below) with more than 1,150 entries on glossolalia including titles in German and French.

———. *The Holy Spirit: A Bibliography*. Peabody, MA: Hendrickson, 1988.

↬ An early bibliographical attempt to bring together in one volume the major works that shape the study of the Holy Spirit.

———. *Speaking in Tongues: A Guide to Research on Glossolalia*. Grand Rapids: Eerdmans, 1986.

↬ A bibliographical collection of major scientific articles published on glossolalia in English from the 1960s and beyond.

General/Edited Works

Arrington, French L., and Roger Stronstad, ed. *Life in the Spirit: New Testament Commentary*. Grand Rapids: Zondervan, 1999.

↬ The first New Testament commentary embodying a distinctly Pentecostal/Charismatic perspective.

Anderson, Allan H., and Walter J. Hollenweger, ed. *Pentecostal after a Century*. Journal of Pentecostal Theology Supplement Series 15. Sheffield: Sheffield Academic Press, 1999.

↬ A series of studies on Pentecostalism as a worldwide, particularly non-Western phenomenon. An analysis of Pentecostal contextualization and indigenous roots from several global perspectives.

Dempster, Murray W., Byron D. Klaus, and Douglas Petersen, ed. *The Globalization of Pentecostalism: A Religion Made to Travel*. Oxford: Regnum Books International, 1999.

↪ An assortment of essays attempting to update the global development of Pentecostal thinking in systematics, missiology, biblical studies, history, and praxis.

Elbert, Paul, ed. *Faces of Renewal: Studies in Honor of Stanley M. Horton*. Peabody, MA: Hendrickson, 1988.

↪ A symposium of biblical, historical, and contemporary studies in the context of renewal.

Hunter, Harold, and Peter Hocken, ed. *All Together in One Place: Theological Papers from the Brighton Conference on World Evangelization*. Journal of Pentecostal Theology Supplement Series 4. Sheffield: Sheffield Academic Press, 1993.

↪ A compilation of essays focusing on Pentecostal responses to racism, sexism, socioeconomic oppression, and the environment.

Ma, Wonsuk, and Robert P. Menzies, ed. *Pentecostalism in Context: Essays in Honor of William W. Menzies*. Journal of Pentecostal Theology Supplement Series 11. Sheffield: Sheffield Academic Press, 1997.

↪ A collection of essays treating biblical, theological, and missiological issues relevant to the Pentecostal movement.

Spittler, Russell P., ed. *Perspectives on the New Pentecostalism*. Grand Rapids: Baker, 1976.

↪ Scholarly assessments of the charismatic renewal by historians, theologians, and social scientists including Walter Hollenweger, Clark Pinnock, Kilian McDonnell, William Samarin, and Morton Kelsey.

Synan, Vinson, ed. *Aspects of Pentecostal/Charismatic Origins*. Plainfield: Logos, 1975.

↪ An early compilation of essays assessing the roots and significance of the young charismatic renewal.

Wilson, Mark, ed. *Spirit and Renewal: Essays in Honor of J. Rodman Williams*. Journal of Pentecostal Theology Supplement Series 5. Sheffield: Sheffield Academic Press, 1994.

↪ A collection of papers focusing on the relationship between Spirit and church revival.

History

Anderson, Allan H. *An Introduction to Pentecostalism: Global Charismatic Christianity.* New York: Cambridge University Press, 2004.

↠ An innovative study focusing on the global origins of Pentecostalism with special attention to historical and theological distinctives.

Anderson, Robert Mapes. *Vision of the Disinherited: The Making of American Pentecostalism.* New York: Oxford University Press, 1979.

↠ The emergence of Pentecostalism portrayed as a radical and dysfunctional reaction to social pressures expressed primarily through escapism and conservative conformity.

Atter, Gordon. *The Third Force.* 3d ed. Peterborough, ON: College Press, 1962.

↠ An early Canadian history focusing on key figures in the movement as well as distinguishing doctrinal characteristics.

Blumhofer, Edith L. *The Assemblies of God: A Chapter in the Story of American Pentecostalism.* Springfield: Gospel Publishing House, 1989.

↠ An exploration of the turn-of-the-century social, cultural, and restorationist impulses that gave rise to the Assemblies of God.

———."The 'Overcoming Life': A Study in the Reformed Evangelical Origins of Pentecostalism." Ph.D. diss., Harvard University, 1977.

↠ An important work citing the influence of nineteenth-century Reformed and Keswick theology upon the origins of Pentecostalism.

———. *Restoring the Faith: The Assemblies of God, Pentecostalism, and American Culture.* Urbana: University of Illinois Press, 1993.

↠ A study of the impact of restoration and millennial doctrines on the shaping of the Assemblies of God.

Frodsham, Stanley H. *With Signs Following: The Story of the Latter-Day Pentecostal Revival.* Springfield: Gospel Publishing House, 1946.

↠ An insider argues for the providential emergence of Pentecostalism.

Goff, James R. *Fields White unto Harvest.* Fayetteville: University of Arkansas Press, 1988.

↠ The first thorough examination of the life of Charles Fox Parham and the importance of his life and ministry for the sociological and ideological roots of Pentecostalism.

Harper, Michael. *Bishops' Move*. London: Hodder and Stoughton, 1978.

> A biographical presentation of six Anglican Bishops involved in charismatic renewal.

———. *Three Sisters: A Provocative Look at Evangelicals, Charismatics, and Catholic Charismatics and Their Relationship to One Another*. Wheaton: Tyndale, 1979.

> A pastoral call for renewed Christian charity and unity by participants within the charismatic renewal.

Harrell, David Edwin Jr. *All Things Are Possible: The Healing and Charismatic Revivals in Modern America*. Bloomington: Indiana University Press, 1975.

> The definitive history of healing and charismatic revivals in modern America marking the methods and impact of the various healing revivalists.

———. *Oral Roberts: An American Life*. Bloomington: Indiana University Press, 1985.

> A sound honest biography of Oral Roberts by a leading historian.

Kendrick, Klaude. *The Promise Fulfilled: A History of the Modern Pentecostal Movement*. Springfield: Gospel Publishing House, 1961.

> One of the first works to emphasize the crucial role of Charles Parham in the early articulation and propagation of the Pentecostal message.

Kulbeck, Gloria Grace. *What God Hath Wrought: A History of the Pentecostal Assemblies of Canada*. Toronto: Pentecostal Assemblies of Canada, 1958.

> An early and officially sponsored history of the providential emergence of Pentecostals in Canada.

McGee, Gary B. *People of the Spirit: The Assemblies of God*. Springfield: Gospel Publishing House, 2004.

> An innovative biographical history focusing upon the shaping of the Assemblies of God through ordinary people.

Miller, Thomas William. *Canadian Pentecostals: A History of the Pentecostal Assemblies of Canada*. Mississauga, ON: Full Gospel Publishing House, 1994.

> A narration of the beginnings of the Pentecostal movement in Canada.

Nelson, Douglas J. "For Such a Time as This: The Story of Bishop William J. Seymour and the Azusa Street Revival: A Search for Pentecostal/Charismatic Roots." Ph.D. diss., University of Birmingham, 1981.

> An examination of the life, theology, and impact of William Seymour and consequently the Azusa Street Revival.

Nienkirchen, Charles W. *A. B. Simpson and the Pentecostal Movement*. Peabody, MA: Hendrickson, 1992.

↳ An analysis of A. B. Simpson's relationship to early Pentecostalism illustrating specific ways his influence touched the complex story of early Holiness-Pentecostal relationships.

O'Connor, Edward. *The Pentecostal Movement in the Catholic Church*. Notre Dame: Ave Maria, 1971.

↳ Reflections upon the historical and theological impact of the charismatic renewal on the Roman Catholic Church

Poloma, Margaret. *The Assemblies of God at the Crossroads: Charisma and Institutional Dilemmas*. Knoxville: University of Tennessee Press, 1989.

↳ A sociological analysis of the ever unfolding relationship between charismatic experience and institutionalization in the Assemblies of God.

———. *Main Street Mystics: The Toronto Blessing and Reviving Pentecostalism*. Walnut Creek, CA: Altamira Press, 2003.

↳ A sociological analysis of the events surrounding a new wave of Pentecostalism to emerge out of the Toronto Airport Vineyard Church.

Quebedeaux, Richard. *The New Charismatics: The Origins, Development, and Significance of Neo-Pentecostalism*. Garden City: Doubleday, 1976.

↳ A history of the origins and development of the charismatic renewal as well as an assessment of its significance to the Church.

Ranaghan, Kevin, and Dorothy Ranaghan. *Catholic Pentecostals*. New York: Paulist, 1969.

↳ An early look at charismatic renewal in the Roman Catholic tradition.

Reed, David A. *In Jesus' Name: The History and Beliefs of Oneness Pentecostals*. Journal of Pentecostal Theology Supplement Series 31. Dorset, UK: Deo Publishing, 2007.

↳ The most complete analysis of Oneness Pentecostals to date. This volume is a thorough update of his 1978 dissertation.

Riss, Richard M. "The Latter Rain Movement of 1948 and the Mid-twentieth-century Evangelical Awakening." M.A. thesis, Regent College (Vancouver), 1979.

↳ A historical and theological analysis of the controversial revival originating at Sharon Orphanage and Schools in North Battleford, Saskatchewan.

Rudd, Douglas. *When the Spirit Came upon Them: Highlights from the Early Years of the Pentecostal Movement in Canada*. Burlington, ON: Antioch Books, 2002.

↳ A popular history highlighting key figures in the formation of Canadian Pentecostalism.

Synan, Vinson. *The Century of the Holy Spirit: 100 Years of Pentecostal and Charismatic Renewal, 1901–2001*. Nashville: Thomas Nelson, 2001.

    ↦ An accessible and comprehensive survey of the Pentecostal and Charismatic movements.

———. *The Twentieth-Century Pentecostal Explosion: The Exciting Growth of Pentecostal Churches and Charismatic Renewal Movements*. Altamonte Springs, FL: Creation House, 1987.

    ↦ A Classical Pentecostal reflection on charismatic stirrings among various traditions such as Lutherans, Mennonites, and Orthodox Catholics.

Wacker, Grant. *Heaven Below: Early Pentecostals and American Culture*. Cambridge, MA: Harvard University Press, 2003.

    ↦ A monumental presentation of early Pentecostalism captured via two parallel impulses: primitivism (a desire to return to apostolic Christianity) and pragmatism (an ability to utilize current cultural strategies for contemporary mission).

Warner, Wayne E. *The Woman Evangelist: The Life and Times of Charismatic Evangelist Maria B. Woodworth-Etter*. Metuchen: Scarecrow, 1986.

    ↦ The most exhaustive study to date on this early female evangelist.

Theology

Alexander, Paul. *Peace, Power, and Pentecost: Nonviolence, Nationalism, and Militarism in American Pentecostalism*. Telford: Cascadia Publishing House, 2007.

    ↦ The definitive trajectory on the early importance of pacifism and its demise within American Pentecostalism as well as a contemporary appeal to revisit a peace ethic.

Althouse, Peter. *Spirit of the Last Days: Pentecostal Eschatology in Conversation with Jürgen Moltmann*. Journal of Pentecostal Theology Supplement Series 25. Edinburgh: T&T Clark, 2004.

    ↦ A solid treatment of the origins of Pentecostal eschatology placed in conversation with current scholars (Steven Land, Frank Macchia, Eldin Villafane, and Miroslav Volf) and the influence of Moltmann upon their respective theologies.

Burgess, Stanley M. *The Spirit and the Church: Antiquity*. Peabody, MA: Hendrickson, 1984. Reprint of *The Holy Spirit: Ancient Christian Traditions*. Peabody, MA: Hendrickson, 1994.
———. *The Holy Spirit: Eastern Christian Traditions*. Peabody, MA: Hendrickson, 1989.
———. *The Holy Spirit: Medieval Roman Catholic and Reformation Traditions*. Peabody, MA: Hendrickson, 1997.

    ↦ A trilogy on theological reflection on the role of the Holy Spirit throughout the history of Christendom.

Dayton, Donald. *Theological Roots of Pentecostalism*. Peabody, MA: Hendrickson, 1987.

↪ An important pioneering analysis on the role of the Wesleyan movement upon the formation of early Pentecostalism.

de Leon, Victor. *The Silent Pentecostals*. Taylors, SC: Faith Printing, 1979.

↪ A survey of American Hispanic Pentecostalism within the context of the Assemblies of God.

Farah, Charles Jr. *Pinnacle of the Temple*. Plainfield: Logos, 1979.

↪ A superb and honest analysis of the Word of Faith movement by a Charismatic scholar.

Faupel, D. William. *The Everlasting Gospel: The Significance of Eschatology in the Development of Pentecostal Thought*. Journal of Pentecostal Theology Supplement Series 10. Sheffield: Sheffield Academic Press, 1996.

↪ An assessment of eschatology as the dominant theological belief in Pentecostalism.

Gelpi, Donald L. *Charisma and Sacrament: A Theology of Christian Conversion*. New York: Paulist, 1976.

↪ An integrative look at the convergence of the sacraments and the gifts of the Spirit.

———. *Pentecostalism: A Theological Viewpoint*. New York: Paulist, 1971.

↪ An early theological critique and statement on charismatic renewal in the Roman Catholic tradition.

Hollenweger, Walter J. *Pentecostalism: Origins and Developments Worldwide*. Peabody, MA: Hendrickson, 1997.

↪ This text reflects the developed interpretation of one of the most influential scholars in contemporary Pentecostal studies.

———. *The Pentecostals: The Charismatic Movement in the Churches*. Minneapolis: Augsburg, 1972.

↪ A detailed guide to the global expansion of Pentecostalism with an emphasis on Europe, Africa, and South America.

Hummel, Charles E. *Fire in the Fireplace: Charismatic Renewal in the Nineties*. 2d ed. Downers Grove: InterVarsity Press, 1993.

↪ A passionate call for Christian charity and mutual understanding among participants in the charismatic renewal.

———. *Fire in the Fireplace: Contemporary Charismatic Renewal*. Downers Grove: InterVarsity Press, 1978.

↪ A popular historical assessment of trends in the Charismatic renewal.

Jenkins, Philip. *The New Faces of Christianity: Believing the Bible in the Global South.* New York: Oxford University Press, 2006.

↬ A historical/theological assessment of biblical interpretation in the global south and its potential impact upon the future of Christianity.

———. *The Next Christendom: The Coming of Global Christianity.* 2d ed. New York: Oxford University Press, 2007.

↬ A provocative analysis on the emergence of Christianity (including Pentecostalism) in the non-white global south and its future against the historically dominant Christianity of the global north.

Kydd, Ronald. *Charismatic Gifts in the Early Church.* Peabody, MA: Hendrickson, 1984.

↬ An analysis of New Testament experiences carried over into the early church era (through the fifth century) thereby challenging cessationist theologies.

———. *Healing Through the Centuries: Models for Understanding.* Peabody, MA: Hendrickson, 1998.

↬ An important historical and theological analysis of various healing models utilized throughout Christian history.

LaBarre, Weston. *They Shall Take Up Serpents: Psychology of the Southern Snake-Handling Cult.* 2d ed. New York: Schocken Books, 1969.

↬ An early analysis of snake-handling and its importance to believers of the Southern Appalachians.

Macchia, Frank D. *Baptized in the Spirit: A Global Pentecostal Theology.* Grand Rapids: Zondervan, 2006.

↬ A call for Pentecostals to respond to the growing displacement of Spirit baptism in Pentecostal and Charismatic theology and praxis via fresh treatment of Christology, soteriology, and ecclesiology.

MacNutt, Francis. *Healing.* Notre Dame: Ave Maria, 1974.

↬ A pastoral perspective offering practical models for healing ministry in the contemporary church.

———. *The Power to Heal.* Notre Dame: Ave Maria, 1977.

↬ A pastoral resource for believers interested in pursuing the ministry of prayer in conjunction with healing.

McDonnell, Kilian. *Charismatic Renewal and the Churches.* New York: Seabury Press, 1976.

↠ A theological reflection on the impact of history and psychology upon Pentecostalism and the Charismatic renewal.

———. *Presence, Power, Praise.* Collegeville: Liturgical Press, 1981.

↠ A collection of formal ecclesial statements assessing the impact of the Charismatic renewal on post-1960 traditions.

———. *The Charismatic Renewal and Ecumenism.* New York: Paulist, 1978.

↠ A pastoral work calling upon Roman Catholics to engage in sympathetic ecumenical dialogue with other traditions.

McDonnell, Kilian, and George Montague. *Christian Initiation and the Baptism in the Holy Spirit: Evidence from the First Eight Centuries.* Collegeville: Liturgical Press, 1991.

↠ An examination of post-biblical writings on Spirit baptism and the sacramental role of charisms in the early Christian era.

McGee, Gary B., ed. *Initial Evidence: Historical and Biblical Perspectives on the Pentecostal Doctrine of Spirit Baptism.* Peabody, MA: Hendrickson, 1991.

↠ An important compilation of essays offering honest and thoughtful appraisals of the historical formation of the doctrine of Spirit Baptism and its exegetical foundations.

Montague, George T. *The Holy Spirit: Growth of a Biblical Tradition.* New York: Paulist, 1976.

↠ A reflective and exegetical analysis of the principle canonical texts on the subject of the Holy Spirit with implications for ecumenical theology and Christian unity.

Pinnock, Clark H. *Flame of Love: A Theology of the Holy Spirit.* Downers Grove, IL: InterVarsity Press, 1996.

↠ An innovative ecumenical study by a Charismatic Baptist that treats the role of the Spirit in relation to Trinity, creation, Christology, ecclesiology, soteriology, and missiology.

Price, Lynne. *Theology Out of Place: A Theological Biography of Walter J. Hollenweger.* Journal of Pentecostal Theology Supplement Series 23. Sheffield: Sheffield Academic Press, 2002.

↠ A superb rehearsal of the stellar academic career of Walter Hollenweger along with implications of his global thinking.

Ruthven, Jon. *On the Cessation of the Charismata: A Critique of the Protestant Polemic on Postbiblical Miracles*. Journal of Pentecostal Theology Supplement Series 3. Sheffield: Sheffield Academic Press, 1993.

⇨ An important study and critique of Protestant views on the cessation of miracles in the post-apostolic age.

Smail, Thomas A. *The Forgotten Father*. Grand Rapids: Eerdmans, 1980.

⇨ An outstanding challenge to the Charismatic community concerning neglect of the role of the Father in the renewal.

Smail, Thomas A., Andrew Walker, and Nigel Wright. *The Love of Power or the Power of Love: A Careful Assessment of the Problems within the Charismatic and Word-of-Faith Movements*. Minneapolis: Bethany House, 1994.

⇨ A sympathetic yet critical pastoral response to serious exegetical, doctrinal, and practical issues of the Charismatic subculture.

Volf, Miroslav. *Exclusion and Embrace: A Theological Exploration of Identity, Otherness and Reconciliation*. Nashville: Abingdon, 1996.

⇨ A challenging proposal calling for embrace as a theological response to exclusion via the New Testament metaphor of salvation as reconciliation.

———. *Work in the Spirit: Toward a Theology of Work*. New York: Oxford University Press, 1991.

⇨ An innovative interpretation of work, including industrial, agricultural, medical, political, and artistic work, in light of the doctrine of the Holy Spirit.

Yocum, Bruce. *Prophecy: Exercising the Prophetic Gifts of the Spirit in the Church Today*. Ann Arbor: Word of Life, 1976.

⇨ An analysis of the gift of prophecy in Pentecostal and charismatic contexts, including definitions, usage, and testing.

Yong, Amos. *Discerning the Spirit(s): A Pentecostal-Charismatic Contribution to Christian Theology of Religions*. Journal of Pentecostal Theology Supplement Series 20. Sheffield: Sheffield Academic Press, 2000.

⇨ A pioneering effort that explores a missiological pneumatology for engagement of world religions.

———. *The Spirit Poured Out on All Flesh: Pentecostalism and the Possibility of Global Theology*. Grand Rapids: Baker Academic, 2005.

⇨ A call for Pentecostals to engage in ecumenical conversation with world religions and culture in order to develop a Pentecostal global theology.

Spirituality

Albrecht, Daniel E. *Rites in the Spirit: A Ritual Approach to Pentecostal/Charismatic Spirituality*. Journal of Pentecostal Theology Supplement Series 17. Sheffield: Sheffield Academic Press, 1999.

↪ An innovative study of Pentecostal worship rites that shape, nurture, authenticate, and transform the spiritual lives of Pentecostal Christians.

Archer, Kenneth J. *A Pentecostal Hermeneutic for the Twenty-first Century: Spirit, Scripture and Community*. Journal of Pentecostal Theology Supplement Series 28. London: T&T Clark, 2004.

↪ A history of Pentecostal interpretative models with a new proposal for a hermeneutic appropriate to the contemporary context.

Bridges-Johns, Cheryl. *Pentecostal Formation: A Pedagogy among the Oppressed*. Journal of Pentecostal Theology Supplement Series 2. Sheffield: Sheffield Academic Press, 1993.

↪ An attempt to place the nature of Pentecostal catechesis and ecclesiology as being prophetic as opposed to tradition as suggested by the educational paradigm of Paolo Friere.

Chan, Simon. *Pentecostal Theology and the Christian Spiritual Tradition*. Journal of Pentecostal Theology Supplement Series 21. Sheffield: Sheffield Academic Press, 2000.

↪ An ecumenical call for consideration of glossolalia and Spirit Baptism in Pentecostal and charismatic contexts within the larger Christian spiritual tradition.

Christenson, Larry. *The Charismatic Renewal among Lutherans*. Minneapolis: Lutheran Charismatic Renewal Services, 1976.

↪ The history, status, and future of the charismatic renewal in the Lutheran tradition.

Cox, Harvey. *Fire from Heaven: The Rise of Pentecostal Spirituality and the Reshaping of Religion in the Twenty-first Century*. Reading: Addison-Wesley, 1995.

↪ A fascinating and sympathetic account that addresses reasons for the success and impact of the Pentecostal movement.

Land, Steven J. *Pentecostal Spirituality: A Passion for the Kingdom*. Journal of Pentecostal Theology Supplement Series 1. Sheffield: Sheffield Academic Press, 1993.

↪ A thorough theological construction of the narrative beliefs and spirituality of Pentecostals.

Parker, Stephen E. *Led by the Spirit: Toward a Practical Theology of Pentecostal Discernment and Decision Making*. Journal of Pentecostal Theology Supplement Series 7. Sheffield: Sheffield Academic Press, 1996.

⤷ An exploration of the psychological and theological dynamics of claims to divine guidance by Pentecostals.

Wilkinson, Michael. *The Spirit Said Go: Pentecostal Immigrants in Canada*. American University Studies Series 7. New York: Peter Lang, 2006.

⤷ An impressive sociological consideration on the formation and sustainability of ethnic Pentecostal communities upon settlement in Canada.

Biblical Studies

Aune, David. *Prophecy in Early Christianity*. Grand Rapids: Eerdmans, 1983.

⤷ A reputable New Testament scholar considers prophetic oracles through the mid-second-century and offers a comprehensive treatment of the place of prophecy in the New Testament.

Charette, Blaine. *Restoring Presence: The Spirit in Matthew's Gospel*. Journal of Pentecostal Theology Supplement Series 18. Sheffield: Sheffield Academic Press, 2000.

⤷ A landmark analysis of Matthew's pneumatology by a Pentecostal scholar. Accordingly, shows Matthew's indebtedness to the Old Testament and the eschatology of redemption that comes as a direct result of the activity of God's Spirit.

Dunn, James D. G. *Baptism in the Holy Spirit*. Philadelphia: Westminster, 1970.

⤷ This classic Evangelical work launched a new era of Pentecostal scholarship concerning the role of the Spirit within the total complex of becoming a Christian. A crucial text for any Pentecostal seeking to understand an Evangelical perspective on Spirit Baptism.

———. *Jesus and the Spirit: A Study of the Religious and Charismatic Experience of Jesus and the First Christians as Reflected in the New Testament*. Philadelphia: Westminster, 1976.

⤷ A New Testament study of the religious and charismatic experiences of Jesus as understood in the life of the early Church.

Ervin, Howard M. *Conversion-Initiation and the Baptism in the Holy Spirit*. Peabody, MA: Hendrickson, 1984.

⤷ A careful grammatical, syntactical, and contextual critique of James Dunn's *Baptism in the Holy Spirit*.

Fee, Gordon. *1 Corinthians*. NICNT. Grand Rapids: Eerdmans, 1987.

⇨ An important commentary by this outstanding Pauline scholar advocating balanced charismatic experience and its contemporary application.

———. *God's Empowering Presence: The Holy Spirit in the Letters of Paul*. Peabody, MA: Hendrickson, 1999.

⇨ An encyclopedic analysis of every Spirit text in the Pauline letters, highlighting Paul's consistent desire that the Spirit must be experienced as a living presence in the church.

———. *Paul, the Spirit and the People of God*. Peabody, MA: Hendrickson, 1996.

⇨ A reliable guide to the recovery of the experienced presence of God in the church via a fresh understanding of the Spirit as proclaimed in the letters of Paul.

Grudem, Wayne A. *The Gift of Prophecy in I Corinthians*. Washington, D.C.: University Press of America, 1982.

⇨ An analysis of the nature and practice of prophecy in the Corinthian church and other New Testament churches.

Hildebrandt, Wilf. *An Old Testament Theology of the Spirit of God*. Peabody, MA: Hendrickson, 1995.

⇨ A guide to the role of the Spirit in creation, in the establishment and preservation of God's people, in prophecy, and in Israel's leadership.

Hovenden, Gerald. *Speaking in Tongues: The New Testament Evidence in Context*. Journal of Pentecostal Theology Supplement Series 22. Sheffield: Sheffield Academic Press, 2002.

⇨ An examination of the phenomenon of tongues from a religio-historical perspective, beginning with inspired speech in the ancient world and then Lukan and Pauline references.

Keener, Craig S. *Paul, Women and Wives: Marriage and Women's Ministry in the Letters of Paul*. Peabody, MA: Hendrickson, 1992.

⇨ An egalitarian study of Paul's understanding of the role of women, with solid exegesis on women in Spirit/prophetic contexts.

McQueen, Larry R. *Joel and the Spirit: The Cry of a Prophetic Hermeneutic*. Journal of Pentecostal Theology Supplement Series 8. Sheffield: Sheffield Academic Press, 1993.

⇨ A hermeneutical assessment of the relationship between the text of Joel, the New Testament use of Joel's themes, and the Pentecostal experience of the Spirit.

Menzies, Robert P. *Empowered for Witness: The Spirit in Luke–Acts.* Journal of Pentecostal Theology Supplement Series 6. Sheffield: Sheffield Academic Press, 1994.

⇨ A valuable revision of a doctoral dissertation promoting a Classical Pentecostal defense of the role of the Spirit in Luke–Acts.

Mittelstadt, Martin William. *Spirit and Suffering in Luke–Acts: Implications for a Pentecostal Pneumatology.* Journal of Pentecostal Theology Supplement Series 26. London: T&T Clark, 2004.

⇨ An exegetical analysis focusing on Luke's ability to hold in tension the roles of the Spirit in contexts of suffering and of victory.

Penney, John Michael. *The Missionary Emphasis of Lukan Pneumatology.* Journal of Pentecostal Theology Supplement Series 12. Sheffield: Sheffield Academic Press, 1997.

⇨ An analysis of Spirit Baptism in Luke–Acts as a unique Pentecost event signaling Israel's eschatological reconstruction for mission to the nations.

Shelton, James B. *Mighty in Word and Deed: The Role of the Holy Spirit in Luke–Acts.* Peabody, MA: Hendrickson, 1991.

⇨ A study of Lukan pneumatology in contexts of conversion, water baptism, the infilling of the Spirit, prophecy, and Spirit baptism.

Solivan, Samuel. *The Spirit, Pathos and Liberation: Toward a Hispanic Pentecostal Theology.* Journal of Pentecostal Theology Supplement Series 14. Sheffield: Sheffield Academic Press, 1998.

⇨ An examination of distinct Hispanic-American issues from experience and suffering to language and culture (including acculturation and assimilation) and the possibilities for a transformed and liberated life.

Stronstad, Roger. *The Charismatic Theology of St. Luke.* Peabody, MA: Hendrickson, 1984.

⇨ A monumental redaction/literary study focusing on the intentional and didactic Charismatic pneumatology of Luke.

———. *The Prophethood of All Believers: A Study in Luke's Charismatic Theology.* Journal of Pentecostal Theology Supplement Series 16. Sheffield: Sheffield Academic Press, 1999.

⇨ The role of the Spirit for vocational empowerment found particularly through the contemporary prophethood of all believers.

Thomas, John Christopher. *The Devil, Disease and Deliverance: Origins of Illness in New Testament Thought*. Journal of Pentecostal Theology Supplement Series 13. Sheffield: Sheffield Academic Press, 1998.

› An exegetical study on the origins of illness by the various New Testament writers.

———. *Footwashing in John 13 and the Johannine Community*. JSNTSup 61. Sheffield: Sheffield Academic Press, 1993.

› A comprehensive study of footwashing in the ancient world providing many fascinating parallels to the early Christian practice as well as contemporary application.

Turner, Max. *Power from on High: The Spirit in Israel's Restoration and Witness in Luke-Acts*. Journal of Pentecostal Theology Supplement Series 9. Sheffield: Sheffield Academic Press, 1996.

› Turner shines fresh light on specific Lukan concepts and provides a coherent understanding of the general shape of Luke's pneumatology.

Wenk, Matthias. *Community Forming Power: The Socio-Ethical Role of the Spirit in Luke-Acts*. Journal of Pentecostal Theology Supplement Series 19. Sheffield: Sheffield Academic Press, 2000.

› A study of the role of socio-ethical dimensions in Lukan pneumatology with particular focus upon Jesus' attention to the marginalized.

Internet Resources

Researchers interested in accessing the internet may start with the following sites.

Organizations

Mother of God Community: A Catholic and Ecumenical Charismatic Community
http://www.motherofgod.org/

Pentecostal/Charismatic Churches of North America
http://www.pccna.org

Pentecostal/Charismatic Peace Fellowship
http://pcpf.org/

Pentecostal World Fellowship
http://pentecostalworldfellowship.org/

Society for Pentecostal Studies
http://www.sps-usa.org/

Research and Archives

Allan Anderson: Home Page
http://artsweb.bham.ac.uk/aanderson/index.htm

Superb links for global Pentecostalism.
http://artsweb.bham.ac.uk/aanderson/Pentecost/articles_and_papers.htm

Assemblies of God: Flower Pentecostal Heritage Center
http://ifphc.org/

Dunamai.com
http://www.dunamai.com/
Includes primary documents online.

Fuller Theological Seminary: David du Plessis Archive
http://www.fuller.edu/archive/

Hollenweger Center for the Interdisciplinary Study of Pentecostal and Charismatic Movements
http://www.hollenwegercenter.net/

International Pentecostal Holiness Church Archives and Research Center
http://pctii.org/arc/

Lee University: Hal Bernard Dixon Jr. Pentecostal Research Center
http://faculty.leeu.edu/~drc/

Oral Roberts University: Holy Spirit Research Center
http://www.oru.edu/university/library/holyspirit/

Pentecostal Assemblies of Canada Archives
http://www.paoc.org/administration/archives.html

Pentecostal/Charismatic Religious Studies Resources
http://ccat.sas.upenn.edu/~kbanner/pentec.html
65 links to various Pentecostal sites.

Pentecostal-Charismatic Theological Inquiry International
http://www.pctii.org/
Includes links to online publications

Revival Library
http://www.revival-library.org
Collection of primary materials available on CD

Swedish Pentecostal Movement: Pentecostal Research and Information Center
http://www.pri.pingst.se/english/pri.asp

University of Birmingham
http://artsweb.bham.ac.uk/aanderson/Pentecost/Bibliographies.htm
Bibliographies for Pentecostal and Charismatic Studies

University of Birmingham: Research Unit for Pentecostal and Charismatic Studies
http://artsweb.bham.ac.uk/aanderson/Main/research_unit_for_pentecostal.htm

Vanguard University: Wilson Institute
http://www.vanguard.edu/wilsoninstitute/

Online Journals

Asian Journal of Pentecostal Studies
http://apts.edu/ajps.htm

Australasian Pentecostal Studies
http://aps.webjournals.org

Cyberjournal for Pentecostal-Charismatic Research
http://pctii.org/cyberj/index.html

Enrich: A Journal for Pentecostal Ministry (Pentecostal Assemblies of Canada)
http://www.paoc-excel.org/A1_pex_05_ENR/a1_05_enr02.html

Enrichment Online (Assemblies of God periodical)
http://ag.org/enrichmentjournal

Index to Pentecostal and Charismatic Scholarly Papers and Periodicals
http://home.regent.edu/ruthven/spspage.html

Journal of European Pentecostal Theology (index through 2000)
http://home.regent.edu/ruthven/eptaindx.html

Journal of Pentecostal Theology (index through 2000)
http://home.regent.edu/ruthven/jptindex.html

Paraclete: A Journal of the Person and Work of the Holy Spirit
http://home.regent.edu/ruthven/parcindx.html
Index: published for 1967–1995.

PentecoStudies: Online Journal for the Interdisciplinary Study of Pentecostal and Charismatic Movements
http://www.glopent.net/pentecostudies

Pneuma: The Journal of the Society for Pentecostal Studies
http://sps-usa.org/pneuma/home.htm#ARTICLEINDEX

The Pneuma Review: Resources of Spirit-Empowered Ministry
http://www.pneumafoundation.com/links_fellows.shtml

Society for Pentecostal Studies Conference Papers (index through 2000)
http://home.regent.edu/ruthven/spspaper.html

Society for Pentecostal Studies Newsletters
http://home.regent.edu/ruthven/SPSNewsletters1990s.html

Link directly to select online publications (indexes, directories, papers, journals, etc.)
http://www.pctii.org/online.html

Modern Authors Index

Albrecht, Daniel E., 189
Alexander, Paul, 184
Althaus, Paul, 49n7, 65
Althouse, Peter, 184
Anderson, Allan H., 14, 27, 33, 33n16, 34, 34ns17–18, 37, 44, 123n1, 124n6, 132n26, 142, 146n5, 169, 179, 181
Anderson, Gordon L., 55, 55n23, 65
Anderson, Robert Mapes, 181
Archer, Kenneth J. A., 74n22, 94, 189
Arrington, French L., 54n19, 65, 71n9, 94, 133n31, 134ns31 & 33, 142, 179
Atkinson, William, 153n24, 169
Atter, Gordon, 181
Aune, David, 190

Badcock, Gary D., 49n6, 65
Barrett, C. K., 147n8, 169
Barrett, David, 162n36, 166, 166n49, 167n51, 169
Barrett, David B., 1, 10
Barth, Karl, 24, 24n21, 27, 30, 76, 78, 78n41, 85n68, 94
Bell, E. N., 15, 27
Berkhof, Hendrikus, 76, 76n31, 77, 77n32, 94

Bloesch, Donald G., 86n69, 92n101, 94, 106, 106n9, 107n10, 119, 119ns13–15, 122
Blumhofer, Edith L., 53n17, 65, 181
Boff, L., 77, 77n39, 89n87, 94
Bowne, Borden P., 86, 86n71, 94
Bradley, James E., 154, 154n29, 155, 169
Bridges-Johns, C., 189
Bruner, Frederick D., 21, 77n37, 94, 101, 122, 153n23, 169
Bryant, M. Darrol, 44, 42n32
Bundy, D., 73, 73n19, 74n20, 94
Burgess, Stanley M., 146n5, 169, 172, 178, 184
Busch, Eberhard, 78n41, 94

Cadbury, Henry J., 103, 103n4, 122, 147n6, 169
Cerillo, Augustus, Jr., 178
Chan, Simon, 22, 22n18, 27, 189
Charette, Blaine, 190
Christenson, Larry, 189
Coffey, D. M., 56–57, 57n26, 58n27, 59, 59n29, 60n31, 61n32, 62, 62ns33–35, 65–66
Cohen, David, 97
Collins, Kenneth J., 51n12, 66
Comblin, J., 89, 89ns86–87, 94

Cox, Harvey, 189
Cross, Terry L., 74, 74ns21 & 24, 75n25, 79, 79n45, 94
Cunningham, Lawrence, 162n37, 169
Cunningham, Scott, 154n27, 169

Dabney, D. Lyle, 47, 47n2, 66, 77n35, 80, 80n48, 94–97
Davis, Derek, 167n51, 169
Dayton, Donald W., 20, 20n15, 21, 27, 53n15, 54n18, 66, 68, 185
de Leon, Victor, 185
Del Colle, Ralph, 82, 82n55, 95
Delling, Gerhard, 103n3, 122
Demarest, Bruce A., 49n7, 50n8, 66
Dempster, Murray W., 16, 17n9, 27, 166n49, 169, 180
Dieter, Melvin E., 53n15, 66
Dorner, Isaak, 74
Dowd, Michael B., 150ns18–19, 169
Duffield Guy P., 33n15, 44, 72–73, 73ns16–18, 95
Dunn, James D. G., 101, 105, 105ns7–8, 122, 124n3, 142, 152, 152n22, 153, 153ns23–24, 154n25, 169, 190
Dusing, M. L., 52n13, 53n14, 54n19, 66, 72, 72n13–15, 95
Dye, Colin, 55n21, 66

Edwards, Denis, 80, 80n48, 85n67, 90n89, 92, 92ns98–99, 95
Elbert, Paul, 151, 151n21, 169, 172, 180
Ellington, Scott A., 74n22, 95
Elliot, Elisabeth, 145n4, 169–70
Erickson, Millard J., 49n7, 50n8, 51n12, 66
Ervin, Howard M., 18, 18n11, 27, 153, 153n24, 170, 190

Farah, Charles, Jr., 185
Farley, E., 86n70, 95
Faupel, D. William, 20–21, 20n16, 26–27, 53ns15–16, 54n18, 66, 185
Fee, Gordon D., 76n28, 91n95, 95, 123, 123n2, 124, 125n7, 128n16, 129n17, 131n23, 134ns31–32, 139, 139n43, 140n44, 142, 153n23, 170, 191
Filson, Floyd V., 149n16, 170
Frein, Brigid Curtin, 156n31, 170
Frodsham, Stanley H., 181
Fudge, Thomas, 16, 16n15, 22, 22n19, 27

Gabriel, Andrew, K., 7–8, 71n8, 76n28, 92ns 97 & 100, 95, 176
Gallagher, Robert, 157n32, 170
Garland, David E., 134n31, 142
Gause, R. Hollis, 52n13, 53n14, 66
Gaventa, Beverly Roberts, 148n11, 162n36, 170
Gelpi, Donald L., 185
Goff, James R., Jr., 30n2, 44, 181
Goldingay, John, 149, 150n17, 151n20, 170
Grider, J. Kenneth, 51n12, 66
Griffiths, Paul J., 43n34, 44
Grudem, Wayne, 49n7, 66, 191
Gunton, Colin E., 70–71, 71n4, 81n51, 84n62, 86, 86n72, 91, 91ns92 & 94, 95
Guthrie, Shirley C., Jr., 85, 85n68, 86, 87ns73–74, 95

Hagner, Donald A., 25, 25n22, 27
Harper, Michael, 182
Harrell, David Edwin, Jr., 182
Hart, Larry D., 33n15, 44, 52–53, 52n13, 53n14, 66
Hayford, Jack, 16, 16n7, 27

Hefley, James, 167n51, 170
Hefley, Marti, 167n51, 170
Hessel, Dieter T., 97
Hezmalhalch, Thomas, 17n8, 27
Higgins, John R., 52n13, 53n14, 54n19, 66, 72, 72n13-15, 95
Hildebrandt, Wilf, 191
Hinze, Bradford E., 66, 77n35, 94-97
Hocken, Peter, 180
Hodge, Charles, 48n4, 50n9, 51n12, 66
Hollenweger, Walter J., 19, 19ns12-13, 20-21, 27-28, 125n8, 142, 179, 180, 185, 187, 194
Holm, Randall, 158n33, 170
Hordern, William E., 77n37, 94
Horton, Stanley M., 30ns3-4, 31ns5-10, 32ns11-14, 44, 66-68, 71, 72n11, 96
Hovenden, Gerald, 191
Hull, J. H. E., 103n3, 122
Hummel, Charles E., 185
Hunter, Harold D., 18, 18n11, 27, 163, 163n42, 172-73, 180

Ice, Laura M., 134n32, 143

Jenkins, Philip, 162n38, 170, 186
Jenney, Timothy P., 53n14, 66
Johnson, Elizabeth A., 70, 77n33, 81, 81n52, 84, 85n65, 87n76, 95
Johnson, Luke Timothy, 147, 147ns7 & 9, 148n11, 170
Johnson, Todd M., 1, 10, 167n51, 169
Jones, Charles Edwin, 178-79

Kaiser, Walter C., Jr., 118, 119n12, 122
Kärkkäinen, Veli-Matti, 35-37, 35n21, 36ns22-25, 44, 70, 70n3, 76, 76n29, 80, 80n46, 95-96

Karris, Robert, 160n34, 170
Kasper, Walter, 77, 77n38, 96
Keener, Craig S., 191
Kendrick, Klaude, 182
Kilgallen, John J., 42n33, 44
Klaus, Byron D., 166n49, 169, 180
Knight, J. A., 53n15, 67
Kulbeck, Gloria Grace, 182
Kurz, William, 148ns11-12, 164n44, 171
Kydd, Ronald, 186

LaBarre, Weston, 186
LaCugna, Catherine Mowry, 67, 83, 83n60, 96
Lamb, Christopher, 42n32, 44
Lampe, Geoffrey W. H., 162n35, 171
Land, Steven J., 21, 21n17, 26, 28, 136-37n37, 139n42, 142, 149n16, 171, 184, 189
Leckie-Tarry, Helen, 126n9, 142
Lederle, Henry, 146n5, 171
Lee, Edgar R., 74n22, 96
Letham, Robert, 50n8, 67
Levinskaya, Irina A., 111n11, 122
Lindbeck, George, 20, 20n14, 28
Lindström, Harald, 51n12, 67
Lochman, Jan Milič, 40n31, 44
Longenecker, Richard N., 126n12, 142
Lord, Andrew, 34n19, 35-37, 35n20, 41, 44

Ma, Wonsuk, 180
Macchia, Frank D., 7, 15n4, 18n11, 24n20, 28, 46n1, 67, 80, 80n46, 96, 119-20, 120ns16-19, 122, 124n5, 129, 129n18, 135n35, 139n43, 142, 175-76, 184, 186
MacNutt, Francis, 186
Maddox, Randy L., 51n12, 67

Marek, Karel, 149, 149ns14–15, 171
Marshall, I. Howard, 75, 75n27, 96, 103–4, 122, 172
Marshall, Molly T., 88, 88ns81–83, 89, 89ns84–85, 96
Marshall, Paul, 167n51, 171
Matera, Frank J., 126n10, 142
McDonnell, Kilian, 77, 77n36, 78ns40–41, 82–84, 82n56, 83ns58 & 60, 84n63, 88, 88ns79–80, 93n103, 96, 180, 187
McGee, Gary B., 162n37, 171, 182, 187
McGrath, Alister E., 51n11, 67
McQueen, Larry R., 191
Menzies, Robert P., 18, 18n10, 28, 55, 55n22, 56n24, 67, 153, 153–54ns23–25, 171, 180, 192
Menzies, William W., 55, 55n22, 56n24, 67, 71, 72n11, 96, 153–54ns24–25, 171
Mills, Watson E., 179
Miller, Thomas William, 182
Mittelstadt, Martin William, 6, 9, 138, 138ns40–41, 142–43, 144n1, 147n6, 153n24, 154n26, 155n30, 156n31, 171, 177, 192
Moessner, David, 165n45, 171
Moltmann, Jürgen, 28, 71, 71n7, 77n37, 78, 79n42, 81ns49–50, 92, 92n102, 96, 165n45, 166n50, 171, 184
Montague, George T., 187
Mühlen, Heribert, 69n1, 83–85, 83n57, 84n64, 85, 85n66, 87, 87n77, 96
Muller, Richard A., 47n3, 67
Murray, John, 51n12, 67

Nelson, Douglas J., 182
Newberg, Eric, 162n37, 172

Nienkirchen, Charles W., 183

O'Connor, Edward, 183
Outler, Albert C., 68

Parker, Stepehn E., 190
Parsons, Michael, 97, 147n6, 172
Pearlman, M., 52n13, 53n14, 54n19, 67, 72, 72n12, 96
Pecota, D. B., 54n19, 67
Penney, John Michael, 192
Pervo, Richard I., 147n6, 172
Petersen, Douglas, 166n49, 169, 180
Peterson, David, 104, 122, 156n31, 172
Pickard, Stephen, 80n48, 97
Pinnock, Clark H., 7, 44n36, 56n24, 67, 74, 74ns23–24, 77ns33 & 35, 79, 79ns43–45, 80n46, 84n63, 85n67, 87, 87n75, 88ns78–79, 89–90, 90ns88 & 90, 93, 93n104, 96–97, 180, 187
Pittenger, Norman, 83n57, 97
Polkinghorne, John, 85n67, 97
Poloma, Margaret, 183
Porter, Stanley E., 95, 126n9, 127n13, 132n27, 134n31, 143
Powell, Mark Allan, 148n10, 172
Praeder, Susan Marie, 148n13, 172
Preece, Gordon, 80n48, 97
Price, Lynne, 187
Prior, Michael, 38n29, 45
Pruitt, Raymond M., 53n14, 54n18, 67

Quebedeaux, Richard, 183

Rahner, Karl, 57, 57n25, 67, 82, 82n53, 84, 84n61, 97
Railey, James H., 74n22, 97
Ranaghan, Dorothy, 183

Modern Authors Index 201

Ranaghan, Kevin, 183
Reasoner, Victor P., 53n15, 67
Reed, David A., 183
Reuther, Rosemary Radford, 97
Richie, Tony, 36n25, 45
Riss, Richard M., 183
Robeck, Cecil M., 163, 163n42, 172–73
Robertson, John C., Jr., 86n70, 97
Rosner, Brian S., 151n20, 172
Rudd, Douglas, 183
Rusch, William G., 49n6, 67
Ruthven, Jon, 188

Sanders, Fred, 75n26, 83n59, 97
Schreiner, Thomas R., 124n4, 143
Schwöbel, Christoph, 75n26, 97
Seymour, William J., 16, 16n8, 28
Shelton, James B., 153, 153n24, 172, 192
Shults, F. LeRon, 81n51, 97
Sirks, G. J., 77n36, 97
Smail, Thomas A., 165, 165n47, 172, 188
Solivan, Samuel, 192
Spencer, A. B., 148n10, 172
Spencer, F. Scott, 148n10, 172
Spittler, Russell P., 76n30, 97, 136n36, 143, 154–55, 154n28, 170, 172, 180
Sternberg, Meir, 148n10, 172
Stott, John R. W., 102, 105, 105n6, 122, 153n23, 172
Stronstad Roger, 7–9, 18, 18n10, 28, 101n1, 104n5, 122, 130n20, 143, 153, 153n24, 172–73, 175–76, 179, 192
Studebaker, Steven M., 8, 44n36, 57n26, 59n30, 67, 74n22, 79, 91, 97, 176
Synan, Vinson, 180, 184

Tabbernee, William, 77n34, 97
Tallman, Frank D., 52n13, 53n14, 54n19, 66, 72, 72ns13–15, 95
Tannehill, Robert C., 148n11, 165n45, 166n48, 173
Tappert, Theodore G., 51n10, 68
Thistleton, Anthony C., 134n31, 143
Thomas, John Christopher, 193
Thompson, John, 82, 82n54, 97
Thompson, Matthew K., 74n22, 97
Torrey, Reuben A., 53n17, 54n20, 68
Tucker, Angelina, 144n3, 173
Turner, Max, 153n23, 173, 193

Van Cleave, Nathaniel M., 33n15, 44, 72–73, 73n16–18, 95
Van Der Maas, Eduard M., 146n5, 169, 178
Volf, Miroslav, 94, 184, 188

Wacker, Grant A., 14, 21, 178, 184
Walker, Andrew, 188
Wall, Robert W., 147n6, 173
Wallace, Mark I., 91, 92n96, 97
Warner, Wayne E., 184
Warrington, Keith, 164, 164n43, 173
Webster, John, 90, 90n91, 91n92, 97
Wenk, Matthias, 193
Wesley, Luke, 162, 163ns39–41, 173
Wessels, Roland, 53n17, 68
Westfall, Cynthia Long, 6–7, 9, 127n13, 132n27, 143, 177
Wilkinson, Michael, 190
Williams, Ernest S., 53n14, 68
Williams, J. Rodman, 33n15, 45, 53n14, 68, 75n25
Wilson, Mark, 180
Witherington, Ben, III, 126n11, 127n15, 134n32, 143
Wright, N. T., 151n20, 173
Wright, Nigel, 188
Wyckoff, John W., 54n19, 68

Yocum, Bruce, 188
Yong, Amos, 6–8, 35n21, 36n26, 37n27, 38ns28 & 30, 43n35, 44–45, 80, 80ns46–47, 96, 98, 129n19, 133n30, 135, 135n34, 137n38, 143, 176, 188
Yun, Koo Dong, 14, 28

Zizioulas, John D. 78n40, 98

Subject Index

Assemblies of God, 2–3, 15–16, 30, 52, 54, 144–45, 146n5, 150, 162, 176
Apocalyptic, 24–25
Augustine of Hippo, 30
Azusa Street, 2, 5, 182

Baptism in the Holy Spirit
   conversion–initiation, 105, 107, 112, 119–21, 133–34n31, 135–36, 152
   distinctive doctrine, 14, 17, 20–23, 46, 80
   empowerment, 15, 22, 26, 29, 46, 53–54, 130–31, 159, 166–67
   entire sanctification, 54
   initial evidence, 2, 16, 54
   Jesus Christ, 113–116
   John the Baptist, 113–114
   Luke, 104–6, 135
   Paul, 124n5, 135
   sanctification, 14–15
   subsequence, 8, 14–16, 46, 55, 64–65, 80, 102, 106, 108, 109–112, 116, 118, 120–21, 124–25, 133–34n31, 135, 136n36, 152
   the Kingdom of God, 24–26, 139n42, 139n43

Baptism in the Holy Spirit (*cont.*)
   tongues, 2–3, 8, 13, 15, 16, 20, 21, 26, 46, 54, 80, 108, 111, 114, 117–18, 121, 123, 131
Bennett, Dennis (1917–1991), 2
Biblical theology, 72, 75
Bredesen, Harald (1918–2006), 2
Brownsville Revival, 3

∞

Calvin, John (1509–1564), 48, 50n9
Cappadocians, 91
Cardinal Suenens, Léon-Joseph (1904–1996), 2–3
Charismatic Movement, 2, 7, 14, 26, 33, 77, 121, 146n5, 163, 165
Catholic Church, 2
Christendom, 4
Christian Science, 32
Christology, 24, 26, 49–52, 56, 58, 60, 63–64, 71, 73, 75, 82–83
   Cross, 15, 48, 50, 52–53, 55, 59, 64, 71, 92, 139, 165
   homoousios, 58
   hypostatic union, 61
   incarnation, 56, 58–59, 61, 63, 71, 73–74
   resurrection, 73n18, 114, 157
   Spirit Christology, 58–59, 137n38

Church of God (Cleveland), 2, 146n5
Church of God in Christ, 2, 146n5
Clark, Stephen (1940–), 2
Classical Pentecostalism, 2–3, 9,
　　37, 52, 56n24, 71n10, 125, 135,
　　136n36, 146n5, 153n24, 159,
　　163, 166

∽

Dispensationalism, 18, 151
Doctrine of God
　Classical theism, 8, 69–71, 93
　Divine attributes, 8, 69–70, 72–73,
　　78, 80–81, 83–85, 88, 91–93
　Divine immanence, 69, 85–87
　Divine transcendence, 85–87, 90
Durham, William H. (1873–1912),
　　15–16

∽

Eastern Orthodoxy, 77, 77n40
Ecclesiology, 27, 80, 83n59
　body of Christ, 35, 118–119, 128–
　　129, 131, 135, 133–34n31, 140
　church, 32, 35, 40, 46, 79, 84, 88,
　　90, 121, 124n5, 126, 130, 138,
　　139n43, 141, 144, 147, 157n32,
　　160–63, 175
　communion of saints, 26, 62–63,
　　89–90
　koinonia, 25
　people of God, 39
　temple of the Holy Spirit, 9, 129
Edwards, Jonathan, 5, 56–57
Eschatology, 18, 21–22, 24, 26, 139
Evangelical theology, 47–52, 55

∽

Finished Work, 15–16
Fletcher, John, 14–15, 53n15
Four-Fold (Foursquare) Gospel,
　　20–22

Full Gospel, 22, 26

Gifts of the Spirit, 6, 8–9, 13, 15,
　　20–22, 26, 30, 34, 46–47, 80, 85,
　　130–32, 130ns20–21
Gnosticism, 32
Good Samaritan, 38–39
Great Commission, 30

∽

Hayford, Jack, 16
Healing, 15, 17, 19, 21–23, 30, 34, 38,
　　125, 137n38, 136, 138, 142, 145,
　　154, 157n32
Health and Wealth gospel, 18
Hermeneutics,
　evangelical, 102, 105, 124
　narrative, 103, 112, 115, 117, 124,
　　126, 128, 136, 141, 147–52, 159
Hinduism, 32
Holiness movements, 14–15, 17, 20,
　　46, 53,
Holy Spirit
　classical theism, 8, 69–74
　creation, 89, 91–93, 137n38
　Creator Spirit, 92
　divine faithfulness, 91
　divine holiness, 90–91
　divine immanence, 87–93
　divine omnipotence, 88–89
　divine passibility, 91–92
　divine relationality, 89–90
　grace, 47, 56–57, 59–64
　incarnation, 58–59, 61
　Luke–Acts, 6, 9, 18, 102, 116,
　missions, 38–39, 41–43, 118, 160
　mutual love, 57–60, 62–63, 79n43,
　　81, 90, 90n89
　Paul, 6, 9, 102, 112
　redemption, 8, 35, 41–43, 47,
　　49–50, 52–54, 56, 58, 61, 63–64,
　　137n38

Holy Spirit (*continued*)
  sanctification, 14–15, 17, 49–50, 52, 53n15, 54–55, 63, 91, 120, 130n20, 137–38
  suffering, 6, 9, 92, 138–39, 146, 154–59
  application of redemption, 50–51, 53, 64–65
  divine attributes, 70, 87–93
  Trinity, 16, 47, 56
  third blessing, 53–54
Hospitality, 38-40, 42–43

∞

International Church of the Foursquare Gospel, 2, 16, 146n5
International Pentecostal Holiness Church, 2, 4, 146n5
Interreligious dialogue, 32–33, 36–39, 42–43

∞

Jerusalem council, 126–27, 140
Jesus Christ, 5, 22, 30, 48, 58–61, 71–72, 106, 117, 119, 126–28, 148, 176
  anointed, 24, 38, 88, 110–11, 113–14, 121
  Justification, 19, 27, 48–52, 54–55, 63–64, 120
  imputed righteousness, 48–50, 52

∞

Kenosis, 85
Keswick Revivals, 14–15
Kingdom of God, 21, 24–25, 36, 108, 128–29, 139ns42–43

∞

Latter Rain, 20–21, 26
Liberation theology, 89
Lim, David, 15

∞

Manichaeism, 32
Martin, Ralph (1942–), 2
Martyrdom/persecution, 144–46, 154, 157–63, 157n32, 162ns35 & 37, 166–67, 167n51
Montanism, 77
Moody, Dwight L. (1837–99), 15

∞

Narrative (and oral theology), 19–21, 124–25, 125n8, 127, 150
Neo-Charismatic Movement (Third Wave), 2–3
New Age movements, 32

∞

Oneness Pentecostalism, 16, 22, 80, 71n10, 80
Open Theism, 74, 74n10
Oral traditions, 125, 127–38, 134n31, 150
Ordo salutis, 51–55, 136n36, 142
Ozman, Agnes (1870–1937), 2

∞

Panentheism, 91–92
Parham, Charles Fox (1873–1929), 181, 182
Pentecost, Day of, 39–41, 103, 106–9, 112, 114–17, 119, 139
Pentecostal Assemblies of Canada, 2, 146n5, 149
Pentecostalism
  distinctive doctrine, 7, 13–14, 17–23, 26–27, 80, 93, 105, 119, 123, 125, 128, 130, 136, 140–42, 153, 159
  ecumenism, 17–18, 20, 26, 35–36, 56, 77, 80, 146
  eschatology, 18, 20–26, 36, 44, 109, 115, 125, 137n38, 139–41

Pentecostalism (*continued*)
  Evangelicalism, 18, 29–30, 46–47, 52–56, 63–64, 75, 102, 118–119, 124, 151
  Fundamentalism, 29–30, 124
  global, 1, 4, 13, 17–24, 34–36, 46, 64, 132, 136, 146, 162–63, 165–67, 177
  missions, 4, 18, 20–21, 29–30, 32–35, 37–38, 40–43, 80, 118–19, 132, 144–46, 145n4, 161–62, 165, 166n49, 167, 175
  spirituality, 3, 33–34, 46–47
  suffering, 6, 9, 145–46, 157n32, 159–67, 177
  theology of religions, 8, 29–30, 32, 35–37, 36n36, 80
Pneumatological theology, 78–85, 176
Pneumatology, 8, 24, 47, 49–52, 54–60, 63–65, 70, 70–80, 82–83, 88, 93, 146, 149, 151–53, 153n24, 155, 176
  Pauline, 6, 9, 123–25, 130n20, 139, 177
  Lukan, 9, 18, 154, 177
  ecumenism, 18
Postmodernism, 4
Pre-millennialism, 18
Promise of the Father, 30, 39, 134n33
Prophecy, 15, 34, 108–10, 112–17, 120, 123, 128, 130–31, 155–56, 167n51
Protestant Scholasticism, 47, 47n3, 51n11

∞

Rabbinic Judaism, 127
Reconciliation, 34, 41, 51n12, 129n19, 188
Repentance, 16, 24, 32–33, 51, 51n12, 106–7, 116, 135

Revelation, 25, 31, 33, 57, 125, 130
  Paul, 125–28, 130
  the Holy Spirit, 107, 110, 127
  general, 31, 37
  special, 31
Revival, 1–3, 5, 14, 16, 18, 20, 30, 53–54, 93, 136, 145, 180, 182–83

∞

Sacraments, 185
Sanctification, 14–15, 17, 19, 21, 25, 48–52, 54–55, 63–64, 120, 125, 129–30, 136–38, 139n42
Second blessing, 14, 176
Second Coming of Christ, 17–18, 21, 139
Seymour, William, J. (1870-1922), 2, 4, 16, 182
Signs and Wonders, 3, 132–33, 133n30, 136, 144
Sin, 31–33, 38, 48, 50, 52–53, 64, 73n18, 89n87, 90, 106, 109, 116, 130, 137n38
Social justice, 34–35, 39, 41, 129n19, 142, 137n38
Soteriology, 34–35, 38, 47, 49, 49n6, 51n12, 80, 83n59, 137n38, 186–87
Spiritual warfare, 3, 137

∞

theologia crucis and *theologia gloriæ* 165
Theology of religions, 6, 8, 29, 32, 35–37, 36n26, 176
Third blessing, 15, 53–54
Tongues (glossololia), 2–3, 8, 13, 15–17, 20–21, 26, 34, 39–40, 46, 54, 80, 108–9, 111, 114–15, 117–18, 121, 123, 130–31, 132n25, 135–36
Toronto Blessing, 3, 183

Trinity, 16, 47, 56–59, 62–63, 65, 71–72, 75–76, 79–84, 90, 93
  economic and immanent, 56–59, 62–63, 71, 81, 84, 90, 93
  filioque, 77, 81
  modalism, 16
  panentheism, 91–92
  perichoresis, 82–83, 83n60
  revival of, 71, 76, 81–83
  social Trinity, 79
  theology of religions, 36
  triune, 8, 69, 71, 74, 76, 79n43, 82, 85

∾

Wagner, C. Peter (1930–), 3
Water baptism, 16, 24, 134n31, 192
Wesley, John (1703–1791), 14, 50n9, 51n12, 53n15
Wesleyan theology, 19, 46, 51, 51n12, 53–54, 53n15, 80
Wimber, John (1934–1997), 3

∾

Zoroastrianism, 32

www.ingramcontent.com/pod-product-compliance
Lightning Source LLC
Chambersburg PA
CBHW070321230426
43663CB00011B/2186